CHESS CHILD

CHESS CHILD

THE STORY OF RAY ROBSON, AMERICA'S YOUNGEST GRANDMASTER

BY

GARY ROBSON

Nipa Hut Press

Seminole, Florida

Cover photo by Yee-chen Robson

Library of Congress Cataloging-in-Publication Data
Robson, Gary, 1965 –
Chess child/Gary Robson.
p. cm. -- (Nipa hut press)
ISBN-13: 978-0-9826682-0-7

www.nipahutpress.com

Printed in the United States of America

First Edition

FOR MY FAMILY

“If one advances confidently in the direction of his dreams . . . he will meet with success unexpected in common hours.” - Henry D. Thoreau

“I have said it: let it go! If I had waited until I acquired the final truth, the ultimate beauty, I should never have said anything at all. I must go on – incomplete. It is the test of the writer – that he is sincere in his imperfections, honest in his limitations.” – David Grayson (Ray S. Baker)

PART I

1

I was sitting outside a library on a cement curb in Taipei, Taiwan. Ray was dozing in and out of a light sleep in his stroller, and Yee-chen was inside the library reading a book. I was thinking about what poems to present to my American Literature students, when a stranger approached. He stopped in front of us and stared at me for a while, and then at Ray, and then back and forth between us. He made a number of gestures with his hands, and I thought he wanted money for food.

At first, I thought to ignore him. His left eye was closed shut, and I suppose the socket may have been empty. He wore army-type clothing which probably came from WWII, and he had flip-flops – only the poorest, only the street people in Taiwan, wear flip-flops outside the home. He was about 5'4" and anywhere from 70 to 90 years old. He carried a duffle bag and five or six plastic bags filled up with unknown things. From his gestures and his grunts, I guessed that he was mute, and for all I knew he may have been deaf as well.

As I said, my first thought was to ignore him. He looked dingy and even a little crazy. He was a strange man, and he was only a few feet from my infant son. In addition, his hands reaching out in wild gestures were drawing attention to me, and I have always preferred to stay in the background of any scene. So I put my head down and ignored him. I could see out of the corner of my eye that he was preparing to go. But then I thought, *Why not see what he wants? Maybe he really has something to say to me. He was trying so hard to communicate with those flying hands. If it's so important to him, why not give him a little of my time?*

When he saw that I gave him my attention – that I wasn't going to turn away – he brightened and again stretched out his hands. This time I realized that he wanted my pen and paper; I gave them to him (not without reluctance, for I thought he might pack them in one of the plastic bags and hike off). On the backside of the page that I had been working on, he began to write.

He wrote Chinese characters from the top of the page to the bottom. I thought that he was probably asking for food or money, thinking that I could read Chinese. He just had a "hungry" look about him – something we shared, for I suppose that, to most people, I look like I could use a big burger, fries, and a shake to coat my own bony frame. But he wrote quite a bit, and I soon realized that he wasn't asking for something. What he wrote looked more like the poetry I'd often seen in Yee-chen's books and elsewhere. After writing each line, he would pause, wheeze heavily, take another breath, and then labor over his next line.

After finishing, he gave the paper to me, and I nodded a thank you and hoped that that was that. It looked like he was all set to go, but then he turned back, added a parenthetical line on the paper, and did a mass of pantomiming about what he'd first written. Perhaps he was acting out the words. As his acting drew even more stares, I tried to distance myself by not paying attention, and when he looked at me as if for some response, I drew a question mark on the page to indicate that I didn't understand and that he was wasting his time on me (yet what I was thinking was that he was wasting my time). And it looked like my plan worked because he made as if to go, but then he returned again.

He gestured for the pen and paper once more, and this time he drew three fish with one head – that is, he drew three fish in such a way that they resembled a three-bladed propeller; the heads were all on top of one another, making them look like one head, but the bodies were laid out in three different directions. With several gestures, he seemed to me to be presenting this picture as a riddle, perhaps playing off of my question mark. When I again showed that I was clueless, he went to great pantomimic pains to solve the riddle for me. I remained unenlightened. And he waved goodbye (again), and then soon after returned (again).

This time he drew something that looked lewd, but by hand-movements gave me the idea that it was a propeller of sorts. Again I was lost, again he tried to pantomime the answer, again I was left unenlightened. And he made as if to go, and again he came back.

This time he wrote something brief opposite my question mark and added his own question mark. And then he went through the act of teaching me, solving the riddle, etc. – all of which was wasted on me. And the departure and the return.

Next he taught me how the Chinese count from 1 to 10 on one hand; this I'd seen before. He went through the numbers at least ten times and emphasized the difference between 3 and 10 five times (3 and 10 have only a slight difference in appearance, and this he seemed to want to emphasize). All of this repetition began to bore me, and I resumed my blank, uninterested look. And the departure and the return.

He then asked me what 8 plus 8 equaled: another riddle. The answer to this one, which I gathered from his pantomime, was a camera. Apparently the 8 in Chinese character form resembles half a camera and by placing one 8 upside down atop another, it forms a box (like a camera). This I think I got. Then he waved goodbye (again) and this time really left.

Yee-chen came out of the library a few minutes later and when I showed her the sentences the man had written, she said: "This doesn't make any sense. Why do you let strange people write in your notebook?"

On the way home, Yee-chen told me about the book she'd been reading. It was by a foreigner (perhaps an American), and it comically related the events which led up to the birth of his daughter. I only half listened, though; I was upset that I'd wasted my time with the bag-man.

That night, still stewing over the incident and not content to let the matter rest with Yee-chen's comment about nonsensical writing, I made her translate the characters that the man had written in my notebook. His first sentences were indeed a riddle: "Holland's hot peppers are improving. There are six or seven colors. If you think about how to cook it (i.e., a pepper), the future will be very good." And in parentheses he wrote: "Show this to your wife." The brief writing with the question mark was also a riddle: "How can three fish have one head?"

And then came the enlightenment: I understood! His numerous gestures to me and Ray, back and forth between the two of us . . . his knowledge that Ray's mother was Chinese . . . this, along with the English translation, made me understand the meaning of the words.

The hot peppers, I saw, were a symbol for people. There are many kinds (shades) of people ("6 or 7 colors"). Yee-chen and I and Ray are all different colored peppers. If we (Yee-chen and I) think about how to prepare/develop/tend our pepper (Ray), the future will be good for him.

The three fish: one is Yee-chen, one Ray, and one is me. But we are one in that something within connects us and makes us somehow indistinguishable or inseparable from one another. It is like the three blades of a fan – when at rest they appear to be three, when in motion they appear as one (his propeller example).

All of this I realized instantly.

Yee-chen said that I read too deeply into the nonsense and dismissed my interpretation. But later she was still interested in the topic, in the mystery, and still later she was awake and energized – a state which she attributed to the old man who she realized was wise, and to his words which she knew were not foolish.

2

Yee-chen and I had spent the last two years of our lives – which were also the first two years of our marriage – in the Republic of China (Taiwan) living simply on the wages from the 10 hours or so per week that I spent teaching English as a second language. Yee-chen was born in Burma but escaped to Taiwan where she attended high school and college. I had made my own escape from the United States in the 1980s by joining the Peace Corps. After a two-year stint in the Philippines, and after quite a bit of wandering with just a pack on my back, I found myself in Taiwan where Yee-chen and I met and married.

It could have been easy to just stay in Taiwan, but, since leaving the Peace Corps, I had established a nomadic lifestyle, always finding excuses to move to another place. In the US, I did my wandering on wheels, driving from north to south and east to west, sleeping in my car and sometimes staying in friends' or relatives' homes for a few days at a time. In Latin America, I used others' wheels as I hitchhiked and walked my way from Guatemala to Costa Rica, spending no more than one month in any one town. I found many beautiful places in which to live during my travels, but each time there would come a morning where I would wake up and, without understanding why myself, pack my few belongings into my backpack, pick a direction, and walk away.

In Taiwan, I had a wife. During our first two years, we went from an apartment in Taipei to a broken-down house at the base of Ali Mountain. At one point, Yee-chen lived in a female dormitory at the university where she was finishing up her baccalaureate degree, and I slept in my tent, alternating between a cow pasture in the hills outside of the city and a slab of concrete beneath the wing of an airplane near the dormitory. I never wondered what a small airplane was doing permanently parked in one corner of the campus, but I was grateful for it.

When I slept in the hills, I was far away from Yee-chen. On campus, however, we shared my 1.5-person tent beneath the plane.

In sum, we ended up living in at least half a dozen places from the very north to the very south of Taiwan, in addition to a lengthy trek through rural China around the time of our first anniversary. As we approached our second anniversary, I convinced Yee-chen to move with me to Micronesia. My argument was simple: she could work on her US citizenship while at the same time remaining close to Asia. I suppose by this time, Yee-chen had figured out that my arguments were mostly meaningless. Like the passionate shepherd who says all the right things to woo the pretty woman, I said whatever I needed to in order to get my feet in motion once again. And Yee-chen, like the pretty woman who knows better than to believe everything she hears, still says yes. There is simply no other answer to give when one is young and in love.

My plan upon our arrival in Guam was to sell hong-cha (the Chinese version of sweetened iced tea) from a pushcart to tourists on the beach. I thought that it would be a nice way to spend my days, walking about the beaches under the Micronesian sun and having all day to think my thoughts. However, we weren't there more than a day before I realized how foolish my plan was. It costs a lot of money to live in a place like Guam, where vegetables are imported and, along with everything else in the grocery store, cost more than I could make from selling tea on the beach. The only thing I could afford was the locally produced goods, but who can live on pickled papaya? So I invested $250 in a wreck of a car – which I affectionately referred to as "the Guam Bomb" – and drove around looking for work. The physical condition of the car accurately reflects our financial situation at the time. The floor mats, if removed, showed the road below; the hatchback – which was for several months kept in place by a wire – eventually fell off; and the roof above the front seats had completely rusted through. I used duct tape (painted the color of the car) to "fix" that problem, but still, if we had a torrential rainfall, as we regularly did on tropical Guam, I would need to drive with a small umbrella over my head.

But I was pretty good at making do with what I had, and I kept that car alive for the two years that we remained in Guam. The Guam Bomb took me back and forth to my initial part-time job as gardener for a family and, a few months later, it took me back and forth to my full-time job as a high school English teacher. The students laughed at my car and, on field trips, refused to ride with me. But once they got to know me, I think they understood that money and appearance meant nothing to me. This last explains why, instead of making tens of thousands of dollars when we lived in Taiwan, I worked just 10 hours a week. I have always thought that work was necessary in order to provide the basic needs and that working more than necessary was foolish; all of the rest of my time has always been for thinking, reading, writing, and for walking and talking with friends – all of the things that make up living for me.

So by the end of the first summer, I had my job as a high school teacher, and Yee-chen had her job as a part-time teacher of Chinese at the Chinese School of Guam. It was a crazy year for me because I had never had to work so much before in my life. I needed the full-time job in order to pay for our apartment, the gas, food, and the other bills; it was no day on the beach handing out cups of hong-cha and enjoying the beauty of the moment. I had no time to think, no time to read, and no time to walk. I had less time for Yee-chen too and, as a result, she grew lonely; it was this loneliness, along with biology, that led her to thoughts of starting a family.

The need for her to have a child eventually grew so strong that, by the middle of our first year in Guam, it was no longer just a thought; instead, it became the main goal of her life. And so we had a son. This is how most of the big decisions in our lives have been made, when one of us has had an overwhelming urge to move in some direction. Always the partner supports the one who experiences the strongest urge. Up until that time, I had a dim vision of waiting out this strange period of constant work and busyness. I dreamed instead of returning in a few years to the life that I once had: traveling, walking, thinking, reading, and spending as little time as possible working so as to support simple needs. A baby does not necessarily change such dreams, but its arrival does make for one nervous dreamer.

Ray Robson was born on October 25, 1994, in the US territory of Guam. He came with Typhoon Wilda – storm number 9435 – at 9:30 p.m. He was one of four typhoon babies born that night in Tumon General Hospital. I was the birthing partner, so I was a part of every second of the birth. I cut the cord and was the first to hold our child in his hands. Up to that moment, I had led an interesting life with many highlights and a few firsts. I was the first male child from either side of the family to earn a college degree. I was one of the one-in-ten applicants who was accepted into the Peace Corps, and I was the only person in my family to join. In the Philippines, where I was a volunteer, I lived in a bamboo hut by the side of a river without electricity. At that time, and at other times throughout my years in Asia, I had what some people have never had in their adult lives: time to think about life and time to live life in a very simple manner in a genuine community. I remember one airplane flight, during the middle of my Peace Corps experience, where I thought about what a plane crash would mean. I decided at that time – I was just 23 – that if I had control over the moment, I would choose to die in someone else's place because I had already lived life deeply and that perhaps some of my fellow passengers hadn't yet really lived. How foolish I was! If I could only have looked a short distance into the future, I would have seen that all the best was still to come and that it started with my life with Yee-chen and continued even stronger with the birth of our son. The richest experiences and learnings lay ahead of me.

Ray's birth coincided with the writing of my master's thesis on the thematic and structural connections between the American thinker, Henry Thoreau, and the Chinese philosopher, Lao Tse. I started the program literally days before Ray was conceived and, as I do with all unfinished tasks, I focused on little else but the final goal – in this case, graduation. I traded my full-time job for an adjunct position at the community college, took an overload of classes, and was already working on the thesis before Ray took his first breath. After he was born, I cared for Ray Monday through Friday and also on the weekends while Yee-chen worked at the Chinese school. My own graduate classes and part-time work were in the evenings, and the night owl schedule that I adopted became in sync with Ray's sleepless nights, so that he was able to have a parent hold him or feed him when he couldn't sleep. I wrote my master's thesis in the middle of the night over a period of months with Ray at my side most every night. We took countless midnight drives over Guam's rolling hills, the motion of the car always a calming influence on him. In the daytime, Ray would be restless inside the home. All I ever had to do was to take a chair outside the apartment and sit with him in my lap. He was interested in, and stimulated by, the simplest of things: the movement of cars, the wind blowing, the ever-present butterflies floating past, the sounds of the nearby ocean.

It was the same when he was older and more mobile. When Ray was eight months old, and we were back in Taiwan, his favorite toy was a tissue box. He delighted in pulling tissues out of the box, and the box itself played a central role in his games. For him, it was a car to drive along the apartment floor or a train to chug up and down the mountains of blankets on our bed. If we were outside, he liked to sit on one of the thousands of parked motor scooters found everywhere in the city. He could see the machines darting about the streets every day, and I am sure that he was seeing himself doing the same in his imagination. If he saw some boxes in an alleyway, he liked to pick them up and maneuver them about. He didn't have, or need, a drawer full of plastic toys. He had one stuffed animal given to us by a friend, and he had one big blue plastic ball, another gift from a friend. That is all. One doesn't need a bag full of toys if one has an imagination and a stimulating home environment. Regarding this, I guess that Yee-chen and I were Ray's main toys. I juggled for him, played with him, read to him, and talked with him. Yee-chen gave him her time as well, with the added benefit that she spoke to Ray in Mandarin. What could be more stimulating than the presentation of the world through two disparate languages? How much time and thought and imagination are necessary to puzzle out such an experience?

Our move back to Taiwan, when Ray was not yet one, was based on our new long-term goal. My old goal – backpacking around the world with Yee-chen and living on a shoestring – was replaced by a new family-based goal of moving us eventually to the United States, where Yee-chen could continue to work on her citizenship and where we might be able to provide a more stable home environment for Ray. Of course, in all honesty, part of the reason for our move also had to do with my need to make a major change every two years. After we'd been in Guam for two years, I felt the urge to do something else somewhere else. This feeling was doubly strong because it was accompanied by the completion of something big. Whenever I finish something big – like my two-year Peace Corps contract in the 1980s – I have an urge to go somewhere else and to engage in something totally different. I had just completed a master's degree in Guam, and I wanted to be involved in something else. I rationalized that the year in Taiwan was necessary in order for me to make the kind of money that we would need to fly back to the United States and settle somewhere, but the real reason for our relocation was that I simply felt compelled to move.

In any event, I knew from before that one could make quite a bit of money if one really cared about work, so Taiwan wasn't a bad decision. The goal was clear: make money. And in just a few weeks' time, I was working four jobs at once: writing educational articles for magazines, editing a digest, editing English-language books, and teaching English as a second language at a college. By the end of one year, I had enough money to fly us to the United States, to purchase a US version of the Guam Bomb, and to settle us into a place in Sarasota, Florida.

It is ironic that, aside from our other reasons for settling in the United States, Yee-chen wanted to make the move for educational reasons. She had had such a terrible experience as a student in the tier-driven test-crazy Asian school system that she didn't want her child to go through the same thing. If we hadn't made the move, I guess Ray would today be representing the Republic of China instead of the United States at chess events, and we would be flying to Mainland China, to Singapore, and to Australia for tournaments instead of to Philadelphia, Chicago, and Nevada. The irony, of course, is that now with No Child Left Behind, we have duplicated the Asian system that we sought to escape, while China and other Asian nations have recently adopted a more Western-style form of education that is less focused on testing.

We decided on Florida because it was closest in temperature to what Yee-chen and I had been used to from our years together in Asia and Micronesia. So Ray turned two in sunny Sarasota, and, aside from a few years in Flagstaff, Arizona, where I studied on a doctoral fellowship at Northern Arizona University, we've been in Florida for all of the subsequent years of Ray's life. Not only have we been in one state, but we've been in one house since Ray was six years old. This is home for him, and if Florida wants to claim him as her own, then that's fine with us.

Once we made the US our home, English quickly replaced Ray's Mandarin – this, despite the fact that Yee-chen daily worked with Ray in an effort to maintain his first language. One-hour lessons simply cannot compete with life in this notoriously monolingual society. And once Ray became interested in letters and in reading English books – around the age of three – Mandarin was permanently moved to the shadows. Still, Ray has managed to develop his skills to the point where he can read and write simple Chinese sentences and where he can understand much of the language. Although his pronunciation is good, speaking in general is probably his weakest point. Naturally shy people are slow to speak in public – especially if they think they might make a mistake. I speak of this from experience, and Ray is just as shy as I am and probably even more of a perfectionist (age, when combined with year after year of myriad mistakes, ultimately gives a once-young perfectionist a well-earned margin of error).

Daily lessons in Mandarin did not make up the only part of Ray's education. Most people I meet on the chess circuit assume that Ray has stayed at home his whole life and has, since the age of one or two, spent all of his time studying chess. On the contrary, Ray's spent seven years in various school settings, including a Waldorf school, a public kindergarten, a public center for gifted studies, and a private Montessori school. I had always wanted to work with Ray at home instead of sending him to school. My wife and I were both teachers; Ray could read, calculate, and focus for extended periods at age three; and it just seemed the right plan for him. It wasn't, however, until these past few years that it was possible – both in terms of economics and of time – for us to make the home-school arrangement a viable choice. When I saw that it could work, that's the route we took.

With our present set up, Ray has more time to study chess than before, but he's also free to explore at his own pace other academic interests, such as math (which he has studied online) and reading (which he does at a college level, choosing books from my bookshelf). We learn about history, geography, language, and culture with every chess trip that we take. Mandarin is still a regular course with his mom as teacher, and he gets far more recreation (mostly Ping-Pong, basketball, and tennis these days) than he ever would in a public or private school setting. Only science and art are lacking. I'm not worried about science, however, for K-12 science, as it's generally taught in this country, is mostly done through reading. Ray can do well on a college entrance exam for any subject that's based on reading passages. It will only be a problem if he decides to pursue science as a profession, but, even then, he'll make up the lost time quickly because he knows, through chess, how to study and how to do research. And art? Well, to put it plainly, Ray hates art. Although he's never loved any course at school outside of P.E., art was the only subject that he actually hated. Even in fifth grade, he couldn't get beyond awkward misshapen stick figures; art just wasn't his thing. His greatest joy in being educated at home was not that he would have more time for chess; it was, I think, that he would never have to have another lesson in art.

Regarding his chess studies, I've read in others' accounts that Ray started playing chess as a seven-year-old, as a five-, as a four-, as a three-year-old, and even as an infant, coming out of the womb, I suppose, with a pawn in hand and saying as his first words, "e4". I have discovered that people report what they want to report; in many cases, facts have made no more than guest appearances in chess articles and blog discussions on Ray. We have laughed over many articles and interviews that just don't get it right. For example, in one article, the author had Ray reading one chess book a day for 365 days. In another article, the author had young Ray either defeating or drawing every grandmaster he faced in a tournament.

And then there is Wikipedia: my bane. The problem with Wikipedia is that any idiot can post anything he wants. Someone reads some of the articles with incorrect information on Ray and then posts the information as "facts" on Wikipedia. I used to go onto the site and edit incorrect information until someone – probably the master of misinformation himself – informed me that Wikipedia has a rule prohibiting persons too close to a subject from commenting on it. I suppose that if Wikipedia had been around during Einstein's time, they would have insisted that third and fourth parties alone be allowed to interpret his Theory of Relativity. Perhaps with this work I can, at the very least, counterbalance the body of misinformation and half-truths about my chess-playing son. And, as the saying goes, the best place to begin is at the beginning.

I taught Ray how to play chess when he was three years old. He learned on the flat tiled floor of our kitchen in a condominium in Sarasota, Florida. I'd bought the combination checkers-chess set at a nearby K-mart for a few dollars, thinking that we'd start with checkers and would have the chess to graduate to after some years. However, Ray was drawn immediately to the chess pieces, and it's easy to figure out why. They had interesting shapes: there were horses and castles and teepee-shaped objects. He wanted to know how to play *that* game, so I set up the board and showed him how the pieces moved. I wasn't expecting him to really get it (even though I already knew that he was sharp), but he learned how the pieces moved almost immediately and, when I'd come home from work, I'd find him squatting Asian-style (flat-footed) on the kitchen floor, moving the knights and other pieces around the board and playing out games of his own creation. And he'd challenge me. Every single afternoon, I'd walk through the door and my three-year-old son would look up from the kitchen floor and say, "Baba, do you want to play chess?" Of course I said yes.

So we started playing chess every day, sometimes playing six or more games a day. The games were played quickly and were over when Ray hung a piece (left it unprotected and open to capture) or allowed me to martial my forces into an attack that ended with checkmate. Over the next twelve months, we played hundreds of chess games; I won every one of them. Of course I did. After all, my opponent was a three-year-old child. I was an adult with a couple of degrees and high marks on the logical/analytical section of the old version of the Graduate Record Examination. How could it be otherwise?

PART II

3

If there is something unique about Ray, then it's his perseverance at such a young age. I suppose that most three-year-olds would have given up on a game that they lost ten or twenty times in a row. Ray, however, lost hundreds of consecutive games during the first year that we played chess, but he kept on playing nonetheless. It wasn't that he never got discouraged; instead, it was simply that he loved playing the game, and the more he played and the more he learned, the greater his desire to beat me grew. And I encouraged him. I told him that every day he was getting smarter and better and that he would one day beat me. After our games, I usually went over the things that I saw that Ray missed – where he could have taken a piece or protected a piece; nothing too deep, just helpful hints, for I knew little to nothing about chess theory or strategy. He was a good student, listening to what I said, thinking about it, and sometimes asking questions. And then with his newfound knowledge and with a growing confidence in himself, he'd challenge me again. And again. And again and again. And finally, when he was just four years old, he beat me at chess for the first time.

My own father had it easy. I never beat him at anything until I was nearly a man. What was I to do now that my four-year-old had just beaten me in chess? Yes, I had been encouraging him and telling him that with practice and study he'd get better and beat me . . . but that wasn't supposed to happen for another decade! Despite all that I had learned (or thought that I had learned) about the evils of competition, about life and a gentle path, I was pissed. I remember thinking about the poem, "My Son, My Executioner," and how a father, upon observing his son's growth and development, realizes that the stronger the son gets, the closer to death the father grows. So that was it then; my own mortality was staring at me, shining out from behind the brown eyes of my little boy who celebrated his win by immediately shouting out the news to his mom.

My reaction – quite natural, I believe – was to resist. I began to put even more concentration into the games. I did not intend to lose again, and I played every move to win. Yet I made sure not to take anything away from Ray's accomplishment, and I let my son know clearly and honestly that he had beaten me, that he had made the better moves, and I congratulated him and told him that this was just the first of many wins. Truer words were never spoken.

My resolution to increase my focus and to not drop a game to Ray worked for several weeks, and it had a beneficial effect: it made Ray work harder to beat me and so improved the level of his play. I'd come home from work, and he'd have the chess set out, going over moves or simply playing against himself. He played dozens of solo games a week. His hard work paid off when he eventually beat me a second time, and then a third, and then so many more times that I sadly (yet proudly) stopped counting.

Whenever I had beaten my own father at something, then that was the end of that father-son activity. What's the point in repeatedly arm-wrestling someone who is daily growing in strength while you are daily growing older and weaker? My father could have gone to the gym and worked out more, but if I had done the same, the twenty-year-old would still best the forty-five-year-old; there's no getting around that. Chess, however, is a mind game, and the mind fades less quickly (and less drastically) than the body as one ages. I foresaw years of chess games between my son and myself, and I thought that I could help him by helping myself. Thus, after dropping more and more games to Ray, my next move was to purchase a second-hand introductory chess book written in 1958: Fred Reinfeld's *Chess in a Nutshell*. I needed to improve my game and in so doing, Ray would surely improve his.

We used the book in this way: I read it first, practiced what I'd learned on the board against Ray, and, after I'd won, explained to him the concepts presented in the book that I'd applied in my win. Ray would then apply those same concepts in his games against me, we'd analyze as best as we could, and then I'd read more and start the cycle all over again. What was most beneficial about this method was that, at an early age, Ray learned the advantage of reading and study. The fact that I was the first reader and practitioner of the knowledge (and so winner of the games) was not lost on him. He easily connected study with success. As he was already an avid reader and in possession of an impressive vocabulary developed naturally over years of living with an English-teacher father, Ray had no trouble reading the chess book himself. He read and reread that book every day, moving from page 1 to page 143. He absorbed what was written, memorized it, repeated it out loud, and played it over and over and over again on the chessboard, and soon he was beating me more often. What Ray did with this first book is the secret to his success. He read the words, played out the moves, thought about the moves, and even at this early age questioned what he read. In other words, he improved because he worked hard and he worked well.

4

It was at about the time when Ray was beating me two out of every ten games that we stumbled onto the world of scholastic chess. Ray was in first grade, when he came home one day with a report about a man who had come to the school to talk to the kids about chess. The man, someone from the local chess community, showed the children some basic strategy, told them there was a chess club in the area, and invited them to an upcoming tournament just for kids. Ray was so excited that I promised I'd take him. It would be his first tournament, just five days before his seventh birthday.

Neither of us knew what to expect as we pulled into the parking lot outside of the playing area. I get nervous when I don't know how things work, like when I'm driving through a big city for the first time or when I'm learning a new language. I don't like to make mistakes, but in such novel situations mistakes happen. The chaos that we encountered in the chess hall made a first-time drive through Manhattan seem like a simple task. There were kids of all ages playing games surrounded by dozens of other kids who hovered inches from the board – all talking at the same time, giving advice or criticizing the moves. There were other kids, mostly little ones about Ray's age, running after one another as if on a playground. There were mothers and fathers (some with babies and other non-chess-playing siblings) all about the room. Some parents were in small groups – chess buddies, I guessed, grown familiar after numerous Saturday encounters. Some kids were gathered around pieces of paper taped to various spots on the walls of the room. And in addition to everything else, there was one long line of kids and parents.

Of everything going on in the room, the line seemed the most familiar to me, so that's where we headed. Once we reached the front of the line, I was handed a registration form for Ray and told how much to pay. Pay? I didn't know that chess cost money. What section? I didn't know there were different sections. What rating? I didn't know what a rating was. What was his USCF ID number? He didn't have one. What?! He has to join an organization today to get a number, and I have to pay for that too?! I was beginning to feel overwhelmed, and if I could judge by the closeness with which Ray clung to me, I could tell that he was feeling the same. Still, we were there, so I paid the tournament fee and the USCF (United States Chess Federation) yearly membership fee and nodded in agreement when the man (who turned out to be the tournament director) told me that Ray would play in the K-5 (kindergarten to grade five) section.

Thirty minutes after it was supposed to begin, the director called for all of the kids to get to their boards. We followed the mass of kids who ran to the papers on the walls. I saw that the papers contained lists of names of kids playing in different sections. I kept Ray close so that he wouldn't be elbowed or squashed by the bigger kids who were crowding around the papers. With my 6' height, I was able to find Ray's name over the heads and shoulders of the kids. Beside his name were the letters "UNR" and beside those letters was another boy's name, the number 715, and a board number. We didn't know about the UNR or the 715, so we focused on the board number, found the place, and I stood by Ray until his opponent sat down so that I could make sure that we were in the right spot. When No. 715 arrived, I moved against the wall with the other parents in a place where I could clearly see Ray and where he could see me.

I watched from my spot about 10 feet away as Ray's opponent pulled out a black case from which he extracted a rolled up board, large black and white chess pieces, a big clock, a notepad, a few pencils, and a water bottle. Even though he was just a kid and perhaps no more than a few years older than Ray, he was an imposing figure. He'd come with a professional case, laid out everything expertly, and placed his water bottle in such a manner that I thought that that water bottle was always placed in that very spot game after game. Ray looked over at me several times with questioning, sometimes pleading, eyes. I just shrugged my shoulders as if to say, "I don't know either, Bud," but I also tried to muster an expression of encouragement. The truth, however, was that I was getting nervous like Ray, and, also like Ray, I was wondering, Does he need a notebook, and, if so, what is he supposed to write in it? And what's with the clock? Do you mean that you not only have to move pieces, but you have to tell time as well? I was thinking about the watch I was wearing, and I wondered if Ray could get by with that.

Fortunately, the director gave instructions that addressed most of our fears. The clocks, we learned, were to be set so that each player had 30 minutes in which to make his moves. Ah, so one clock gives the time for both players. Good. Ray doesn't need my watch now. Players who had a high rating were expected to notate the game, but it wasn't a requirement for unrated players. So that's what the notepad was for. And the "UNR" must mean "unrated," and Ray's opponent's rating must be 715. Round Two (of five rounds) was to begin at 11:30. Five rounds? Wow! This last was a surprise, but at least other things were beginning to make sense and seem not so overwhelming. I still had questions, though. How did a player get a rating? And what kind of a rating was 715? Was a higher number better or, like in golf, was a lower number better? I had no clue. At any rate, I didn't have much time to ponder those questions or to seek answers because the players were instructed to shake hands and begin the game.

The clock was started, and the first moves were made. After Ray's first move, however, No. 715 just sat and stared at the board with an amused look on his face. I couldn't figure out what was going on, and I wouldn't have been able to explain things to my equally confused son even if I had been allowed to talk with him during the game. I felt that Ray was doing something wrong, but I just couldn't figure out what it was. After several minutes, a man who was standing right beside me and who had been watching the same game walked to the table and whispered something to No. 715 and immediately the boy told Ray to hit a button on the clock. The man, No. 715's father, returned to my side and told me that he knew that Ray was a novice and that he didn't think it was fair for his boy to win on time. So, if the 30 minutes run out, you lose. I had just learned more. I thanked the father and said apologetically that neither Ray nor I knew anything about clocks or notations or ratings.

The game ended after a short while – 10, maybe 15, minutes. Ray was checkmated. I watched as No. 715 put out his hand, and Ray shook it. Ray walked over to me, but I sent him right back to help put away his opponent's equipment, and so he cheerfully helped re-pack the professional-looking set. We had time before Round Two, so we went outside, took a little walk, and talked about the game. I told Ray not to worry because it was his first game. I told him to just try his best and have fun. I said we'd stay for another game if he wanted but that I wanted to go home soon because our friends were coming over for a visit, and I hadn't planned on staying very long.

Ray wanted to stay for another game, so at the appropriate time, we fought our way to the wall chart (experts already) and found the appropriate board. His second opponent's rating was 268, but this information didn't help us, for we still didn't know if that meant that he was better or worse than No. 715. At any rate, the game began, and a few minutes later, it ended. Another checkmate. Ray's second loss.

On the way home, I told Ray not to be discouraged, that the kids with ratings had more experience and that with practice he'd soon be winning games too. I told him that I was sorry that we couldn't stay longer, that I had no idea there would be five rounds and that the tournament wouldn't end until after 5:00. I said next time we'd stay longer. Ray understood. I could tell that he would have liked to have played more games, to try for that first win, but he knew that we'd be back, just as he knew that he'd be better prepared for the next one. He'd see to that himself.

5

One needs more than intelligence to excel in a game, a sport, or life; one needs focus and determination. Even at ages 2 and 3, Ray had focus. If he was interested in something, he could patiently work at it for hours on end. I remember that his fascination with numbers began at an early age, and over several months, he familiarized himself with numbers by counting. When he reached unfamiliar territory, he asked me for help. "Baba, what comes after 29?" When he had the names and patterns down for two-digit numbers, we went through the same process for numbers with three digits, four digits, etc. His goal was to keep on counting as far as he could.

When he entered kindergarten at age 4, Ray was still fascinated by numbers and often did his calculations while doing some of his lessons in class. His teacher called me in to discuss the matter. I knew what she was worried about, but I wasn't concerned because . . . well, because I am a counter too. I count steps. I also count the letters in the words on signs that I pass by when driving and find the midpoint of each word. When I was younger, I even counted seconds, eventually turning it into a subconscious process whereby at any moment of the day I could tell the time accurately within five minutes.

I knew from personal experience that there were a great many benefits to having this characteristic, such as attention to detail and the ability to focus intensely – not to mention lower electric bills and a secure house at night. These skills are essential when one lives in my home, where my wife is a human "ON" switch. In the morning, I follow Yee-chen from room to room, turning off each light that she leaves on. In addition to lights, I have either turned off or closed fans, televisions, stove burners, drawers, cabinets, computers, faucets, garden hoses, showers, refrigerators, tea pots, ovens, front doors, side doors, back doors, car doors, garage doors – in short, anything that has a switch, a knob, or a handle. So I wasn't worried about Ray; in fact, I was looking forward to the assistance.

In addition, I saw that Ray's counting branched into addition, subtraction, multiplication, etc. and noted that he was already well ahead of his classmates in mathematical ability. Equally important was the fact that he was genuinely interested in numbers and math, and, indirectly, in patterns. Although I didn't know this at the time, all of this would benefit him as he studied chess, learned opening moves, and understood the geometry of the board. To placate his teacher, however, I told Ray to do his counting, but to do it silently until he got home.

He had the same intensity when it came to reading. When he started, he threw himself into it, reading everything in the house, everything we brought from the library, and reading every sign, cereal box, poster – whatever – that his eyes passed over. Even as a four-year-old, he could sit quietly and focus for extended periods on a book. His interest in reading in general was later replaced by a fascination with the arrangement of the letters and this, in turn, moved him towards spelling. He would ask me over and over to give him spelling tests. "Ask me to spell a word," he would say, and if he misspelled a word, I only had to correct him once. We'd sometimes do the spelling games at home, but usually we did them when we were out in the car – on our way to a fishing hole or off to the market. Wherever and whenever didn't matter much: it was always a good time to practice.

At the time, what I did seemed the natural course to take; however, I realize today how very important my actions were. Instead of playing the spelling game over and over with Ray, I could have shut him down completely by saying something like, "Why don't you just watch TV for a while?" Instead of encouraging him, I could have stifled his creativity and his fascination with the manipulation of numbers by giving him a pill. I wonder how many kids have been switched off in the midst of some genuinely creative process? As it turned out for us, when Ray was old enough for school, he was soon identified as gifted and put in an accelerated program. Even in the accelerated program, he was in a class by himself. By the time that we took him out of school – after fifth grade – he had been teaching himself math for the last few years. He had other skills too. Between the ages of 12 and 14, Ray edited all of his mother's assignments for the graduate program that she was enrolled in. This is what happens when a child is supported in his interests and is allowed to develop at his own pace.

I mentioned fishing above. Most people who know about Ray probably imagine that he's some sort of a non-athletic human chess program. Or perhaps, when they read about him on the Internet, they imagine that he's an average kid who happens to have one special talent: chess. But that's not Ray. Ray loves all sports and is a fierce competitor. Our Ping-Pong matches in the garage are on the scale of intergalactic warfare. Screams, shouts, and trash-talk come from both ends of the table. I come up with shots that move Ray from one side of the table to the other, and he does everything short of diving onto the cement floor to get the ball back. It's the same when we play net-less badminton on the street in front of our house, where just about any shot is considered "in" and it's up to the opponent to get to the birdie. The badminton games are far better for us than the Ping-Pong because no one keeps score. Neither one of us can stand to lose to the other, and it makes for a more agreeable dinner when we both sit at the table as winners.

In addition to what we always did at home, Ray played sports when he was still in school: cross-country, soccer, and flag football. Since leaving school, he's taken classes in yoga, tai chi, and, most recently, tennis. In addition to the sports, he's always read daily and studied Chinese each night with his mother. I think that the multiple activities that Ray has participated in have enhanced his ability at the chessboard, for he has been stimulated in a number of ways that have all led to good physical and intellectual health. And so when Ray came to study chess, he already possessed key qualities of a good student: interest, self-motivation, physical and intellectual health, concentration, determination, stamina, a good vocabulary, good reading comprehension, and the support of his parents. I point this out because Ray soon jumped multiple levels in chess ability with few chess-related aids. All that he had were games with one average player (i.e., his dad) and one introduction-to-chess book.

* * *

After finishing in last place in his first tournament in October of 2001, Ray used his two resources to prepare for the future: he studied his chess book more carefully and played dozens of games with me to test what he'd learned. Yet another resource came in the form of a few basic skills lessons that a local chess tutor presented at Ray's elementary school. As a part of the latter presentations, there were informal games among the students, so he got to practice against others besides me. This last was most beneficial because Ray had already begun to see patterns in my own play; he knew where I was most likely to move in particular positions. He needed to see different styles, and that's just what he got from the games at his school.

Ray's hard work paid off in the form of 9 wins out of the 10 tournament games that he played in over the next few months, in addition to an undefeated record against the chess club kids at his elementary school. During these months, he seemed to be improving on an hourly basis. He was also soon winning more games against me – 3 or 4 wins out of every 10 games. By the time that he was seven, Ray was winning at least as many games as I was, and it was obvious that he would soon pass me by. I was reflecting on this one day, and it occurred to me that maybe I should find a chess tutor for Ray. I mean, if he could do so much with so little, what could he accomplish with more (and better) support, someone with a more extensive knowledge of chess than I had? This wouldn't be a quick decision for me, for I had been Ray's main educator in nearly everything since he could walk and talk. I wasn't sure if I was willing to put his education into the hands of another.

While I was struggling with the decision to hire a tutor, one of the things I did was to learn more about the rating system and where Ray stood in relation to others in the chess world. When I struggle over a question, I have a habit of thinking about it and very little else until I come to a conclusion. I am not comfortable with unresolved issues. To answer my questions, I seek out as much information as I can – items directly related to the decision and even peripheral items – and I include everything into a goulash-like mental mix. I then mentally stir and stir and stir this mix through waking and sleeping hours until I know how to act. Ray's rating was probably a peripheral piece at this time, but I considered it anyway.

After the initial tournament, where Ray lost to two players, his first official chess rating was 120. In order to get a sense of what that meant, I searched the United States Chess Federation's (USCF) website and found that players were categorized in the following way:

Rating	**Rank**
* 3 GM Norms	Grandmaster (GM)
3 IM Norms	International Master (IM)
2200 –	National Master (NM)
2000 – 2199	Expert
1800 – 1999	Class A
1600 – 1799	Class B
1400 – 1599	Class C
1200 – 1399	Class D
1000 – 1199	Class E
800 – 999	Class F
600 – 799	Class G
400 – 599	Class H
200 – 399	Class I
100 – 199	Class J
	Unrated

* A player earns a norm after achieving a certain level of play against other top players.

Ray looked to have an Everest-like climb ahead of him. He was, in fact, at the bottom of the list. Even after his 10-game winning streak and a bump in rating up to 677, Ray was much closer to the bottom than to the top.

I used the chart, and Ray's place on it, to further motivate him. I told Ray that after just a few tournaments, he was already moving up the chart, and that with more practice and continued success, he would shoot up the chart in no time. And when he asked, "Do you think I'll ever be a master?" I replied without hesitation, "Yes, you will be a master." His next question was, of course, "When?" I said what I always said when Ray asked this question. When will you beat me at basketball? When will you run faster than me? When will you become a master in chess? The answer to each of these questions was the same: "It all depends on how hard you work and on how well you work."

It's noteworthy that Ray asked the "master" question in the first place. It shows that he was already thinking ahead and aiming high, and, as Thoreau said, "In the long run men hit only what they aim at." Better for Ray that he was aiming so high, overcoming fears and doubts of failing miserably. And if failure was limited to the lazy, then Ray had nothing to fear; he proved by his actions over the next several weeks and months that he was determined to improve. My response to Ray's question is also worth noting. I wasn't trying to boost my son's ego with my words; I genuinely meant it. I knew from the time that Ray was three that he was an exceptional child – that he could master things quickly and understand at a deep level. So it doesn't strike me as odd that after only three tournaments my son was asking about being a chess master, and I was telling him matter-of-factly that he would be one.

I decided that the best way that I could help Ray was to continue to support him psychologically; to continue to be his training partner (or, as was more often the case, his punching bag) through dozens and dozens of games played from the time I got home from work until Ray went to bed, every day, for week after week; and to provide for him whatever tools seemed necessary. The one book and a father's support seemed enough for a while, but in February of 2002, when Ray was 7 years old, I had finally stirred the mix long enough and come to the conclusion that I needed to add another ingredient. Now that Ray was beating me more and more frequently, I finally decided that it would be best to put him in the hands of someone who played better than I did.

Why did I wait so long to allow him to work with another? I was Ray's first teacher, and I would have liked to remain his only teacher. Part of it was ego. I didn't want to admit to myself or to Ray that I could no longer help him. To him, I was the smartest person in the world. I could answer every math question, spell any word, and figure out how to fix whatever got broken. Added to this was my own personality quirk of wanting to do everything on my own; I hate having to rely on anyone else. This attitude has its benefits, for over the years I have learned to work with tools, fix cars, and solve a number of problems on my own without the expense and without the (oftentimes inept) services of another. One more item to throw into this mix is that I was a damn good teacher. I knew how to illustrate the main ideas from the book for Ray; I could devise sample problems on the chessboard for him; and I could analyze positions and variables fairly deeply. But the fact remained that Ray's ability was increasing at a disproportionately fast rate, and he was beginning to ask the kinds of questions about tactics and theory that I couldn't answer without becoming a full-time student of chess myself. I so much loved working with Ray and our new life in chess that I seriously considered this last option. Why I couldn't do it takes a little explanation and perhaps will reveal more about our family and how we function.

Part of our reason for moving from Asia and Micronesia to the United States was that it seemed to be the environment that might offer the best future possibilities for Ray and also for Yee-chen, and anything that was good for Ray and Yee-chen – that would add to their happiness or security – would also be good for me. As the one who was fluent in English and who knew his way around, it was up to me to secure the job that would pay our bills. And because this wasn't Asia, where I could find a cheap and simple place for us to live and where I could support us with minimal labor, I had to give up on some economically shaky jobs that I thought might be more fun to hold. For example, before returning to teaching, I tried out as an environmental activist, where I would have the responsibility of educating persons in various neighborhoods about environmental issues close to home – the pollution of a river, the plan to sell off park land to an industry, etc. What I particularly liked about the job was that it involved walking from door to door all afternoon. I would have all of that time in between homes and neighborhoods to walk and to think. The pay, however, would not sustain a family of three – not even a family that was living very simply, with combined material goods that could be contained in three suitcases.

I also pursued what I considered to be an ideal job for me: a mailman with a walking route with all the time I desired to think my thoughts and to analyze to whatever depths I could manage. I took the postal exam – which appeared to be nothing more than a test of one's ability to memorize a number of objects as quickly as possible – and my score put me at the top of the list. I found out when I received the first postal job offer, just a short time after taking the test, that all new employees were part time only and had to supply their own vehicle for the first year. The part-time work without benefits killed it for me; in a country such as this one, one should not live without health insurance or a regular source of income. And this is how I ended up as a teacher in the United States, and it was from a job as a middle-school teacher that I returned home to find my son on the kitchen floor, waiting all day to challenge his dad to a game of chess.

I managed to teach in Bradenton, Florida, for two years until a recurring "ailment" kept me from continuing. I guess the best name for this disease from which I suffer is "Peace Corps-itis"; it is characterized by the inability of a former Peace Corps Volunteer to be satisfied with any job for more than two years. Symptoms include an unrealistic and unrelenting desire to do something else, someplace else. I picked up this bug in the Philippines in the 1980s, and it was still with me, stronger than ever, a decade later. All I can say is that – by the end of 1998, my second year of teaching in Manatee County – I could not stop thinking about doing something else somewhere else. As always happens in these situations, something else somewhere else appeared – this time in the form of a doctoral fellowship at Northern Arizona University in Flagstaff, Arizona.

We had just reached the point where we had enough savings to consider buying a small home – the final piece of the security that Yee-chen, as a woman with a young child, desired more than anything else. We had been married long enough for her to know that I cared less about the doctorate itself than I did about doing something different somewhere else. She said, rightly so, that the degree would mean something to anyone else but that I would probably end up teaching high school or something similar. Still, I had become so enthusiastic and positive about the opportunity to do something different that I was able to win out and move us all to Flagstaff – 7000 feet up and everything that Sarasota wasn't: rural, cold, and surrounded by mountains, lakes, and hiking trails.

I completed my doctoral degree in good time – just under two years in fact – for three reasons: I have always been able to focus deeply on a task and give all of myself to it; the fellowship, which was initially designed for three years, turned into a two-year fellowship; and Peace Corps-itis kicked in. It was in the kitchen of our tiny unit in the family housing quad where Ray, as a four-year-old, beat me in chess for the first time. A decade later, he still remembered the game and how he doubled his rooks in an attack which he says I could have escaped from had I seen the right move. I, too, can see his doubled rooks bearing down on my king, but I remember even better how he joyfully shouted the news of his win to his disbelieving mama. My dissertation and work duties at the university did not keep me from playing chess with Ray every week. I also made the time to teach him how to ride his bike without training wheels, to teach him how to throw and hit a baseball, to play catch with a football, to go hiking and camping dozens of times, and to go fishing at a nearby lake. When you want to share something with someone, it doesn't matter how busy you are: you find the time or you make the time. That's all there is to it.

After becoming Dr. Robson, I moved us back to Florida. The move back exhausted the little savings that remained from my two years as a graduate student. In fact, I had to take cash off of a credit card in order to buy a suit for an interview and to pay for our first month's rent in an apartment. The money was well spent because I got the job – at a local university – and in almost no time we had enough money for the down payment on a house of our own in Seminole, Florida.

I took a winding route, but I have brought us back to where I started: why I struggled with the decision to pursue my own studies in chess so that I could continue to be Ray's teacher. Although we all enjoyed Flagstaff – particularly the family hiking and camping trips – we were there for me. Yee-chen had put off having a home for an extra two years, and it was time for me to do something for her. By February of 2002 – the time when I was struggling with the decision to get a chess tutor for

Ray – we were less than one year into a 15-year mortgage on our "new" 30-year-old house. My job at the college was the only way we had of chipping away at the mortgage while paying the rest of the bills at the same time. The job that I held in the winter of 2002 was administrative in nature – practically identical to sales – and I hated it. It ate up too much of my time and energy and gave me nothing back aside from money. But, in truth, and this is contrary to everything I had ever believed up to that moment in my life, money was what we needed at that time. Yee-chen and Ray both deserved a home, and that is what I gave them. The decision also meant that it was time for me to see what someone else could do to help my son progress in chess.

So I hired a tutor, but, of course, I never gave up entirely. Like Thoreau, the most influential of my deceased mentors, I continued to work on improving myself. I sat in on every lesson, studied our chess book on my own when I had a few free minutes, and put more of my energy into this game that my son loved so much, so that even though I would no longer be his only teacher, I would still be an integral part of the process.

6

"How many a man has dated a new era in his life from the reading of a book" (Henry David Thoreau). Over the next several months, I began to add to Ray's "library of one" by purchasing from second-hand bookstores books on strategy, tactics, opening theory, endgame, and whatever else I could find. And Ray, as with his first text, studied these new books from cover to cover every day over and over again. He was now rarely without a chess book. If we just drove to the post office and back (no more than fifteen minutes for the round-trip), he would still grab a chess book and read it – lines of play and all – as if it were a novel.

A page from the old chess books that we had looks something like this: 1. P-K4, P-QB4; 2. Kt-KB3, P-K3; 3. P-Q4, PxP; 4. KtxP, Kt-KB3; etc., where the first letters stand for chess pieces and the letters/numbers stand for the 64 squares on a chessboard so that P-K4 represents the movement of a pawn to the K4 square on the board. There are pages and pages of these moves with a few illustrations of key positions along with very little annotation. In order to make any sense of a 50-move game, one would either need an illustration showing the position of the pieces after each move, or else one would need a chessboard at one's side on which to play out the moves. I discovered during our drives that Ray had a chessboard in his mind and that he was able to play out the moves he was reading on this mental board of his, keeping track of where the pieces were even in complicated positions.

I always thought that I was the one in the family who had a great memory. Yee-chen, in perfect Zen fashion, begins each day with no knowledge at all of what she said or did the day before. She is notorious in our family for not being able to remember . . . anything! I, on the other hand, can recall in detail dreams that I had as a seven-year-old, conversations from 20+ years back, or the words to any song that I have ever sung at least once all the way through. My Achilles's heel, and this is something that Ray has no patience with, pertains to sports games: for some reason, I cannot recall the details of any game I have watched on TV. Ray will say, correctly but with too much sarcasm, "The 76ers are playing the Celtics again. You won't remember this, but this was a great game that we already watched last year." I always answer his jab at my memory weakness with what I believe is the perfect response: "Great! I get to watch it again, and it will be as if I'm watching it for the first time!"

Aside from this memory lapse, I really do have an exceptional memory and I am, in fact, the keeper of the family history: all of the dates, the trips, and the details of each trip are in my mind. I can tell Yee-chen what I said to her on our first day together 18 years ago. I can remind her when it is our anniversary, when it is her birthday, and also how old she is. However, I cannot do anything like what Ray is able to do with the chessboard. Ray is able to keep track of all of the movements of the 32 pieces on the 64 squares regardless of how jumbled these pieces become in the course of a game of chess. Most people can keep seven objects in mind with some effort. We need visual aids, notes, and mnemonic devices to keep track of more than this. I am getting so used to the unusual things that Ray can do that I have to remind myself that mentally keeping track of 32 interchangeable objects on 64 squares is really remarkable.

* * *

With more books at his disposal, hours of practice per day with his dad, and one hour per week of basic skills instruction with his Expert-level instructor, Ray began to tear up the local scholastic scene during his first year on the "tour" as a first grader. After less than a dozen events, Ray's rating was 1188: a solid Class E player. At this point, I felt that Ray needed even more support to move up another level, and I decided to create a new plan for Ray. My first act – part one of the new plan – was to cut his tutor, for it soon became clear to me that the student was going to catch, and then pass, the tutor.

Ray's first paid tutor, a local expert, was a likable man. He had a sharp wit that sometimes included jokes or comments best heard by adults alone, but he never said anything around Ray that made me cringe. Ray definitely liked the expert, and spending an hour with him was one of his favorite weekly activities. We would drive down to the local chess club after I got home from work, and I would sit right beside Ray so that, in effect, two of us were getting a lesson for the price of one. Of course, I let the expert and Ray do all of the talking during the lesson; however, on the way home, I would go back over the lesson with Ray, focusing on what I thought to be the most important parts.

Although the expert didn't show anything new to Ray – nothing that wasn't in our first chess book – he was invaluable in that he could be asked questions directly. The best chess authors are able to anticipate readers' questions, but they can never anticipate all of the questions that a student needs answered. Also, the expert recommended books and encouraged Ray to read and study. He was definitely a positive influence on Ray, and he helped to move him to another level. One of the most useful parts of each lesson – and probably the one that Ray enjoyed the most – was when Ray and the expert sparred. Since Ray was playing in the K-5 section of scholastic events, he never had the chance to play an expert-level player. I think that part of what motivated Ray to work so hard between the one-hour weekly sessions was his desire to beat his instructor in these short mini-matches at the end of each lesson. After 20 hours of instruction, when the student had drawn the tutor a few times, I knew it was already time to move on.

Dropping a tutor is a hard thing to do. To the tutor, the parent is automatically the villain. The question that is always asked is why. *Why are you dropping me?* And there is no easy way to tell someone that you think another person would do his job better. This is basically the message that is received by the tutor no matter how gently and skillfully the message is delivered. The expert was extremely hurt when we moved on. Ray was his best student – a kid who actually listened to what he said, thought about it, worked on his game, and came back an improved player every week. Ray read when asked to read, studied when asked to study, and always came to the session prepared. In the expert's eyes, Ray was the kind of student that comes around once in a lifetime. I can only hope that the expert – along with the others we have worked with and then replaced – can look at Ray's progress as a chess player, and, more importantly, his progress as a human being, and realize that Ray is as good as he is today because of the decisions that we made. I hope that all of his former tutors can see that they played an important role during the time that they worked with him, and I hope that that is enough for them – to have been part of his development, a part of the process. It doesn't matter what they think of me; it is always about Ray and what I can do to help him. The expert served as a complement to what Ray was learning from his self-study at home, but Ray now needed "more." It took some trial-and-error over the next several months to figure out what that "more" should consist of.

Part two of the new plan came directly from part one: find another tutor who could go beyond where the first one had left off. Until I found a replacement, I took on the role of tutor. I had more time for this role – and to improve myself as a player – because I'd left my administrative job at the university to return to public school teaching. In so doing, I had fulfilled Yee-chen's prediction that a doctorate would be wasted on me. She had it right – all the way down to the high school teaching job.

The doctorate that I had earned in Flagstaff before returning to Florida had prepared me for a role in academia, but I wasn't cut out for suits and big offices and meetings about student enrollment and how to generate money. Lao Tse and Thoreau (friends from my early twenties) were screaming at me during those days, and I finally listened to them and gave up what seemed to be my best shot at financial security. If I care deeply about something, then I am your man to hire. The reverse is also true: if I don't care about something, then there is simply no way that I can do that thing for very long, and I certainly will not do it very well. I took the position at the university and kept it for as long as I did – no more than two years (of course!) – because my wife deserved a home and because I wanted to give one to her. Once we had the home and I knew exactly how much we needed each month to pay the mortgage and the other bills, it was an easy decision to take a $15,000 pay cut in order to return to a more meaningful job – something, at least, that I could care about. Working with humans to help them in some way is something that I can care about; money, business, and profits – and all of the people and tasks associated with them – well, none of that is for me. While I did give up a portion of our security, one thing that I got in return was invaluable: more time with Ray. I had an entire month before the school year started, and I spent much of those days playing chess with Ray and helping him to understand the books we'd picked up.

Still another part of the new plan for Ray was to increase the library, which we did by visiting used book stores on our own and also with the help of Ray's grandparents who picked up books and sent them to us. It is true that most of these books were written in the 1950s and 1960s and contained a lot of chess lines that had subsequently been refuted. Still, there was much to be learned from these old books. At the very least, we had dozens of games played by masters to study, and some of the games had detailed annotations which allowed us to see what a master focused on in his own games. Also, even if the books were outdated, by studying them, Ray would still have an edge over most players his age. I don't think there could've been more than a handful of children going into second grade who were daily studying from chess books, regardless of when they were written.

With a few dozen more (and newer) books on chess theory and tactics, Ray was soon spending a minimum of 25 hours a week studying chess on his own. He was reading everything we found and analyzing masters' games every day. The study time had nothing to do with my plan; instead, that was Ray's own doing. I never had to tell him to study chess. I'd come home from work, and he'd have a position set up on the board – one that he'd worked out himself – and he'd ask me to find mate in two, or he'd tell me to find the pin (when one moves a piece to a place that prevents his opponent from moving a piece or risk losing material) or find the fork (when one moves a piece to a place that attacks two pieces simultaneously), etc. He was using the books he had as a springboard for creative thought. In the end, it all added up to mastery, and the mastery led to success.

All that I needed to do was to show interest in what my child was doing, to try to solve the puzzles that he created for me, and to talk with him about that which he loved. How easy such things were for someone who already enjoyed spending time with his son more than anything else.

* * *

When the 2002/2003 school year started, Ray and I both went back to school. He began Grade Two, and I revisited my years as a Peace Corps Volunteer by returning to the classroom to teach non-native speakers of English. Now that I was home earlier and free on every weekend, I had more time – not to mention more energy – to take Ray to chess tournaments. It was during the next four months, while Ray was still playing in mostly scholastic events, that I learned what I was like as a chess parent.

During any given round, I stand as if on a perch, hawk-like, in various positions about the room eyeing my chess child. I cannot read or write while the game is on. Even if I remained outside of the playing hall, my thoughts would be too locked on the battle inside to allow me to concentrate on anything else. I stand and watch entire games from as close to the board as the tournament director will allow me. I shut down bodily functions and remain standing motionless and expressionless in one or two spots watching my child's game for hours. At such times, I am reminded of a line from *Siddhartha*, one of my favorite books. Siddhartha was asked what it was that he could do – what his special talents were – and he replied, "I can think, I can wait, I can fast." When I am watching Ray play chess, all that I can do is think of the myriad possibilities of the game in progress. There is nothing else that I need to do; I can wait for as long as it takes, and I become unaware of the passage of time even. I control bodily desires and bodily functions: I do not eat, I do not drink, I do not go to the bathroom. It is nothing that I attempt; it is just how it is. I find a place, and that is where I stay. Ray looks up and expects to see me there, and that is where I am. I simply cannot do anything else. I've tried reading, but I end up reading the same page several times, and even then not comprehending what I've read. Occasionally, I've jotted off a disjointed letter to a friend, but the letters often focus on the chess game being played, so it's as if I wasn't really free from the game.

At one of Ray's first tournaments, I noticed that he was frequently looking up from his game to stare at me. I thought that I might be making him nervous, so I walked outside and waited until the end of the round. After the game, when he found me outside, he asked me why I wasn't watching. He said that he liked me to watch, that he liked it when he looked up and saw me in the room. Those words were just as good as, perhaps better than, "I love you," and I have remained in the room within visual range ever since.

It's a powerfully strong feeling for me to see my son battling on his own a few feet away. There's nothing I can say or do to assist him. I have to watch and hope that he'll be successful. When he's down a piece and fighting back, my eyes are riveted to the board. What will happen next? Will his opponent fall into the trap he's just set, or will he play his Knight to h5 and spoil the whole thing? When I'm watching, I try to read Ray's mind. I study the board and think about what I would play, and when Ray plays something else (which he usually does) I try to figure out why he played it – why his move was better than mine. Once I do this, I then look at his opponent's options and try to find his best moves, or I'll find blunders for the opponent and begin to hope that he'll make the bad moves. It feels like I am living for a few hours through my son, but I still know who is who. He's put in the hours; he's read the books; he's the one sitting at the chess table battling another. He's the star, and I am the cheerleader. For me, a chess match featuring my child is as exciting as being courtside for the seventh game of the NBA finals – even more exciting, for one of the stars of the event will be riding home with me that night.

7

As soon as Ray learned what it meant to be a master – someone who had a superior understanding of the game – he began working toward a number. The magic number that separates a master from the rest of the world is 2200. To reach that number, Ray would have to move from beating the lower-rated children at the scholastic tournaments to matching or defeating masters in tournament play. In order to make this greater goal less daunting, I worked with Ray to develop intermediary goals.

The first of these goals was for Ray to become the number one player in his grade (he was in second grade then) both in Florida and in the United States. This, I thought, was manageable, for at 1188 (Ray's rating at the end of the summer of 2002), there were not many ahead of him, either in the state or in the country. And considering the consistently upward path that he was moving in as a result of his study habits, I thought he'd make both goals within a reasonable amount of time. To Ray's questions about "when," I had the same response: "It all depends on how hard you work, Bud."

Of course, in order to get the rating points, it meant that Ray would have to play in tournaments, so a second goal developed: hit as many events as possible. I figured that the more exposure Ray had to different styles of play, the more he could learn. And with Ray, the more he "could" learn was nearly always synonymous with the more he "would" learn. So over the next year, we began increasing the number of events until at one point we were going somewhere almost every weekend.

I watched Ray's progress firsthand, and I observed his study habits daily. He was intelligent, he was motivated, and he was focused. He was poised at the board, and unlike many of the kids – even the top kids – he was rarely distracted. After his improvement over the course of the last year, others began to watch him along with the regular scholastic stars, and many parents commented to me about Ray's ability to attend to what he was doing and to seem oblivious to distractions. He was focused and sitting up straight concentrating at the board for several minutes; he stood out among the other kids who were staring at the games next to them or even walking around the room between moves. I just saw something in him at such times that made me feel with certainty that he was going to be one of the best. His recent excellent performance and his rapid rise in the ratings supported that feeling. Regarding the latter, after just a few dozen tournaments he was well above nearly everyone whom he had played earlier that year. Success wasn't somewhere in the beyond; it was in the house.

As we moved into a new scholastic year, I began to think about what else I could do to help Ray to continue in his upward path. I decided, once more, to turn to an outside tutor. This time, however, I sought out a master, one whose rating and ability were well above Ray's first tutor. I wanted to see if Ray's work ethic and serious approach would be aided by working once every week or two with a genuine master. Even though, as before, the lessons would only be for a few hours a month to Ray's 100+ hours of self-study, they might still prove to be a useful supplement.

With sporadic outside assistance, his dad for a punching bag, a growing library, his regular devotion to study, and a tournament nearly every weekend to learn from, Ray was soon meeting his goals and needing replacements. We could best gauge his progress by his tournament results. Between September and May, Ray played in events in St. Petersburg, Sarasota, Miami, Tampa, Boca Raton, Orlando, Odessa, Ft. Lauderdale, Clermont, Gainesville, and Cocoa Beach. As I was mastering Florida's highway system, Ray was doing the same with the local talent. Along the way, Ray graduated from the beginner's section, moved into the K-5 section, continued on to the K-12 section, and finally came to a stop at the end of the line: the adult section. As soon as Ray showed promise in one section, I played him up. I thought that he would learn more by playing tougher opponents; one doesn't improve by beating up on novices. And Ray, to his credit, was never trophy-hungry. Certainly he was happy to bring home a big trophy, but he was always more interested in playing better, and so, for example, he just nodded his head when I said that once he made it to the K-12 section, he would have more losses until he got better. And when he did get better, he agreed that it was time to tackle the adult events.

And as Ray played up and got better, his rating increased rapidly. By September, he was a Class D player; by February of 2003, Ray was the number one ranked 8-year-old in Florida as well as the number one ranked second-grader in the United States; and by May, he was on the verge of becoming a Class B player. To reach such heights, Ray had to move from defeating the top-ranked elementary kids to defeating the teenagers and the adults. Once he began playing with the latter two crowds, he was faced with a new set of lessons.

Ray had his first experience playing against bigger kids at a tournament in Miami. He played uncharacteristically poorly, and I learned during the tournament that the main reason was that he felt intimidated by the older/bigger opponents. He was assuming that older or bigger meant better. The problem was clear, so I began working with him on being confident against any opponent. My task was to make Ray believe as strongly as I did that he could beat anyone. I didn't have to look far to find a convincing example. "Remember when we used to play," I said. "I used to crush you every game. But then you got better, and you beat me. You really beat me." He got the point. It helped that he thought that I was the smartest guy in the room because if he could beat me – and how he could beat me! – then he could easily see himself beating anyone. That was what I had hoped would happen, and that's just what did happen. He started with the teens at the smaller tournaments and then graduated to beating adults of all ages at a variety of events.

I always knew that Ray was going to be an exceptional player. I knew that he would continue to improve, just as I knew that one day he would be number one in the state and in the country, yet still I always marveled when he did what he did: when he went undefeated in only his third tournament; when as a seven-year-old he drew or beat the high-school Goliaths; when he won a K-5 scholastic event with less than a year's experience in tournament play; when he tied for first in a K-12 section just a few weeks later; when he had back-to-back wins over Top 100 youths; and, just a short time later, when he won four out of five games against players who were all rated well above him. Before every game of every tournament, I told Ray in convincing language that he could beat whomever he played, that he was going to do well regardless of the rating or experience of his opponent, but despite my own words, he always amazed me with his success.

I guess part of the amazement came from the fact that Ray had been so consistently successful with very few setbacks. And part of it was that he seemed so domineering at the board, so fearless, so composed – even against the adults. Yes, he would look up from the board to see if I was watching him and to simply reassure himself that I was near at hand. But when he played, he was a part of that board. His eyes were locked on the pieces, darting from one imagined combination to another, moving up to stare into his opponent's face, into his eyes, to discern his secrets, to seek answers to silent questions about weaknesses. And when he moved, he moved with authority. When he picked up a piece, he knew where it was going and why it was going there. He would often fold his legs under himself so that he could sit up higher and see the board better, but even when he sat regularly, his small and skinny child's body seemed the dominant one at the table. I think that's part of it: you could just see that he was there to win. Maybe that's why one of the adult players at an event said to me, "It just feels right when Ray wins."

He carried a confidence about him that was genuine, nothing affected about it. Very early in his career, I had taught Ray how a confidence backed up by good moves could unnerve a scholastic opponent. How much more, then, was the pressure on the men who were my age and older? And more pressure still when there would be crowds watching the little boy in the adult section who was holding his own against a man who'd been playing chess for 20 or more years! In any event, Ray's continued improvement and success during the 2002/2003 academic year made me realize that what I had been telling Ray again and again was true: that he was an exceptional player who was only going to get better.

What it all boiled down to, I thought, was that Ray loved the game. There was no better way to describe it. He'd worked so hard, paid attention during chess lessons, had played so well and improved so quickly, and had spent hours each day studying chess books. His love of the game moved him to throw himself into it; his studies resulted in successes over the board; and his play had brought attention to himself. He had become – on a local level – a chess celebrity. By the end of grade two, kids and adults regularly watched his games and followed his progress. He was becoming the mark to shoot for. "He wants to play like Ray." That's a comment I was beginning to hear often at the events. Older kids and adults he'd played were greeting him at tournaments. As a naturally shy kid in social settings, he was handling this aspect of the game well too. He was confident, yes, but he didn't brag. I helped to make sure of that. Despite my constant emphasis on playing good moves, manners and sportsmanship were just as important as playing well. If you talk with people about Ray and ask them to speak outside of his chess ability, they will most likely tell you that he's simply a nice kid – very likeable and quite kind. There's a reason for that.

With his work ethic, his behavior, and, of course, his level of play, Ray hoped to win a national title – one of our biggest goals at that time. And so after achieving his "number-one status" goals, after raising his rating to close to 1600, and having graduated from the local scholastic events to the adult tournaments, Ray's new goal became this: win the 2003 National Scholastic Championship.

8

In February of 2003, Ray played in a Tornado (a one-day tournament with a relatively accelerated – 60 to 90 minutes – time control). He won all four games, finished first, and raised his rating to 1577. Continuing on through March, Ray had wins and draws against players in the 1600s and 1700s. While he was certainly playing at a higher level than ever in his career, he eventually seemed to have leveled off, his rating floating up and down between 1575 and 1625. Although it had only been five weeks since his strong showing in the Tornado, still it was the longest period to date in which Ray didn't make a large upward surge in rating. He'd already shown that he could, on occasion, defeat a 1700-level player, but I wasn't sure what he needed in order to consistently defeat players at that level and to contend with those rated even higher. I began thinking about what I could do to help him over this hurdle.

As an educator, I knew that children had cognitive leaps and bounds – that they could attain levels of understanding when it was the right time. His up-and-down performance through most of February and all of March, despite his continued study at home and his work every week or two with his new tutor, suggested to me that Ray had reached his level for the time being. Analyzing his losses with the local master who had replaced the expert as Ray's tutor, yielded little change in his performance during those weeks. Ray had the beginnings of ideas as to what to play in certain positions, but he wasn't quite ready to see those positions every time he played a game. I had the feeling that he was going to stay where he was for some time and that additional training wouldn't help much; it was something that only time would aid. The result of my feelings, my observations, and my educational expertise was that, for the second time in Ray's chess career, we dropped a chess tutor.

Ray was going to be in for a slow struggle with or without the master.

One immediate benefit from the decision to drop the master was a great savings each month. We had been living on a public school teacher's salary for the past year. Lessons were expensive, and now that we were spending more and more on tournaments (entry fees up to $100, one or two nights in a hotel, gas, and food for the two-day events that Ray was beginning to play in), it was nice to save on lessons that no longer seemed productive. Lessons didn't really cease, though, for we didn't drop the tutor so much as we replaced him.

Some weeks before the final lesson in March, I had purchased a computer chess program which included instructional lectures, game analysis programs, and, of course, practice against computer opponents of various levels. Prior to the final few lessons with the master, I analyzed on the computer program the games I knew he would go over during the lessons. What I learned was that the master made some of the same recommendations for lines of play as the computer program, but that the program provided more options, at a greater depth, and in just a few seconds. The cost of the entire CD was less than it cost me in time and money to drive Ray out to the tutor for a one-hour lesson. This realization justified for me my decision to remove the tutor from our training program.

While the computer software could have been a waste of time, Ray straightaway showed that he intended to use it wisely. He rarely played against the artificial opponents; instead, from day one, he went directly to the tutorial section and studied high-level tactics and strategy. In addition, he went to the database and pulled up classic games from the world's best players to study and learn from. In short, he used the software as any good student would: as a means of strengthening his own level of play.

The downside to leaving a tutor was, of course, the emotions involved. Although Ray had only spent 22 hours with the master, two more than he had spent with the expert, Tutor 2, like Tutor 1 before him, owned responsibility for Ray's success. And having Ray for a student was good for business. It's helpful to say to interested parents that one of your students is Number One in the state for his age group. The fact that Ray rose to Number

One in the United States for his grade level was just gravy. The master was understandably upset when he learned that he was losing Ray, whom he called his best student. His immediate response was to say that he thought I was making a mistake, that Ray was at a level where many players flounder and never emerge from, and that it was important for Ray to have a tutor (himself, of course) to get him through the barrier that lay ahead. Another local tutor, comparable in level to the master, gave a similar warning to me after he had learned that Ray was no longer studying with anyone. I was told that I was making a big mistake to let Ray work without anyone, that maybe (with great emphasis on the word maybe) Ray could think about going solo when he had reached the 1800 level, but to do so prematurely would be to halt his progress altogether.

I took both masters' words lightly, for both protestors made their living by tutoring students and to have one boy go it alone and be successful wouldn't help anyone in the business of teaching chess. Actually, the warnings of both masters served to strengthen my resolve to let Ray work without a paid tutor. Wasn't that the approach taken by the old grandmasters – to study the greatest games available to them and so improve their own understanding of the game, and, consequently, raise their level of play along with their chess rating?

Neither of Ray's two tutors knew him beyond a few dozen encounters. They didn't understand that the one hour of instruction Ray received was merely a fraction of the study time that he put into chess each week. Also, I never liked the ownership that both of Ray's tutors claimed for his success. I wanted to say this to them: "Ray excelled because he worked hard. You helped, but in no way was he your "product." Ray will be a master with anyone's help or without any help at all." The tutors were over-valuing the lessons and grossly undervaluing Ray's own ability and determination. Ray had so thoroughly studied the games of the grandmasters in his books that if I began playing out a game from one of the books, he could tell me which grandmasters were playing the game, what the next moves would be, and what the strengths of the various positions were. A kid with his drive, study habits, and intelligence would flounder for only so long before rising high once more. At least that's what I thought. In the event that I was wrong, I left intact the bridge to the tutor so that we could return if my experiment failed. But I put a lot of faith and trust in my son; I expected him to succeed even if all he had to rely on was a stack of books, a database of games, his own natural gifts, the passage of time and its accompanying maturation process, and the support of those who loved him best.

9

I have never wanted many things in my life, but whenever there has been something that was of particular interest to me, I pursued it with passion; it would be impossible for me to act in any other way. That's just how I am. When I first read Thoreau's *Walden* and connected with it, I knew where to direct my energies. Over the years, I read and reread that book with the same attention to detail and passion for understanding that Ray brought to the first chess book that I gave him. I owned *Walden* and transformed my life to mirror those elements that I found that mattered most to me. I joined the Peace Corps, built a bamboo hut, planted a garden, and lived my own version of a life of simplicity. I experimented with diet, roamed the hillsides for days at a time, meditated by a river, and poured over the philosophies and religions of the world in my own take on Thoreau's quest for understanding. I later wrote my master's thesis on *Walden*, incorporated elements of Thoreau's philosophy into papers written in a doctoral program, and even made a pilgrimage to Walden Pond one summer, swimming in the sacred waters, walking in the footsteps of my mentor, sitting in silent contemplation in a lonely spot in the hills.

"Crazy" most folks would say about this kind of behavior – about this kind of focus – but it's this very intensity of purpose that I have found most rewarding in my life. Those things and thoughts and people that I have hurled myself towards have provided the basis for any meaningful understanding of life and of myself that I have. So when Ray resolved to step up his own already accelerated study of chess in order to move toward mastery and, in the process, become national champion, I wasn't at all surprised. What else could he do? It was in the blood. He had an intensity of purpose that could be seen in the eyes and observed in all of his actions over the next twelve months. My only task was to support him in his quest for mastery; that's what a father does.

Part of my support was to help him identify and work through the problems that he faced during his next season of tournament chess. The first of these problems was poor opponents. The better Ray got, the more difficult it became for him to play against someone who was poorly prepared. Once the opening moves were played and Ray had a large advantage, he would grow bored with the game at hand and would then wander over to other boards and begin to analyze those games that were more interesting. The result was that he'd become so preoccupied with the better games, that he played his own game half-heartedly and so drew or even lost games that he was winning.

I sympathized with Ray. If I were in a conversation with someone who was telling me about his difficulty in finding the perfect pair of shoes for a particular pair of pants, and if seated next to me were two people talking intelligently about the relevance of Taoism on modern Chinese thought, well, I know where my own thoughts would be. My conversation partner would soon be faced with a blank stare, a wooden smile, an unnatural nodding of the head, and an occasional "uh-huh." To assist Ray, I explained that in order to get to play the more interesting games – those with the higher-rated players – he would have to improve his own rating. As long as he stayed in the middle of the pack, he would only have a few chances to play the better players, to get the better games. This was enough for Ray. The idea of being engaged in a challenging, intricate position with a skillful player was enough to bring him around. He didn't stop observing other interesting games; instead, he let himself enjoy the complexities of the good games as a sort of a break from his own board, but when he was seated in front of his opponent, he was all there. And when he was all there, he won.

Another way to secure better games was for Ray to play up. For example, when he was a Class C player, he always played in the Class B section, but this at first created another obstacle for Ray. At that level, nearly all of his opponents were adults – usually middle-aged men. In his first try in the Class B section, Ray lost three straight games – something he had never done before. It wasn't that he was in over his head, for in each of the three games he had winning chances. Instead, the problem was psychological; he was thinking that Class B automatically meant "better than him" since the players were all rated higher than he was.

The key, I thought, was to convince Ray that he could compete with this new group, and it was very easy for me to come up with the right approach, for I had been contemplating a related theme ever since Ray had beaten me at the age of four. I pointed out that most of the players in his division were adults who had probably been playing for 10 or more years. I told him that a grown-up who had been playing for that long and who had been rated 1700 for the past five years wasn't going to get any better; he'd reached his peak and was, if anything, beginning a backward slide. They were rated 1700 but were often playing at a 1600 or lower level; Ray was 1600 but was playing at a higher level. I reminded him of the higher-rated players of all ages who he had beaten over the past few months. I told him that he had the ability, and then I pointed out the games he'd played that proved it.

And then came the question that I knew he would ask because that very question was in my mind: "What about you? Does that mean that you can't get any better – that you're going to get worse?" I told Ray that those other guys had studied for years and that they had reached their peak; they simply didn't have what it took to play beyond a certain level. I assured Ray that my own lack of ability at the board came from a dearth of study and that had I, like Ray, devoted four or five hours a day to study, then I would be better than these guys too – just like I knew Ray was.

I am only human and, as such, one of my weaknesses is that I do not wish to appear vulnerable to my son. The truth of the matter is that for some months I had been questioning whether or not with equal study I would be able to achieve as much as Ray had, and the more time that passed and the better Ray became, the more I began to doubt that I was my son's equal. I could respond to these doubts in a few ways. I could turn it into the kind of scenario that ends with me towering over my little boy and saying menacingly, "So, you think you're better than your old man, huh?" I could also have quit my day job and taken up part-time work in order to free myself for full-time study – to work at becoming a chess master myself and to prove whether or not I had the stuff that it took. Neither of these responses worked for me – the first didn't reflect who I was as a person and the second directly interfered with what had become my main goal in life: to support my son as he took the first steps down his own path and to provide the security that the family needed. Our earlier competition – when the blood stirred whenever Ray challenged me to a game – was no longer needed now. Ray didn't need a father whose goal was to outdo him; he needed me to work with him. If that meant that I had to follow behind him, then I was prepared to do it. In fact, I was doing it already. What parent doesn't want his child to pass him by, to reach greater heights, to achieve his own firsts, and to burn brighter? The honor for the parent lies in being part of the ashes – an older piece of kindling that once fed the flame and that now sits smoldering beneath it all.

* * *

There was more for Ray to learn from the adults than that bigger didn't mean better. For example, I pointed out the difference in attitude between kids and adults because I thought it important for him to understand. When Ray played a kid and captured a piece, the kid would crumble, give up, make more blunders, and Ray would walk away with a win. However, an adult who was down would fight to the very end. No forty-five-year-old man whose friends are standing around the board watching him wants to lose to an eight-year-old kid who needs to sit on his knees in order to see the board properly. They'll lay traps, they'll fight off attacks, they'll forget that they've been sitting down for the past three hours and forgo a restroom break to focus on the board and the position at hand. Against these adults, I taught Ray to maintain his focus and to seek out even more ways to dominate the board in order to ensure that the wins would remain his.

I also talked with Ray about trusting in himself and in his ability in order to start winning against the next level of opponents. This last brought me to a theme that I had always focused on with Ray: the strong finish. During the tournament where he lost three straight, for example, I told Ray that the losses were over and that they couldn't be changed. What he could do, though, was to learn from the losses. He needed to believe that he could beat these guys and then he would. He needed to stay focused throughout the entire game and to remember that the opponent is most dangerous when he's losing. He had plenty of games ahead of him and ample opportunity to finish the summer with success if he would just finish strong. I believed in him, but it was up to Ray to do it.

He did go on to finish strong and to win more games, and in so doing helped to convince himself that what I was saying about his ability was true. He believed that he could beat the "B" crowd, the "old" guys, and then he went ahead and did it. I don't know which of our talks was the key for Ray. We had our pre-games pep talks, our post game analysis talks, and our before bed "summary of learnings" talks. Ray paid attention to everything I said. Maybe his continued improvement and success wasn't due to any of our talks; maybe it was his own sense of responsibility. He knew how much the events cost – the entry fees, the hotels, the gas, etc. – and he knew that we didn't have a lot of money (for one school assignment, Ray was asked to list his three wishes: one wish was for him to become World Chess Champion, another wish was for him to be kind to people, and the third wish was for more money for his parents because "they don't have as much as most other people I know"). I wouldn't have been surprised to learn that Ray felt obligated to give his best simply to justify the expense. Certainly part of the answer, though, lay in his own dislike of losing. He was a competitor and although I had worked with him on how to be a good loser, he did not like to lose. That is why in many games he played – games in which another might have resigned due to the position – he played on and often salvaged a draw or even got the win. At any rate, he began finishing stronger and stronger, and he had been convinced (or he'd convinced himself) that he could play against the Big Boys. All that remained was for me to get him to the events and let him do his thing.

10

When I first taught Ray to play chess, and, a year later when he was four, when we started playing several games a day every day, our routine didn't interfere much with our family life. At least we were at home. Yes, Yee-chen did hint more than a few times that we were playing too much chess, but she saw that Ray loved the game, and I was usually able to convince her of its benefits – the help with focus, the connections with geometry, how it was great for problem-solving, and whatever else I could think to say at the moment.

The more time that passed, the more the game became a part of our lives. Ray still went to school, he still studied Chinese with his mother, he still went to Chinese school on Sunday, and he still had other activities: basketball in the park, bike riding, and reading, among others. It wasn't until Ray started the tournaments that chess started to take Ray and me out of the house.

The scholastics weren't too bad, though. They were only one Saturday a week. Also, Ray had all day with his mom at the Chinese school on Sundays, so it seemed appropriate that he have a day just with me, too. But then Ray got good, and I started presenting arguments about the importance of one excelling to one's ability – how it was important to give Ray a chance to see how far he could go. "And you see that he loves it, right? I mean, he's doing something that he's really interested in. Isn't that a good thing?" Blah-blah-blah. All true – yes – but still, my wife was sharp enough to see how much fun I had on these days with Ray, and she (rightly so) suspected that I just wanted to increase the fun.

Had Ray performed poorly, or had he stayed at the same level for months on end, we probably would have stuck with the local Saturday events. But Ray had an early success – and not just one, but a series of successes – so that it just seemed to make sense to continue with the tournaments, to expand to bigger and longer events, and to expose him to as much chess as possible.

During the first year of chess, Yee-chen would regularly bring up objections. "He's focusing too much on chess." "He needs to do things with other people." "Sometimes the ordinary person lives the happiest life." "How is this chess thing going to help him when he's older?" "You spent *how much* on the weekend in Boca?" "Can he make a living in chess?" "He should do something where he could make more money." And there were many other comments, questions, and observations like these.

I am glad to have someone not steeped in the world of chess – someone who sees it from the outside and can point out its limitations while at the same time providing alternative activities. I am just like Ray (or is it supposed to be the other way around?) in the sense that I like to focus on something and see it through to as far as I can take it. If Ray had only me for a parent, I know exactly what our life would look like. We would be living in a tiny trailer. The house would have been sold, and I would have used the funds to supplement the income from whatever part-time job I took to replace my full-time work. The move from full-time to part-time work would be necessary in order to provide time for studying chess with Ray, for working with him on all subjects outside of chess, for playing sports and games, and for playing in as many tournaments as possible. The trailer walls would be lined with shelves of chess books, philosophy books, and religious texts from the Far East. When we weren't playing, studying, thinking, or discussing, we would be watching ESPN interspersed with Star Trek and Kung Fu reruns. We would both be too lean and too hungry-looking. And what a sheltered life that would be for Ray! I hope that when Ray reads this scene, it will help him to appreciate everything that his mother brings into his life. If Ray had only me as his parent, then he and I would have both lived chess for too much of each day, and, consequently, Ray would have been sorely underdeveloped in many ways and probably not as good a chess player either.

Yee-chen, who had had the oftentimes difficult experience of living with an overly intense husband, was not happy about having a son with an overdeveloped ability to focus. In fact, when Ray was still very little and I recognized what he might be capable of, Yee-chen immediately said that what she wished for was an average child. She said that an average child would have more friends and would be happier in general. A life filled with too much thought would only lead to unhappiness and dissatisfaction.

Yee-chen saw to it that Ray had plenty of non-chess-related activities in his life. Through her efforts, Ray continued to learn Chinese, he participated in school activities, and he became a part of the neighborhood group that played football on the street in front of our house most nights. With her push, Ray attended parties, read non-chess books, did his homework every night, and had plenty of hours and days when he was just an average child.

Early on, Ray tried to include his mom in his chess world by teaching her how to play, but though she did finally learn how the pieces moved, she was hopeless in terms of understanding and applying basic strategy, and she just never clicked with the game – it wasn't something she could see spending more than a few minutes on. It was just a game (and not a very interesting one) to her. Our Saturday trips were nearly always father-son because Yee-chen didn't want to lose both her Saturdays and Sundays (she was already teaching Sundays at the Chinese school). She also had private students to prepare for, and, later, when she became an assistant at a local Montessori school, she had even less free time and didn't think it worthwhile to use her valuable time standing beside me for hours staring at two figures too far away to discern anything from.

The weekend trips, though, really changed things. Yee-chen didn't like us being away for the whole weekend – wasn't one day bad enough already? And she really couldn't attend these because she had those Sunday classes and her responsibility to her students. These all-weekend events – the ones where we'd leave Friday afternoon and come back at midnight on Sunday – were the ones that made her feel the most like a chess widow. We missed more than a few tournaments because Yee-chen was feeling lonely and left out. I agreed to skip this event or that one so that we could all be together for part of the weekend. I have no regrets about any missed event. The family unit is always what's most important, and when someone has a very strong need, we adjust to meet that person's need. Yee-chen did it for me during our various two-year moves, and she did it for Ray every time she stayed home when we were out at a chess event. I did it for Yee-chen when I bought a house and put money in the bank, and Ray and I were both doing it for her every time we gave up an event when she needed us to be together. The family has to come first. If that is preserved in a positive manner, then everything else has a better chance of working out.

The missed events that Yee-chen "forced" on us probably helped Ray anyway. One needs a break – even if it's a break from a favorite activity – so that one can return to it refreshed and hungry for more. The days spent at the beach or at a show instead of in a tournament hall helped Ray, I am convinced, as much as his time at the board. And I'm not talking about numerous breaks. By June of 2003, the end of grade two, Ray had competed in over 40 events. Certainly he was getting in his playing time.

And after the summer of 2003, Yee-chen even joined us on a few weekend trips. She enjoyed the beach or the hotel's pool, while I stood all day long staring at Ray at his board and while Ray sat all day with chess on the brain. But we had meals together, and we always had some time as a family at the end of the day. My only problem with the family trips was the effect on Ray's performance. Ray has a unique relationship with each of us. With Yee-chen, it's all soft and squishy and even babyish; with me, well . . . it's playtime but with a very competitive edge and no babies allowed. We had a routine down with chess; he was serious about it, focused, and determined. Yee-chen's "Oh, just have fun," or, "You should play in the lower section so you can play with the kids and win the big trophy" didn't fit with the route that Ray had been taking himself along and that I had been supporting. Of course, Yee-chen could always say what she thought – *and she always did* – but I would work doubly hard to make sure Ray knew why he was there (to focus, to win his games, to become better and better) and to keep him feeling hungry for more – for better opponents, for bigger tournaments, for more challenges. So, once again, my wife – simply by her presence – helped me to become a better mentor to Ray by keeping me on my toes.

As of this writing, there is no question in Yee-chen's mind that chess plays – and will continue to play – a central role in Ray's life. She knows that there will be more long trips away from home, and she knows that he's at a level now that demands that he play more games against the strongest players. Her objections continue to flow, however, and they always serve to check me (and to sometimes checkmate me); Yee-chen makes me stop and think about where we're going with this.

PART III

11

My plan for the summer of 2003 was to read through certain chess books along with Ray to ensure that he was getting everything he could from them and to see that he was fully understanding the vocabulary, the patterns, the tactics, and the strategy. I found, though, that he'd already learned most of the games in the books thoroughly. I'd no sooner get the board set up and make the first 7 moves than Ray would say, "Isn't that the game where Znosko-Borovsky's black? He plays the Stonewall Attack. On his next move he plays Knight b4. It's a good move because it attacks the Bishop." We went over several games in June and July with the result being that I became a much better chess player after Ray walked me through games he knew very well. But no one learns the subject better than the teacher, so our arrangement also helped Ray to deepen his own understanding of the games he'd studied. Another benefit was that our sessions improved my play enough so that I began to draw and win the occasional game against Ray (I had always won games, but over the preceding year my wins went from five out of ten, to three, to one, to once a month). My own improvement more than anything else seemed to spur Ray on in his studies, for he couldn't stand to drop a game to his dad.

Ratings-wise, things were looking okay, too. He was still ranked Number 1 in the United States for his grade level. In an effort to increase his rating and to keep up with his chess training, Ray played in as many summer events as we could manage. My move to the public schools was both a blessing and a curse. We now had time – all summer in fact – where we were free to travel, but we were handicapped by our budget. After mortgage and bill payments, I had little left for chess; however, all that I had went towards entry fees and hotel rooms. My bank account balance during these years always hovered precariously just above zero. We planned the summer around six events (all but one in Florida) plus attendance at a five-day Florida chess camp in Gainesville.

In the very first tournament, I learned what Ray's next obstacle would be: time. Part of my mantra – the words I whispered to him before the start of each game – included a few words on time. Specifically, I reminded Ray again and again to take his time. After several tournaments, a year-and-a-half of study, and several cognitive advances, he had finally reached a level where taking his time was not the problem; instead, the problem was making moves before his time ran out. Even in games with time controls of two or more hours per player (such as the first event of June), Ray struggled with time. He had developed so much that he was able to mentally follow multiple lines to a great depth of analysis. The problem, of course, was that while he was considering every move until he found the perfect one, his clock was running. There were several games where I stood expressionless to the side – just a few feet from the board – watching Ray's clock click off the time – 120 minutes down to 100 minutes down to 80 minutes – and still not a move. Sometimes he'd tease me by positioning his hand over a piece, letting it hover just a half-inch above the piece for two or three minutes, only to remove it and return to his mental calculations. At such times I wanted to scream. In fact, I was screaming, only it was inside of my head. There was a Sam Kinison-like voice screaming, "Mooooooove! Mooooooove! Move the piece! Ahhhhhhhh!"

Actually, I could appreciate Ray's actions. He was a perfectionist, and he wanted to make the perfect move every time. Or, looked at from the other side, he did not ever want to make a mistake. Earlier, when he was a weaker player, Ray had fewer options to consider. He literally could only see one or two possible moves and so never struggled with time. Now, however, he was beginning to see more and more possibilities – mostly in the form of sharp tactical moves, often involving piece sacrifices. Such sacrifices took careful calculation because if the plan to give up a piece (i.e., a knight, a bishop, a rook, or even a queen) did not lead either to checkmate or to the recapture of material, then the game would usually be lost. Ray began to see possibilities everywhere on the board; his level was such that he had too many options to consider before he could satisfy himself with "the" best move. There's great beauty in striving for perfection, and, in a way, the greatest chess game ever played might be one that never ended, where each player had a lifetime (or lifetimes) to contemplate his moves. There is something to that. On another level, the level I operated on whenever these games were in progress, it was extraordinarily frustrating for me to watch Ray lose games on time to players I knew he could beat.

Ray could completely lose himself in the moment – through contemplation of the position at hand – and, in so doing, would become oblivious to the passage of time. I'd seen him lose himself to the outside world in this same way when deep in thought over one of his chess books. For example, Ray and I drove in my ailing '85 auto from our home in Florida to an out-of-state event that summer. Somewhere in South Carolina, a deer crossing the highway ran into the car; *I* did not run into *it*. It was 8:00 a.m. and the sun was lighting up the land. The deer was standing on the edge of the highway – easy for me to see, and easy for it to see me in my bright red auto. And then, bull-like, it took off across the highway and charged the car. I swerved as best I could, but there was no escaping it. My headlight and one corner of the car were smashed in, but we were safe and the car still worked. And the psycho-deer returned to the side of the highway from which it had come. After the meeting with the car, I didn't think he'd be charging anything else that day. Worse than the dent that the deer had left was the non-stop ringing of the door buzzer on Ray's side of the car. With hundreds of miles ahead of us, it's a wonder that we didn't both go crazy from hour upon hour of high-pitched ringing. I suppose, though, that Ray would be too focused to lose his mind. When the deer hit his side of the car, he was completely immersed in a chess book and barely took notice. Without looking up from his book he said, "I think a bird might have hit the car."

In order to help with Ray's time situation, I had to adjust the mantra – to turn it into an oxymoron. Now, after telling him to take his time, I would add, "But not too much time." His question, of course, was, "How much time is too much time?" I answered by saying that he needed to trust in his ability, that he could look at two or three lines but that he would have to trust himself to make a good move. I was careful not to say the "right" move. I told Ray that there were many good moves and that he just needed to find one of them. I also worked with him on time strategy. I told him to think on his opponent's time. If the position was a complicated one that demanded a lot of time and attention, then I told him to think about what his opponent's best moves might be and then to consider his own responses while his opponent was using his own clock to consider his move.

Too many times I had watched Ray labor over what must have been lengthy combinations, only to see him take an equal amount of time on his subsequent move. I was certain that in his calculations, he must have considered the move his opponent actually made and so should have been able to play out his own response in the line that he had just taken 25 minutes to think through. Why did he have to re-think the position after each of his opponent's moves? His answer to the question hearkens back to what I said about his perfectionism: he said that he wanted to re-evaluate the line to ensure that he hadn't made any errors in his original calculations (or, in his words, "I didn't want to make a mistake").

Despite the change in mantra and despite my coaching, Ray lost some games that summer because he was thinking too much. Although I never gave up on the talks, I suspected that the problem would work itself out over time (no pun intended). I knew that Ray did not like to lose, and enough losses on time, I thought, would finally get him to speed up his play. The irony of the situation was never lost on me either. I knew very well that most chess-parents would have loved it if their child had Ray's "problem," because it's even more frustrating to watch your talented child give away games because of two-second moves – moves that look good at first sight but, with a little more thought, prove to be losing moves. I had observed that it was far more difficult for a speed player to develop into a slow player than it was for the slow to develop some speed.

Despite the time trouble, Ray played some excellent chess in the summer of 2003 and gave me glimpses of what to expect in his future. In his first three events of the summer, he had a combined record of 11 wins, 1 draw, and 3 losses. Over the entire summer, he had wins or draws against higher-rated players. If not for his losses on time and the rare blunders, he would have had an even faster surge in rating. As it was, though, he made steady progress throughout the summer – all the way, in fact, to the August supplement of the USCF ratings where he was listed as a Class B player.

* * *

The most exciting event for Ray that summer was definitely the chess camp he attended in July. The camp, however, was only one of two highlights; the other one involved his cousins. Ray had his school friends (he was attending the Montessori school where his mother taught at this time), and he had the neighborhood friends who he played basketball and football with. In addition, he was just beginning to develop friendships through chess, but his closest friends have always been his cousins – the Kempers – in Gainesville. The Kempers stayed with us in Sarasota for several weeks when they were between moves, and we stayed with them near Gainesville for about a month when we were between moves. During other times, we always found a way to visit. Even when we lived in Arizona for two years, we made our way out to see them, and they made their way out to see us. Once we had settled back in Florida, we made a plan where one family would visit the other every month. Melanie and Danica, both of whom are close in age to Ray, along with their younger brothers, Sullivan and Livingston, are the closest friends in Ray's life. With the Kempers, Ray is just Ray and not "Ray the chess player" as he is defined by most people who have come into his life. He is as comfortable in their home as he is in ours, and that pretty much says it all. Ray ate and played with his cousins each night, and each day he would spend at the chess camp.

The camp sessions were run by a half-dozen grandmasters and masters, and Ray was the only eight-year-old in a room dominated by teenagers. Still, he had so much confidence in the chess arena that he participated in the discussions and both asked and answered questions. The sessions themselves weren't particularly noteworthy. What excited Ray was just seeing the grandmasters and interacting with them. They were what he wanted to be. More instructive than the class sessions were the impromptu games that he was able to have both with the grandmasters and with some of the top teens in the country. Every night, he had tournament games with his fellow classmates, and he did well against the teens. He also benefited from the post-game analyses conducted either by the grandmasters or by the players themselves.

It was at the camp where I learned more about Ray's memory. I knew that he had a good memory just from his recall of passages from dozens of chess books he'd read and from his recall of positions of games either he'd read about or he'd played himself. He didn't have total recall, but what he had was the next best thing. During a lunch with one of the top Florida kids, I watched as the two played mental chess. I'd seen Ray do it before, but I didn't know how accurate he was. His opponent this time was an expert-level player, and he would be able to call Ray immediately on incorrect moves or the movement of pieces to squares already occupied. But this never happened, for Ray seemed to be able to see the board and the pieces as clearly in his mind as if they were on a real board in front of him. I suppose that all of that time reading chess books like novels on our drives to and from tournaments – where he had to visualize the lines that were played out since he couldn't play out the moves on a board – helped him to "see" the board and the pieces when they weren't there. I've read chess books where the authors have said at the outset that a good memory was not necessary to become a master; however, I couldn't help but think that it was a great advantage. How helpful to be able to identify a position from the game before you with a position from a Capablanca game played in the 1920s, and then to recall Capa's line of play! I don't know if Ray did that in his games, but he certainly had the memory for it. At the very least, I thought that this ability might make him an even more formidable opponent as he matured and reached higher and higher levels.

With the end of the chess camp and the start of the school year, Ray was ready to begin another year of chess. He hadn't been competing for two full years yet, but he was top in the state both for his age group and for his grade, and he had raised himself from an "E" to a "Class B" player. He ended his up-and-down summer (great victories, occasional blunders, and losses on time) with a solid rating. He had beaten a national champion from India at one event, he had played well against some of the top teens in the country, and (at the chess camp) he had had his first games against grandmasters. He went into the fall season hungry for more, ready to compete, and as much in love with the game as ever.

12

When I stopped the chess lessons six months earlier, I did so thinking that Ray would eventually be able to progress satisfactorily on his own. I thought also that he was at a cognitive chasm that only time – not costly instruction – would cure. I was never 100% certain that I had made the right decision, and there were times in the summer when I worried that I had made a mistake. Although the flashes of greatness were there and Ray had had some tremendous games, he'd also had some mediocre performances. True, he had gained 77 rating points between the end of March and the beginning of August, moving himself from a C player to a B player, but I wondered if he could have done even more. Our work together consisted of walking through grandmasters' games, regular games against one another, and a few analyses of games that Ray had played with the help of our computer program. It didn't seem like much when I thought about it; however, there really was much more training going on than that.

For example, Ray did have some formal training through the five-day chess camp, and he also had one-on-one lessons every time he went over his losses with his opponents. Every time Ray lost to a higher-rated player, I encouraged him to analyze the game with the victor. We found that most players – at least those who had won – were happy to go over the moves and point out what they thought the best moves in certain positions were. These were very interactive sessions, for Ray often challenged his opponents' suggestions and played out the moves that would refute lines just suggested. These refutations would lead to deeper analyses and more discussions, all of which benefited Ray who, sponge-like, would absorb the information and talk about it with me afterwards. I did my part, too. I'd remind Ray of the lessons of his latest loss – "Remember not to block in your pieces. Remember what happened when you played Barley and you had nowhere to move? You've got to avoid that" – and we would sometimes go over the games together on the computer to see if we could get more, and better, advice.

Ray was using the computer on his own, too. He frequently listened to (or re-listened to) the advanced chess lectures on the program. I'd remind him to cover up the move list to the left of the on-screen board and to pause the lecture so that he could think about what moves he would play and then compare his moves with the moves of the masters who had actually played the game. He also often went to the database and pulled up classic games to study. He'd call me into the room and say, "Look at this position. Who do you think is better?" And after I'd guess (wrongly, most often), he'd play out the moves to show me how Black – which was a piece down and seemingly under attack – was really in a better position and just a few moves from checkmate. But he didn't just show me the moves; he explained them to me ("See, no matter what White plays, Black has Bishop to h3 which pins White's Rook to his King. Then, he just has to find a way to get rid of the g pawn, and he'll crush White"), so I knew that he was really understanding what he was looking at.

He was also still studying from texts, and I bought more books for him that summer, as did his grandparents. Every day he read or reread sections of a chess book. He'd set up positions on the board in the living room and ask me to play for White or Black, so that he could show me the latest combination or strategy he'd learned. He studied tactics, openings, end-game theory, middle-game theory, general strategy, collections of best games of various grandmasters, and in-depth analyses of specific styles. The lessons were there in his head. It was all there; I was just waiting for it to come out consistently at the board. And then it happened: he just got good. Everything clicked, and I no longer doubted my decision to let him work on his own.

From the first tournament of the 2003/2004 academic year all the way up until Nationals in December, Ray was on fire. In the first nine tournaments, Ray's focus and ability helped him to earn wins over twenty players, some rated 200 to 300 points above him. By November he was playing in the Class A section of tournaments, and even in this advanced group, he was winning more games than he was losing. Just two years before, unrated Ray Robson had lost to two low-rated boys before dropping out of the tournament at my request. In just two years' time, he had competed in fifty-three tournaments and in so doing had raised himself up to a Class B player, Number One in the state, Number One in the country, and playing now almost exclusively with adults and other Top 100 youths.

When Ray got good, the less necessary I became. There wasn't anything on the board that I could see that he couldn't see both faster and in greater depth. We played fewer and fewer games together, and, when we did play, Ray was barely present. Instead of studying the board when it was my move, Ray would read a book or even watch TV. When it was his move, he would look at the board for a mere second before moving. Sometimes he didn't move at all; I'd move for him. He'd be in his room reading a book and when I'd call out that it was his move, he'd answer, "Did you take the Knight on b4? Okay, then play Queen to d6 for me. It's mate in two." As polite as he was, I could sometimes see a look of frustration or exasperation cross his face when I played an inferior move. I was no longer challenging him in any way; it was no longer fun for him to play against me.

I recorded some of this experience in the journal that I was keeping at that time: *Last night when we got back, Ray played out his Round 1 win for me. When he got to the 11th move – a move which he had spent nearly forty-five minutes on – he began showing me all of the variations and sub-variations that he mentally calculated and pondered based on the position. I quickly got lost in his rapid analysis and became frustrated and cranky. When he asked me what was wrong, I told him I was tired, and he said he'd skip the sub-variations and just finish out the main lines. I asked him to just finish out the line he was in the process of showing me, saying that it was time for bed. I've found of late that I do get frustrated by my lack of understanding. And if Ray spoke what was in his mind, I'd hear comments such as, "You probably don't see why that's a threat" or "You'd never make that move." Knowing that he's even thinking that is upsetting, but the truth is that he's right: I can't follow most of his analysis – it's too fast, too detailed, and I simply lack the tactical skills to see the multiple hidden threats that are imbedded in the calculated positions which he shows me. My limitations are present to both of us, and Ray is wondering why I don't try to improve. I don't study on my own, and it's weak of me to continue to use "I don't study" as an excuse for playing poorly or not understanding. If I don't drastically improve my own level of play and understanding of the game, in just a few short months I'll be out of the loop entirely – no longer coach even; nothing more than chauffer and check-writer. The real fear, of course, is that even with study, I'll not meet Ray's level. But that's a part a life and something that I need to embrace. Children are more intelligent than their parents. There were a few times when my father came to me for advice – when he said that he couldn't understand something and needed help. It was uncomfortable for me to hear that, and I felt sorry for him. But I was in my twenties when that happened; Ray's a child! And I suppose that makes it harder. But I should not let these feelings interfere with Ray's development. And if I can improve my game, then it will make Ray a better player too. For me to surpass him – to even approach his level – as a player would probably be devastating for him, but there is almost no chance of that happening. I just want to reach a place where I can communicate about the game on a more equal level with him – so that at least I can follow an analysis and be able to make an occasional contribution myself. We'll see. For now, though, there's this tournament to work through, and my job is to be a provider and a cheerleader. And these roles I can handle.*

I was becoming obsolete, unnecessary. Wasn't it just yesterday that I was teaching Ray how the Knight moved? And suddenly, what seemed like just a few moments later, I couldn't even make a suggestion without him shooting it down immediately with no fewer than three very precise lines of play to back up his words. I had to adjust to Ray's leaps and bounds. I was forced to let go of our father-son games and to instead focus on whatever else I could do for Ray. With Nationals just around the corner, I felt pressed to figure out ways that I could help my son without becoming an obstacle myself. The one thing that I knew for certain was that I wasn't going to help Ray by growing irritated with him for passing me by so quickly. I needed to celebrate Ray's advance and keep the mood light and merry. Negative emotions have an awful effect on a child; I needed to be a bright spot for Ray.

13

Aside from the big two-day events, Ray's main tournaments were the one-day adult tornados. We had a routine that we followed religiously on chess weekends. I would wake up an hour before Ray, shower, brush my teeth, and dress. I'd quietly walk into Ray's room and pull out his clothes for the day – shorts, socks, T-shirt, sweatshirt in case the a/c was too cold, and usually a red cap that he liked to wear. Then I'd make sandwiches and put them in a bag with some apples for lunch. I'd add other food to the bag for an on-the-road breakfast. Next I'd pack his chess bag (board and pieces), his clock, his score-pad, and a few pens into my own backpack and place the pack plus the food-bag in the car. When I would hear Ray waking up, I'd wait until he'd gone to the bathroom and then wrestle him fully awake – I mean literally wrestle him. Once he was up and feeling happy from the wrestling, I'd toss him his clothes and tell him to dress, brush his teeth and grab something to read because it was time to go. Fifteen minutes later, Ray (with four or five books in his hands) and I (with the football in hand) would hop into my 1985 deer-dented car and take off for Clermont or Orlando or Kissimmee or wherever there was chess to be played. On our way, Ray would read and I would listen to Alejandro Escovedo, Greg Brown, or James Taylor – Ray usually taking a break from his reading an hour into the drive to eat the breakfast I'd prepared and to sing along with me and whoever I had in the CD player.

At the tournament hall, we'd register and pay the fee; then we'd grab the football – if time – and play catch up until a few minutes before the start of Round One. On our walk to the tournament room, I'd begin my pep talk. "Hernando and Bruce are here – both strong players. You'll get some good games, Bud. Just take your time and make good moves." At the table I would help Ray set up the board and the clock – not because he needed help, but because it was one of my few windows into what he was doing; it was a way of being a part of the process. He'd arrange his bottle of water, his notepad, and pen as he liked, and then he'd don his red hat. I'd whisper into his ear my final words – the mantra that had evolved to fit Ray's changing needs over the years: "Take your time but watch the clock. Focus. Make good moves." And then I'd stand nearby as the game got underway.

That was the routine leading up to the Scholastic Nationals in December. Ray's past few weeks' performance – his games after he got good – had brought his rating into the 1800s. Going into the 2003 Nationals, Ray was the only Class A player in the Grade Three section. He was also one of only thirty-three youths under the age of 19 with a performance strong enough for him to be named to that year's All-American Youth Team. He'd done his work, and it had paid off. Ray was ready for the big event: a win at the National Championship that we'd set as the main goal one year before. The only hard part remaining was for us to get through the final days before the tournament.

While Ray still slept and awakened and went through his days as he always had, I couldn't get chess off of my mind. I thought about Nationals as I lay in bed at night, I dreamt about it, and it was in my mind when I awoke each morning. I was just ready for it to happen, ready for Ray to win his games and finally – after his year-long preparation – become a national champion. The final 18 days were the toughest for me to get through.

Most teachers start to complain after returning from Thanksgiving Break. At that time, and on up until Christmas Break, the kids are more inattentive and hyper than usual, their thoughts on the upcoming break and on the presents they'll get. I didn't complain at all; in fact, I was grateful to have something that would mentally occupy me for 8 hours of every day. When I worked, thoughts of chess were pushed to the back of my mind, and the hours passed a little more quickly.

After school and on weekends, I found other ways to occupy my mind and to assist time in its passing. I completely cleaned and then cleared out the garage, and in so doing chased out the squirrel that had moved in a few weeks before. With everything out of the garage and the squirrel gone, it was easier for me to spot the mice that had taken up winter residence in our attic. By observing their travels between the attic and the garage, I was able to find their entrances to the attic, and, after catching and evicting the unwanted guests, I killed more time by sealing their entrances to the attic.

Other activities that helped me to pass the time included nailing up a section of drywall that was coming down from the garage roof, repairing the motor of the garage door opener, cleaning the entire house, and repairing a toilet that had needed fixing for about three months. The time of year also helped me out, for I got to set up our artificial tree, lay out our 40-year-old train set around the base of the tree and ensure that it was working properly, and, finally, string up the outdoor lights.

On school days, I had an afternoon routine that helped pass the time. When Ray came home from school, he and I would throw the football around out in front of our house. After an hour or so of that, we'd go to the garage where I had set up our Ping-Pong table, and we'd play a three-game tournament. After dinner, we'd sit down and go over a chess game. This last was the major preparation that Ray had before Nationals. I'd pick out a grandmaster game, play White's first move, and ask Ray to think about a good response for Black. If his response didn't match what the grandmaster played, I'd ask him to think about other responses until he hit the right one. We'd play through the opening in this way with Ray picking the moves for both sides. Ray knew the opening lines well, and we would often play through them fairly quickly. We'd slow down when we got to the middle game. I'd ask Ray to think more about each move. If he couldn't figure out what the grandmaster played, then I'd make the move for him and ask him to think about why it was played. I'd compare Ray's reasoning with the annotations from the grandmasters, and then we'd play on in the same way: thinking about best moves, comparing Ray's thoughts with the grandmasters' play, and using the annotations to deepen his understanding of the minds of the grandmasters. If Ray saw moves that weren't addressed in the annotations, then I'd ask him to try and figure out why they hadn't been played or even mentioned in the book.

That was the program. In addition to working with me, Ray also continued to go over games on his own and to read chess books. He had a pile of books by his place at the table for reading during breakfast and dinner. He had a pile of books beside the chessboard that was always set up on the table in the living room. He had chess books on the table beside his bed for reading before sleeping and immediately upon rising. He had books in his school bag for reading on the 15-minute drive to and from school. Between his own studies and what we were doing together in the afternoons, I couldn't think of a better way to prepare him short of putting him in the hands of a grandmaster.

And then, at just the right time, a chess mom in a neighboring town arranged for a grandmaster to visit the area. I found out through a forwarded email message and immediately reserved two back-to-back hour-long private sessions for Ray. I thought that the best way to spend Ray's time with the grandmaster was to have him play his favorite openings and to let the grandmaster play against him with a variety of responses, pointing out throughout the games any weaknesses he saw in Ray's moves. The same could be done with the grandmaster playing White; he could play various openings and advise Ray both on Ray's responses to the openings and on his subsequent moves. The session was scheduled on a Sunday – just five days before Round One.

We made the hour-and-a-half drive, and a few minutes after entering the grandmaster's host's home, the lesson began. Before going over the opening variations, Alexander Goldin, the grandmaster, said that he needed to test Ray's tactics first. He set up a problem and told Ray that he had three minutes to find checkmate, and then, after considering the position, he advanced the time limit to five minutes. Twenty seconds later, after Ray had solved the problem, Alex announced that they were through with tactics and could begin looking at openings.

It had been nearly a year since Ray had had a one-on-one lesson, and I was curious to see how the session would go. The only difference between Ray's behavior with Alex and his behavior with his tutors from before was that Ray lacked the confidence that he always showed with the latter during lessons. Instead of picking up a piece and planting it where he knew it should go, with Alex he reluctantly took a piece and, with an I-doubt-this-is-the-right-move expression on his face, waved the piece hesitantly over various spots before setting it down with no resolve whatsoever. I think that he was intimidated by the grandmaster – that he knew that the person sitting across from him could wipe out just about anyone he played against. Still, Alex said that the moves – reluctant as they were – were generally good ones.

We learned a lot in the two-hour session. We learned that Ray played outside of the "normal" or prescribed opening lines but that, according to Alex, Ray's decisions were fine. The grandmaster said that at Ray's level, one didn't need to be bound by opening lines. I was surprised by Alex's comments. Ray had learned his openings from books and did, in fact, follow the opening lines in his preparation for playing both sides of the board. Perhaps what Alex was seeing was Ray's unfamiliarity with the myriad opening sidelines – most of which Ray had not yet encountered over the board. I guess to a grandmaster, any novice – even one as studious as Ray – would seem to have a limited opening knowledge. I was also surprised when the grandmaster commented that Ray was sometimes playing too passively. I think that if he had had time (or, rather, if I had had the money to pay for more of his time) to look over Ray's previous 20 games, he would have changed his assessment. Still, it was good for Ray to know that in the positions studied with the grandmaster, he had options – aggressive yet sound ones – that he could employ in the future should he find himself in similar positions.

When we walked out at the end of the session, Ray said to me, "I thought that went well" – echoing what I had been thinking to myself. Five days before Nationals and Ray was working out against a grandmaster; things couldn't have been better.

* * *

The final four days were tough on me. On Monday, after I got home from school, I killed time by mowing our large corner lot by hand. I had a 1970-something riding mower that I had got running, but I used our little push mower instead. It would take longer that way, and that was just fine with me. I'd cut a section and then take a break by tossing the football around with Ray. I worked until darkness and then, after a shower, I went over a grandmaster game with Ray until bedtime.

After work on Tuesday, I found more yard work to do – more mowing, some weeding, filling in a rabbit hole that had needed filling for about six months, and tending to our citrus trees. In between jobs I tossed the ball around with Ray, and we ended the day by playing Ping-Pong and going over more chess games. Ray, for his part, was simply Ray – his usual self, doing his usual thing, aware that Nationals was approaching but sleeping well just the same.

On Wednesday, I went through all of our clothing to find the warmest ones to bring to Illinois. The weather report said that it was going to be in the 20s in the daytime! Ray still had a winter coat from the two-year period when we lived in Flagstaff, Arizona, and it fit him well enough. I, on the other hand, had nothing warmer than a rain-jacket. It was going to be layers of T-shirts for me. After arranging the clothes, I watched some TV until Ray got home from school. We played our usual Ping-Pong match, went over some chess games, and then played a game of Chinese chess which lasted until bedtime.

Chinese chess is much like "Western" chess in that strategy and tactics are necessary in order to win. It differs in that there's a General instead of a King, there's an imaginary river in the middle of the board that only some of the pieces can cross, and there are other restrictions on pieces and other rules peculiar to the game that distinguish it from chess, but in many ways it's at least as challenging as chess. Ray and I used to play a lot of Chinese chess a few years before – right around the time that he started playing in tournaments – but "Western" chess took its place. It was nice to return to Chinese chess and re-learn the game together. After Ray was in bed and more time had passed – when I was still awake – I washed and ironed some clothes. It wasn't until late in the evening that I fell asleep; chess, of course, was on my mind, solidified in its place by the episode of *Frazier* that I had fallen asleep to – one in which the main character works through a range of emotions after losing to, and then ultimately defeating, his dad at – what else? – chess.

And suddenly it was Thursday; a year had passed. Last minute packing, leaving the house in good order, and Ping-Pong with Ray filled up the morning and the afternoon. When Yee-chen came home from work, I loaded up the car, and the three of us drove to the airport. We were finally on our way. Or so I thought. After standing in line to get our electronic tickets, and after standing in line to have every inch of our luggage and our bodies and even our removed shoes analyzed (the result of all of their sleuthing was that they flagged my backpack, thinking Ray's chess clock might have been a bomb), we were through all of the checkpoints and at our gate only to learn that our flight was delayed by two hours due to engine trouble. The good news was that the tournament wasn't until Friday, and I could congratulate myself on having anticipated such delays and scheduling a flight a day in advance.

There was another surprise advantage, too. There were three or four kids around Ray's age who were headed for the same tournament via the same plane, and Ray got to play a few practice games. One of the kids was a good fifth-grade player – a nice boy whom Ray had played on a few occasions in tournaments. I watched in dismay as Ray lost, for despite the other boy's talent, I was expecting Ray to win as he usually did. And then when Ray dropped his Queen in his next game – this one against a vastly inferior player – I started to worry about what had happened to Ray. Was it nerves? Was he sick? It wasn't this last because I had just had him checked out by the doctor a few days before (I had wanted to make sure that Ray was 100% and that nothing physical would disturb him during the event). Within myself, I worried. With Ray, I turned the incidents into positives. I said that it was good that he lost to his friend – that it would remind him that a decent player, if given the chance, could beat him. He needed to focus and play his best moves against everyone, regardless of rating or perceived ability. And the second game (the one in which Ray lost his Queen) was also useful, for Ray managed to win the game, and I used this as a lesson that he created for himself: never give up. "Even when you were a piece down," I said, "you never gave up, you made a plan, you found a way to make it work, and you won. That's what you've got to do at Nationals." Of course I ended by telling him that he'd have even better chances if he didn't drop any pieces during his tournament games.

When the flight finally arrived and we were safely seated, while Yee-chen slept, Ray and I looked at chess games from one of the three books he had brought with him, using a miniature magnetic chess set to make the book moves. He was working on his game all the way to the final minute; he wanted to prepare, and I was willing to go over as many games as he wanted. We put the books away only because the plane was landing in Chicago.

14

The hotel where the games were to be played cost $100 per night for four nights, and as the flight for the three of us had already cost $450, I looked for, and discovered, a way to make the trip affordable. I found a Chicago-based couple who were listed in my host-family directory for Returned Peace Corps Volunteers and secured a free room in their apartment for our stay. It was a two-block walk from their place to the city train and about a thirty-minute train ride to the hotel (followed by another two-block walk), but it was manageable, and it saved $400 that we had many uses for. Ray and his mom slept on the foldout couch-bed in the room, and I slept on a blanket on the cold hardwood floor. I could have squeezed onto the bed, but we would have been very uncomfortable, and Ray was the one who needed the good night's sleep. Besides, I wasn't doing much sleeping that first night, and I anticipated (correctly) even less sleep on subsequent nights.

We had until early afternoon (the start of Round One), so at Yee-chen's request, we did some site-seeing, getting off the train in downtown Chicago, walking the streets in 20-degree temperatures, and seeing our new "home" from the top of the Sears Tower. After our mini-trip, we headed all the way to the other side of town and made it in time to grab a quick lunch before the start of the tournament.

First rounds of large tournaments are always delayed. There are hundreds – in this case, thousands – of kids and parents rushing around to find boards and pushing and shoving one another to get a look at the pairing sheets. I used the "mob time" to take Ray aside and toss around the football (I'd squeezed a light and squishable foam-version of a real football into my backpack so that we could maintain our usual routine of tossing a ball before and between rounds). After we'd had our toss and the mob had dissipated, we walked to the pairings sheet unmolested to see who Ray was playing and where he was to sit.

* * *

Ray had a spot at one of the "Top Players" tables, which were in the front of the auditorium and removed from the general playing area. I sat with Ray until his opponent arrived, kneeling down beside him and whispering an extended mantra while he sat, eyes-closed, focusing on my words and taking in their significance: "This is it, Bud. This is what you've worked so hard for for the past year. Do you remember when we started planning for this one a year ago? Well, here we are. This is your year. I guess you know what you have to do. You have to take your time, but you also have to keep your eye on the clock. You need to think about your moves, but you can't use too much time. You just have to trust yourself to make strong, winning moves. You will make good moves. I already see it. Most important of all: focus. Focus. Focus. Focus. You're going to do great, Bud. Just play your game and everything will be fine."

I stepped aside with the parents of the New York boy who Ray was to play. When I answered their question about Ray's current rating, the dad said with a smile, "Well, this'll be a short game" and walked off. Although his son was ranked 55th out of 194 players, his rating was well below Ray's. Still, the father's prediction couldn't have been more off. Ray and his opponent were the last to finish of all of the 97 games being played in the Grade Three division.

When I left Ray at the board as the game commenced, I wasn't feeling good about the way he looked. He appeared to be nervous, and he had commented that his stomach felt funny – butterflies, I was sure. I said not to worry about it, that it was good to be a little nervous because it would keep him from making lazy moves and that he should just focus on his game, but I worried about it from my place just a short distance away. Ray was usually so composed and fearless at the board; that was one of his greatest strengths, for it simultaneously kept him focused and, without any guile on Ray's part, unnerved his opponents. Would things even out if Ray had lost his focus?

I also worried about the setting. The parents were not asked to leave, so hundreds of them stayed and the noise was really too much. Several times I saw Ray with his fingers in his ears trying to keep out the din of the crowd. Worse than the crowd was the Tournament Director who would irregularly blast "Shhhhhh" warnings over the loudspeaker system which scared or rattled the players far more than the steady din did. Besides the noise, there were the visual distractions to contend with. While the Top Tables had been set apart from the other tables in order to honor the best players, the placement of the tables couldn't have been worse: smack dab in the heart of the biggest conglomeration of talking parents and right in the middle of the route that many of the players and parents took to go from inside to outside the tournament hall. Both the players and their younger brothers and sisters walked or ran within inches of Ray's table throughout the course of the game. Still, I reminded myself, both players had to endure the same conditions; if Ray was suffering because of the distractions, then so was his opponent.

One good thing about most first rounds is that they pass more quickly than later rounds. The better players usually finish off their opponents relatively quickly, and other pairs, who have first-round jitters, play quickly and finish out their games in less than an hour or, in some cases, in 15 minutes or less. So while Ray was doing his usual routine of analyzing various lines of play – a process that eats up the clock and keeps the pace of the game relatively slow – scores of noisy kids and their parents were exiting the playing hall. From my position at about a dozen feet from the board, I watched the game in the spaces between passing persons and saw Ray go up a Pawn and then, some ten moves later, go up another. Once he had the second Pawn, I saw how Ray, in his typical fashion, simplified the field by trading off most of the pieces. When he had the game down to a Queen, a Rook, and a Knight on each side (with Ray still maintaining the two-Pawn advantage), I finally relaxed and thought that things were going to turn out well. And that's when he dropped his Rook, and by "drop" I mean he let his opponent capture his Rook without winning any piece in return.

It was on his 29th move. He had been sitting in deep concentration, playing out one line or another, and somehow –

either due to his own mental meanderings, the butterflies, the passing crowd and their din, or some combination of it all – Ray forgot about his Rook that was under attack; when he didn't move it to safety, his opponent quickly snapped it off the board. When it happened, Ray stared at the board for a second and then turned all the way around in his seat to where I was standing and gave me a frown and a look that said, "I just screwed up."

After the dropped piece and the look, I wanted to sit down and so made my way to some spectators' chairs a few feet beyond the playing area. I wondered if this was it. All of the training – all of his hard work – for a year even! – lost after a beginner's blunder in the very first round of the tournament. I figured that Ray must have just been too nervous, and I began to wonder what that meant. Had the nervousness always been there? Had I imagined the poise? Did this whole process put too much stress on him, and, if so, what does that say about the hours of time spent over the past year? Was it all wasted or harmful? And what about the aftermath? What will such a loss to a low-rated player in the first round of a tournament that Ray felt convinced he was going to win do to his confidence? Would he be shattered? Would this one incident prevent him from moving forward? What did it all mean? And then came the big question: Have *I* done something wrong?

Yee-chen, who was seated some aisles away and who was adding to the noise level by talking with another chess mom, saw me in my reverie and walked over to ask what was wrong. I skipped the psychology and said simply, "Ray's down a Rook, and there's a very good chance that he's not going to win this game." She replied, "Don't worry. He'll figure it out," and then went back to her conversation oblivious to the destruction that was at hand. That's a typical Yee-chen comment. She didn't understand the situation at all – hadn't even looked at the board and wouldn't have understood the position had she looked at it in any event. For a moment, I was annoyed, but then it hit me: she is absolutely right. What was I worrying about anyway? If Ray still had a Pawn on the board, then he had a chance to win. He wasn't a quitter, and I knew for a fact that he always played his best when he was losing a game. He became more focused and intent. I'd seen him work miracles before – had watched just a day ago in the airport as he came back after losing his Queen. And if he did lose this game? Well, then that was something that we would have to deal with. Ray had a great strength of character, and we would turn this into something positive if we had to. It wasn't yet time to start repairs. The game was still on.

With my own resolve returned along with my faith in my son, I moved closer to get a better look at the board and watched as Ray attempted to pass one of his two extra Pawns (i.e., move it across the board to where it could be promoted to a Queen). Before making any moves, he sat for dozens of minutes staring at the board, figuring out his plan, seeing the moves that he had to make to see his plan through to the end, and calculating the risk of every move made. When finally he moved, it was with the rest of the game mapped out; he was now just going through the motions and ensuring that the mental game he had just played was mirrored on the board in front of him.

Just as Ray's skill, experience, and poise helped him to move along the Pawn while protecting it and guarding his own King from attack at the same time, so too did his opponent's inexperience help Ray, for the New Yorker did not know how to stop the advancing Pawn. He made a series of moves that did nothing either to stop the Pawn or to capture Ray's King. I watched as, remarkably, the boy turned his attention away from Ray's passed Pawn and captured instead a more sedentary Pawn. In the end, the boy was forced to trade back the Rook he had won for Ray's passed Pawn which evened the game to a Queen and three Pawns apiece. Not until this happened did I really breathe easier, but still I reminded myself that the game wasn't over until it was over – that anything could happen. I just had to be patient and wait to see if Ray would do what he knew well how to do: win what seemed to be an even game.

The wait was brief. Six moves after Ray had evened the game, he "Queened" another Pawn – this time with check, which forced his opponent to give up his own Queen or else be checkmated. With the last obstacle (the opposing Queen) clear of the board, Ray went to work picking off his opponent's Pawns and ended the game a few moves later. Game One was over – the last game of the third grade section to come to an end. Ray was one win closer to his goal.

I'd talked with the New York boy's mom off and on throughout the game (I don't remember seeing the dad return after having made his one cryptic remark), and I kept her informed of the progress, including her son's great advantage after winning the Rook. I watched with her, though, Ray's comeback and the defeat of her son. She was nice and her son seemed nice too, so immediately after the boys shook hands, I told Ray to go over the game and to show the boy what he could have done to win. Ray did this and more. He showed the kid how even after Ray had equalized the game, he could have been forced into a draw by threefold repetition (both players moving their pieces in such a way that the same position on the board is repeated three times in the course of the game). Both boys and parents parted on good terms and wished the other luck in the future rounds.

When we were alone, I gave Ray a two-sided speech. I told him that he shouldn't expect to win any game in future rounds if he was going to drop a piece – that he was lucky that his Round One opponent lacked the experience to win a won game. On the other hand, I congratulated him on his win and told him that he did a great job of maintaining his focus and not giving up after dropping his piece. I reminded him of how others we had both seen fell to pieces when they blundered, and I focused on how Ray's determination and concentration won him the game. Maybe his loss of a Queen in the airport and his recovery during that game was in his mind and helped him to carry on. I didn't know and, frankly, it just didn't matter. The fact was that he had won a lost game, that he had had the heart and the skill to do it. It was success. We celebrated (after a quick meal) by tossing the football around in the little time that we had before the start of Round Two.

While throwing the ball around, I thought about luck. Was Ray's Round One win luck? In one way it was. His opponent had a win that he couldn't capitalize on, and had he offered Ray a draw immediately after taking Ray's Rook, Ray probably would have accepted. Ray was lucky that his opponent chose to play on and luckier still that the boy couldn't find the winning moves. But there were also elements that had nothing to do with luck – composure, for instance. Ray kept his usual cool and stayed focused enough to keep his opponent from having many good options. Also, Ray was quick enough to see his own defensive options and to play his best moves in the time that he had left on his clock. There are some players – most of whom have lost to Ray at some time – who would say that Ray has had an inordinate amount of good luck over the years, but, if each situation were looked at carefully, one would find poise, skill, focus, and timely moves behind each of the "lucky" wins.

* * *

Enough people had complained about the poor location of the top tables that the Tournament Director decided to eliminate the tables altogether and move the top boards back with the rest of the players. Thus, for Round Two, Ray was seated at the end of a long row of tables placed side-by-side. His place was right beside the Number Two board, with last year's national champ, Christopher Heung, seated on the other side of the table from Ray and just one seat over. Ray and Chris both knew that if they continued to win, it would only be a matter of time before the two would be seated directly across from one another.

While my wife window-shopped outside of the playing area, I accompanied Ray to the playing table. As we reached Ray's new seat, we heard one of the other players, at age eight already a notorious trash-talker, telling those around him that after he beat this round's opponent (here he pointed a finger at a small boy seated across the table from him) then he would beat the reigning champ. About Ray (whom I was just helping to get set up a few boards down) he said, "I don't even think we're going to have to play *that kid*. I saw his game, and he was lost." Ray and I shared a secret smile and left the trash-talker to carry on his soliloquy.

To the New York crowd, Ray certainly was "that kid." New York has always been the heart of the chess scene, and many of the top players and coaches lived in, or near, New York. Several of the players at Nationals either went to school together or at least saw one another each month at the local tournaments. They shared the same coaches, represented their schools in team events, and generally shared a common history. Ray was an outsider. He came into this tournament from – of all places – Florida, and this kid unknown to the New York chess scene, and without a coach, had somehow made his way to the top of the national list. I know from having spoken to some of the New York crowd that they considered New York chess to be at a higher level than chess in the rest of the country. I had no reason to argue with them. If this caused any of them, or their children, to underestimate Ray's ability, then all the better for Ray.

Ray's new board location made me a little concerned about the possibility of distractions. One distraction would be the nearness of the games of last year's champ and the other top players; Ray enjoyed looking at others' positions and trying to figure out traps and escapes in every game he saw. Another distraction, though, would be the champ himself, for he was a pretty jumpy kid – out of his seat often and frequently moving about the room, looking at others' games, walking here, walking there. I worried, too, about the trash-talker. I had remembered seeing him at another tournament the year before and noted at that time too his bragging at the board. I wondered if such a kid would employ other – more physical – tactics (like making excessive noise at the table or moving back and forth in front of others, or maybe even kicking his opponent under the table) during the game. I wondered to what degree he, or the champ, or both would be a distraction for Ray.

If any problems arose, I wouldn't be there to assist or to support Ray because I had to leave the room with the rest of the parents prior to the start of Round Two. Apparently, the complaints of the parents or the players about the noise during Round One moved the Tournament Director (TD) to decide to kick everyone out for the first thirty minutes of the round. I stayed with Ray up until his opponent – another New Yorker – appeared with his mother. They were easy to spot because the mother arrived voice-first, complaining as she walked up to the table and continuing to complain while her son got settled. What were her complaints about? Everything. The room, the noise, this player, that player, the TD, etc. etc. She directed most of her comments to the trash-talker's dad who had come up at about the same time to check on his son, but it appeared to me that she would have carried on in the same vein without a listening ear.

Her tirade died down only after she had left the room, leaving me and the trash-talker's dad as part of the last group of parents to leave. The dad came up to me and remarked on Ray's luck during the first round, and he said a few words to try to put a scare into me about the general strength of the New York kids. It was easy to see how the trash-talker came to be; the apple did not fall far from that tree. I didn't respond to the scare tactics and instead, as the trash-talker's dad literally swaggered out of the playing hall, I gave Ray a wave and a nod and left him to his game.

While the TD repeatedly warned the straggling parents and coaches that he was not going to let the games begin until every single one of them had left the room, I stood just outside of the playing area and peeked through the curtains that separated the players from the parents, searching across hundreds of tables and thousands of players to the other side of the room until I spied Ray's bright red cap. It was enough for me just to see the bright red dot. I focused on the dot for about thirty minutes until I saw a wave of parents and coaches filter back into the playing hall. I quickly joined the crowd and made my way to a spot near Ray's board and stood with other spectators behind the silver duct-taped line that the directors had placed around the playing area. As soon as I had taken my place, Ray's opponent shot his hand into the air, calling for a TD. When one arrived, I saw the boy speak rapidly to the TD while looking in my direction. Ray later confirmed what I thought the problem was: the boy didn't want anyone observing the game. The TD, however, informed him that as long as I remained quietly behind the line with the other spectators that I was allowed to watch the game. Nothing was ever said directly to me, so I stayed where I was and continued to watch.

The game appeared to be dead even and very drawish. I stood trying to figure out how Ray could break into his opponent's territory. Perhaps he could force an exchange, though I couldn't see how. Maybe he would have to make a sacrifice, but he would have to have a better follow-up plan than I could devise to see the game through to a win. Ray must have been thinking along the same lines as me, for his clock was ticking and he wasn't moving any pieces. He was down a full thirty minutes in time in a position that was presently drawn. That worried me. While I was thinking about this and about options for Ray, I first heard, and then saw, the opponent's mom. I looked away from the boys' board to see her charging towards me across the playing area, on the wrong side of the tape, bellowing, "You have *got* to be kidding me. You've been standing here the entire time!" Before I could reply, she flew past me and marched to the nearest TD to lodge her complaints. Apparently, she didn't get the response she desired, for I saw her march up to another, and then another, and still others. I supposed that they were all saying the same thing that I was thinking: "Just relax. Look around. There are dozens of parents and coaches in the room watching the games. As long as they keep their mouths shut and their bodies behind the silver tape, it's okay. Relax." It didn't look like she was relaxing, but that was not my problem. My only concern was with the game in front of me and, specifically, with how Ray was going to change the position from a draw to a win.

I was getting concerned about Ray's time; I worried that even if he had found the win, he might not have the time left to see it through. Chris, last year's champ and familiar with us from several events, had already finished his game and had returned to see how Ray was doing. He noted the low time, too, and even came up to inform me, before cheerfully departing, that it looked like Ray was going to lose on time. The trash-talker, too, was doing his own reconnaissance. I watched him walk right up to the board and then gleefully depart in a labored trot all the way to the exit to give his report to his father. Apparently, he had missed some key information, for I watched him lumber all of the way back for a second look and then return to the exit in the same fashion. Like Chris, the trash-talker probably thought that it would be a game lost on time.

I wondered if they would be right. All of the other games in his section had finished long before, and Ray's clock was still ticking. Ray had to alter the position on the board, and he had to act fast. As it turned out, though, it wasn't Ray who changed the position; it was his opponent. The boy blundered on move 35 by moving away a piece that had been protecting a Pawn. With the piece gone, Ray immediately pounced on the Pawn and, in doing so, created yet another benefit: a "won" exchange (capturing a Rook for a Bishop or a Knight). With a material advantage and a board no longer closed to his attack, Ray did a quick study of the position, created his plan, and checkmated his opponent a dozen moves later, seemingly oblivious to the mere seconds that remained on his clock. Two down.

It was a rocky start – what with the blunder in game one and the time trouble and tricky position in game two – but Ray ended the first day 2-0. We found Yee-chen, and the three of us walked through the cold to the train and made our way home (Ray and I playing thumb-wars throughout the thirty-minute ride). By the time we reached the house, it was 11:00 p.m. Florida-time – a full two hours past Ray's usual bedtime. He was exhausted by the day's events and was asleep almost immediately.

* * *

On Friday night, I was asleep at a reasonable hour, but while Ray slumbered on until 7:00, I was up and alert at 2:00 a.m. It wasn't the coldness or the hardness of the floor, and it wasn't the heating vent aimed at my head (keeping my head several degrees warmer than my icy feet); it was a combination of excitement and nervousness that kept me up. I knew that the only role left for me was one of support person and that the best way to perform that role would be to get a good night's sleep, but I also knew that that wasn't going to happen. My thoughts were all on Round Three and when I am too excited about something, I am thrown off balance and everyday patterns, habits, and rhythms become meaningless. That's when sleep doesn't come when it should. At least Ray was sleeping like a baby. It didn't matter if I went completely without rest provided that Ray was rested and ready to play. That thought comforted me as I lay awake waiting.

At breakfast the next morning, Ray's butterflies had reappeared. He complained that his stomach felt funny, and he didn't want to eat anything. Still, I made him eat a small bowl of cereal. I thought that having something in his stomach might mean the difference between a loss from a poor move from a hungry and weak Ray and a win due to a strong move from a healthy Ray. It was a little thing, but I was looking for ways to keep contributing, and this was one of the few things I could do.

Yee-chen went shopping that day, so it was just me and Ray playing thumb-wars all the way to our train stop. When we got to the playing hall, we learned that Ray was paired with yet another New Yorker. I guess this shouldn't have been a surprise since New York has such a strong chess program, where many instructors have formed long-term connections with specific schools within various school districts. New York scholastic squads would sometimes come to such events with a coach – a paid grandmaster – on hand to help prepare the team.

After our football toss and while we were setting up at Ray's board, we learned from Chris's mom that, of the nearly 200 kids in Ray's section, there were only 28 with two wins going into the third round. In a seven-round tournament, this meant that Chris, or one of the other top five kids, would face Ray before the seventh round. I whispered to Ray that none of that mattered. All that mattered, I said, was the game that he had before him, and all that mattered in that game was the first move. He needed to focus on one move, or line of moves, at a time and not get caught up in "what if" scenarios of future rounds. After the usual mantra and my nod goodbye, I left with the other parents for our hour-long wait outside (the TD was displeased with the noise level caused by some of the parents, so he had extended our time in the "holding cell" by thirty minutes). Once more I took a place where I could keep track of Ray by his bright red hat.

While I was waiting and hoping, the trash-talker's dad, whom I had been purposefully avoiding, swaggered up to try again to instill in me fear of the New Yorkers and, in particular, of his son. I didn't give him any opportunities to extend the conversation, and my only response to his pumping me about Ray's play was to tell him that Ray never played against people through computer chess sites and that, instead, he learned by studying books – at which point Mr. Swagger began to extol the virtues of Internet chess (which his son played prodigious amounts of). I finally got rid of him by saying that it looked like the parents were going in. They weren't, but it got him moving toward the door and as soon as he was a few steps away, I made my own move in the opposite direction.

Once the parents really were allowed back in, I quickly made my way to my spot beyond the tape – just six feet or so from Ray's game at the end of the long table. Even though many of the others' games had already concluded and Ray was still there with clock ticking, I could see from the position on the board that it would all be over soon. Ray had coordinated his pieces into a forceful attack, and, after sufficient thought and re-thought, he checkmated his opponent on the 25th move. It was Ray's shortest game and the easiest one thus far.

* * *

The win left us plenty of time to play football both before and after lunch. As we hadn't had much "real" exercise, I let Ray run as much as he wanted to. He ran long patterns ("the bomb" and "the fly" to those who know football), and he worked up a good sweat. When it seemed like he'd had enough without having overdone it, I took him to lunch. With his butterflies still present, he only managed to get down a bowl of soup and a few crackers. It wasn't that much, but I thought that it would be enough, and it was certainly better than playing on an empty stomach. After lunch, we played more lightly – mostly just passes back and forth – for I didn't want to tire him out with two rounds ahead of him that day.

Back in the chess hall, we learned (again from Chris's mom) that there were only 14 kids who had three wins going into Round Four. Included in this group were Chris, the trash-talker, and T.J. – Ray's next opponent. Unlike the first three opponents Ray had faced, T.J. was not from New York. He hailed from Arizona and, other than that he had come into this tournament ranked in the top half, there was nothing else that we knew about him. Ratings don't tell much and can even be deceptive. This is true for players in certain states (Washington, for example) that have their own rating system independent of the USCF system. A player from such a state might have a USCF rating of 1300 from one USCF tournament played a year before but had, perhaps, a current rating of 1500 based on his performance in his state's independent system. We didn't know anything about the Arizona system – whether or not, like Washington, they had an independent league – so I told Ray to play T.J. as if he were playing Garry Kasparov, the former World Champion.

And while the trash-talker talked his trash and while Chris and some of the others fidgeted or goofed around, Ray sat with eyes closed listening to the mantra and seeing himself winning. When his opponent arrived, I left the table with the others. I couldn't come back until the top of the hour this time (yet another time extension created by the exasperated TD), so I divided my time between talking with some of the Florida fathers, staring at Ray's red hat, and imagining in vain what was happening in Ray's game. When I was finally allowed to return to my spot, I saw a complicated position on the board and much less time on Ray's clock than on his opponent's. I saw that T.J. had given up two Pawns in order to create a vicious attack consisting of a Queen and two pieces practically in the face of Ray's King. In addition to this, T.J. had a Rook on a partially opened file (yet another threat to Ray's King). What was most amazing to me was that the boy had done all of this by move 15!

While Ray's clock ate up minute after minute during his strategizing, I tried to find the right moves too. Although I couldn't find a good plan after a long think, I knew that Ray had better find one soon or else he would certainly lose on time. Many things happened during the forty minutes that Ray was lost in thought over the position. I watched Chris and several others finish off their opponents and leave the hall. I watched as the trash-talker burst into tears and then left the room wailing when he managed no better than a draw against his opponent. While Ray thought, I watched as every other game ended. But mostly what I watched was the ticking of Ray's clock. True, he did have about 20 minutes left for the rest of his game, but this was nothing compared to his opponent's remaining time, and Ray, just like anyone, would need time to finish the game.

However, when finally he moved, Ray had found more than just the next move; he had found the entire line, and his next series of moves came rapidly with little loss of time. More important than having finally made a move, thereby saving his remaining precious minutes, was the fact that the next move and the subsequent moves were the right ones. Ray's 40-minute think resulted in the complete deflation of T.J.'s attack, the absolute protection of Ray's King, the exchange of his Rook for T.J.'s Queen, and the outright capture of another piece. After more forced exchanges of pieces, down a Queen and a Knight, and with checkmate just a move or two away, T.J. resigned. Not many minutes remained on Ray's clock, but that no longer mattered. Despite the uncharacteristic butterflies, Ray was playing that day like he had played since he got good a few months back. I could see it in the moves he was making. I could see it in his face, and it was there in his upright body for everyone else to see. He was on; it was to be a good day of chess for him. You could just see it.

* * *

Yee-chen returned from her day in the city in time to join us for dinner. It was soup and crackers for all of us. Ray ate what he could and then in the few minutes remaining, we tossed the football around once more. Yee-chen decided to explore the nearby shops in the Convention Center while Ray and I set up for the fifth and final round of the day.

Going into Round Five, due to a series of draws and upsets, there were only four players with five wins: Ray, Chris, and two Top 100 boys – one from the Northwest (Chris's opponent) and the other from New York (Ray's fourth opponent out of five from that state). While we were waiting for Ray's opponent to arrive, Ray pointed to the table and asked where the spots were coming from. I didn't see any spots, but I told him they were caused by the lighting as it reflected off of the table. My guess was that Ray was nervous. Actually, it was more fact than guess, for Ray had just moments before mentioned the butterflies again. "Don't worry about being nervous," I told him. "It will keep you from getting too relaxed and from making lazy moves." As Tamir, Ray's opponent, approached the table, I whispered the mantra once more: "Take your time, but watch the clock. Trust yourself to make good moves. Focus. Focus. Play your game, and all will be well." Then I stood up, wished Tamir good luck, nodded to his father and left Ray at the table.

It was getting more and more difficult for me to wait out the first hour on the sidelines. Something that made the wait easier was the absence of Mr. Swagger who, after his son's tearful finish in the last round, kept his distance. For one hour I watched the red dot far away, sometimes seeing the dot float across the room and then return a minute or two later: a bathroom break. Most of the time, though, the dot seemed as immobile as I was. I didn't have many thoughts other than an occasional "Come on, Ray!"; all that I could really focus on was the dot and the ticking of my watch.

Years later, when the parents and coaches were allowed back in, I hastened to my usual spot and saw what was becoming a familiar sight: Ray leaning over the board deep in concentration with very little time remaining on his clock. The position seemed to be even, and once again I worried about the time pressure in a drawn position. Ray's time was rapidly slipping to the ten-minute mark. If he didn't find his line soon, he might not even have enough time remaining to get the draw. Once a player's time runs out, regardless of the strength of his position, he loses the game – a fact I'm sure that Tamir knew and perhaps was even counting on.

Tamir, however, inadvertently assisted Ray by blundering, which allowed Ray to win a Pawn on move 22, simultaneously opening up the position and creating weaknesses which Ray was quick to exploit. By move 26 he had won Tamir's Knight. Still, the clock was ticking, and by the time that Ray managed to exchange Queens (move 39), his time was down to five minutes. Even with the material advantage of a Pawn and a Knight, it wasn't going to be easy to win the game with so little time.

That was my thinking anyway. For his part, Ray seemed to be the calm and focused expert that on so many occasions in the past I had watched masterfully pull off wins with much less than five minutes on his clock. His natural poise, along with the past year's worth of several games played under similar circumstances, helped Ray to stay focused and make his carefully calculated moves. His plan, I saw, was to push his passed "c" Pawn. Once he'd gotten his remaining forces in position to see the Pawn safely to the Queening square and had, in fact, pushed the Pawn to within one square of its destination,

Tamir resigned. It was his 50th move; the time on Ray's clock showed just a couple of minutes.

When the boys walked to the sidelines, I congratulated Tamir for having played a good game, and Tamir's father, who had been watching from a few feet beyond me, shook my hand and gave his congratulations to Ray. I took Ray aside a minute later, congratulated him, and said something about the little bit of time he had remaining. "What?" he said calmly. "You don't think I could have won in that position? I had plenty of time left." I couldn't argue with him. He had won the game after all, and he was the one who had spent nearly 90 minutes of his own time and 60 minutes of his opponent's time analyzing the position. If anyone could predict what was going to happen in that game, it was Ray.

The three of us (Yee-chen had joined the party near the end of Ray's last round) walked out of the playing hall and into a light snow. We made our way to the train where Ray and I had our thumb-war matches. I didn't tell him that Chris had won his game too and that the two of them would be squaring off in Round Six, the only players with five wins apiece. Ray had just played some excellent chess – from his one easy win to the great defensive game to his marathon match in the final round. He had had a full day, and I didn't want to make him nervous with thoughts of his upcoming match against the two-time defending national champion the next morning.

Once we reached our stop and had walked out of the train station and into the streets, I was grateful yet again for Yee-chen's presence. Had it just been me and Ray, I would certainly have shuttled Ray directly through the snow-filled streets to the apartment and put him promptly to bed. The hour was late, and Ray had his toughest matches ahead of him. But instead of letting me direct the end of the day, Yee-chen started a snowball fight. It wasn't a long one, but it was fun, and it was just the kind of release that Ray needed after a long day of thinking on a fluttering stomach. We arrived home covered in snow 15 minutes later than planned with Ray appearing to be purged of the day's events, and, after a small snack, Ray was in his usual deep sleep beside his mom by 11:00 p.m.

For me, well, I had most all of the night to contemplate Saturday's completed games and to imagine what would happen on Sunday during the final two rounds. My nervousness surfaced when I dozed off for my two hours of rest and then awoke from dreams of Ray losing at chess. I was just worried, I knew, and I was glad that if someone had to worry, it was me and not my son. But the dreams kept me from sleeping again, and I was already dressed and ready to go by the time Ray awoke from his eight hours of sleep.

* * *

Once again Ray didn't want to eat breakfast, and once again I made him eat a small bowl of cereal. If he wasn't going to have ten full hours of sleep, then he at least was going to begin the day with something besides butterflies in his stomach. Since Yee-chen decided to stay near the apartment to take a walk through the snow-filled streets, it was just the two of us on the train to the playing hall that morning. While we were playing our umpteenth game of thumb-wars, I told Ray that he would be playing Chris in the next round.

Ray surprised me with his next question: "What if he beats me?" I couldn't be angry with Ray for asking this question, for it was one that I had been thinking about since the night before. It was normal for Ray to question his ability at such a time – near the home stretch of a national tournament in which one move in one game could decide who the chess community would call the best. Instead of answering the question, I told Ray not to worry and that he would do fine just as long as he played his game. Then I challenged Ray to a thumb-war match, and for the moment he forgot his doubts in his effort to pin my thumb.

After the train had stopped and we had walked through the snow to the playing hall, I took Ray to one of the near-empty warehouses beside the tournament room. There were only a few people there – a small run-off from the masses piling into the tournament room for the day's first round. I sat Ray down in a quiet part of the warehouse, right on the cement floor, and talked with him about his next game. "First," I said "Chris has jump-butt; he's all over the place during a game – watching other matches, walking all around, moving from here to there. But you have focus. While he's jumping around, you're concentrating on the board. You'll see things that he won't. Second, you want this more than he does. You've been working on your own to win this tournament for the past 365 days. I know that I haven't been in Chris's home, but I am certain that he hasn't studied like you have every day since last year's tournament. I think you're going to win because you are more determined than he is. And if those two reasons aren't enough for you, Bud, here's the third one: you're a better player. Your rating's above his because you've played better than he has over the past year. You've played nearly every tournament in the last six months in the section above Chris's. If you play your regular game, there's no way that he's going to beat you."

Seated there in the warehouse, we did an extended version of the mantra – meditation-style with eyes closed and with Ray's hands in mine: "Take your time, Bud, but don't take too much time. Chris is a good player. Even if you find the win, if you don't leave yourself enough time, Chris might find a way to shelter his King until your clock runs down. Use Chris's time to think about your moves, too. But the important thing is to move. You can't lose on time. Trust yourself, Bud. You're going to make winning moves. Take your time, watch the clock, make strong moves, and focus. Focus. Focus. Focus. You're going to play a good game, Bud. I see it."

We tossed the football back and forth for a few minutes before the start of the round, and then we joined the mass of people and made our way to Ray's seat at the edge of the table. After wishing Chris good luck, I bent down and whispered an abbreviated mantra to Ray. In addition to the usual advice, I reminded him that this was the game that he had prepared for for the past year. "This is your game," I told him. "This is why you're here." With nothing more to say, I filed out of the room with the rest of the parents and coaches, leaving Ray to battle on his own.

As I exited the room, I heard the TD announce to all parents and coaches that upon our return at the top of the hour, we would have to stand behind a barrier well back from the playing area. This meant that I would no longer have my ringside seat for the game that I expected to be the most exciting of the tournament. As there was nothing I could do, I made my way to the curtained area and stared once again at the red dot that represented my son.

If you added all of the hours of sleep I'd had from the past three nights, it still wouldn't make one full night's sleep. During a part of my latest sleepless night, I had thought back to a talk I'd recently had. It was during one of the larger events a short time before Nationals. Chris was there, and while the boys were in the tournament hall, Chris's mother approached me and asked what I thought about the boys agreeing to a pre-arranged draw should they meet at Nationals. She said that in this way both boys could be the national champ and no one would go home a loser. It was a surprise to receive such a humane and non-combative suggestion, for chess is generally dog-eat-dog with no pity for the other guy. I didn't think she'd understand it if I told her that Ray would have felt like a loser had he "won" the title in that manner. Also, it wasn't as if the boys were equally matched. During the past twelve months, Ray had worked hard to ensure that he was well ahead of Chris in wins and in rating points. Also, Chris had had the title two years running; it didn't seem fair to me that he should be given a third title. If he was the best player, then he would have to prove it. Those were my thoughts. Of course, I didn't say everything that I thought. All I said was that the boys ought to give it their best and if Chris won, then he should be champion, and the same for Ray.

And now the two were playing, and finally, after another lifetime of waiting, the parents and coaches were allowed back in. I took my place in the area behind the barrier after finding a corner spot that gave me a full view of Ray but that left Chris out of sight, hidden behind a column. I didn't need to see Chris, though. Ray's body language was telling me the story. I saw that Ray was sitting up high on his knees, leaning over the board, and intent on the game. I saw that the focus was there, and that was all that I needed to know. On two occasions when Ray walked past the barrier to go to the bathroom, he looked into the crowd, found me, and gave me a quick reassuring smile.

What had happened on the board that I couldn't see was that Ray had won a Pawn by move 10; he had forced a Queen exchange on move 23; he had won a piece a short time later; and then he had scooped up a few more Pawns before Chris, with no hope of win or draw, resigned on move 42. It was the second fastest game that Ray had played in the tournament. When I saw Ray's hand shoot up to signal the TD that the game was over, I knew that he had won. No one who loses a game is anxious to share the result with the TD or with anyone. When Ray walked up to me at the barrier, he said simply and quietly, "I won." That was it. He had just beaten the defending champion and his biggest obstacle to the 2003 title, and all he could say was "I won." And all that I could say in reply was, "I knew you were going to win. I knew you could do it."

* * *

The tournament wasn't won yet. Although Ray was the only player going into the final round with six wins, there were two who had five-and-a-half points. One of the two would be playing Chris, and the other one would face Ray. If Ray lost, then his opponent would win the title with 6.5 points to Ray's 6.0 points. If Ray drew, then he would either win the title for himself or else share it in the event that Chris's opponent defeated Chris. While it was nice to know that Ray had a draw option that could still give him the title (or at least a share of the title), he hadn't spent so much of the last year working hard to settle for anything less than a sweep. He was there to win.

Since Ray's last-round victory was comparatively short, we had more time than usual before the next round. Thus, we did what we always did when we had time on our hands: we played football. I threw long passes to Ray in the near-empty warehouse where we had had our pre-game meditation. The repeated throws and catches helped both of us to work off some of the pressure that had come with the day's events, and I was feeling about as rejuvenated as Ray looked when we finally stopped for lunch. We met Yee-chen for a bowl of soup with crackers and shared the good news with her. While Ray and Yee-chen ate, I played out Ray's game against Chris on the miniature magnetic set that I had in my backpack. It wasn't as good as seeing the game up close, but it was all that I had, and it helped me to understand why the game had ended as quickly as it did.

After lunch, while Yee-chen explored the shops around the area, I tossed the ball some with Ray and then returned with him to the meditation spot for our final pep talk. With my hands holding his, I reminded Ray of all that he had gone through during the past year; in addition, I recounted his tournament games: his comeback victory in Round One, his win from a drawn position in Round Two, the easy Round Three win, the great defensive battle in Round Four, the time pressure victory in Round Five, and the crushing win over the defending champion in Round Six. There was one more game to win, I reminded him, and he needed to stay focused to do it. It wasn't the time to celebrate yet. He would need all of his focus in order to play his best game and finish the event as the only undefeated third-grader. I told him that he could do it, that I saw it happening, and that all that was left was for him to make it so.

A few minutes after our talk, Ray was sitting at his spot at Board One, and I was giving him a firm nod as I walked out of the playing hall with the last of the parents and coaches. While departing, I reflected on the calmness of Ray. It seemed to me that he sensed that the tournament was going to be his – that the worst had passed. Ray's calm didn't make me feel any better. I preferred it when he was a little nervous, for it helped to keep him focused and alert. Too much calm and peace of mind might result in a lazy move, and lazy moves were losing moves. Whatever his calm meant, there was nothing I could do to either encourage it or shake Ray free from it. Everything was in Ray's hands.

Yee-chen came back from her shopping, so instead of taking my usual spot by the curtains to stare at the red dot, I sat with Yee-chen in the nearby warehouse. She showed me some simple hand-made jewelry that she'd bought nearby. It was amazing to me that she could even think about anything but the chess game that was being played one warehouse over, but this was an advantage for her; Yee-chen would never die of either heart failure or high blood pressure. Hers was the healthy response; mine was the dangerous one. Still, I was who I was, so I sat there thinking-thinking-thinking about a game that I couldn't even see.

A few of the chess dads that I knew saw me and came over to kill a few minutes off of their own clocks. From them I learned of a deal that had been made among four of the older players. Rather than play their games and risk losing the title, the two pairs agreed beforehand to draw one another and so guarantee themselves a share of the national title. It was a shame that one of the boys didn't have the courage or the belief in himself to try for the win. I imagined Ray in a similar situation seven or eight years in the future and knew that he would be the one to say no, thereby forcing the other three to play their games honestly or risk losing the title. What those boys did, though, was their business. My only responsibility was to my son, and he already knew where I stood on such deals.

After a sufficient chunk of time had inched past and the parents and coaches began to flood into the room, I left Yee-chen in the warehouse and returned to my spot behind the barrier. My first sight of Ray was of him walking from his board to neighboring boards to spy on others' games. I reasoned that he had either lost his focus completely in the excitement of the final round or that he was so secure in his position that he didn't need much thought or concentration to play out his last game. I hoped with all of my heart that it was the latter, but, of course, I had no way of knowing. When Ray saw me on one of his bathroom trips, he gave me a short smile. I didn't fully relax, though, for the game was still on, and I had seen many players – Ray among them – lose a won game. "Focus!" I shouted to Ray, but it was a silent shout made by the voice within my head – the voice that was reminding me that nothing was over until it was over.

A reporter from a New York newspaper helped distract me from my thoughts by asking me questions about Ray. He was there to cover Chris during his third title bid but turned to us after Ray had won their match. *Who is his coach?* He doesn't have a coach – unless you count me. He has spent the past year working on his own, playing out grandmaster games every day for 365 days. *What makes him so good?* He has a focus and a determination that others don't seem to possess. He has natural intellectual ability, yes, but he works hard every day to improve himself. *Why do you spend so much of your own time and money on this activity?* Ray is my son, and I love him. When I learned that he was truly good at chess, it was only natural for me to support him and to do as much to assist him in his development as I could. I wanted him to succeed at something that he really enjoyed. *Do you think he's going to win?* I hope so. He has worked so very hard since the last tournament. He truly deserves to win.

I left the reporter after the last statement – there really wasn't anything more I could say – and moved to the side of the father whose son had beaten Ray in the airport before we left Tampa. He had just come from getting himself a cup of water from the water jug near Ray's board. He gave me the scoop: Ray was up a Pawn and an exchange (a Rook for a Knight), but the Queens were still on the board. Queens on the board meant that the game wasn't over; the Queen was the most deadly piece and could always make trouble. Seeing my anxiety, the father returned to the cooler for another cup of water some minutes later and came back with this report: Ray had forced a Queen exchange and then had purposefully given back the Rook/Knight exchange he had won earlier so that he could go into a King/Pawn endgame (only the two kings and some pawns on the board), with Ray having one extra Pawn.

This was when I breathed more easily. Ray could win such a King/Pawn endgame in his sleep. I could see by his body language (he was standing up now in a dominant position) that he was working his King and Pawns to create a passed Pawn. I watched Ray make several quick and forceful moves and knew that he was guiding his Pawn safely to the Queening square. When Ray's arm stretched all the way across the table a few minutes later, I knew that he was reaching for the Queen his opponent had captured earlier so that Ray could replace his passed Pawn with it. When I was sure that that had happened, I knew that it truly was all over. Moments later Ray confirmed my guess when he shot his hand into the air to call over the TD to verify the result of the game.

Yee-chen, who had joined me near the end of the game, turned to me and said, "Congratulations, Baba. You worked so hard for this." And then she gave me a hug. We both watched as Ray and his opponent packed their pieces in the bags the TD had provided and returned the bags and the board to the front of the room. When this final task was done, Ray walked up to us and gave us each a hug. I leaned down and whispered to him, "This is what you came here for. This is what you worked so hard for. You did great, and now you're the champ. 7-and-0. You did it, Bud. You did it."

* * *

After the awards ceremony later that afternoon, after we had carried Ray's four-foot-tall first-place trophy down the snowy blocks, onto the Chicago train, and up the stairs of our temporary home, we all ate a huge dinner. Ray took second helpings of everything and ate no fewer than five servings of salad. Butterflies gone, he was making up for all of the bird-like meals he had eaten since Friday. Other than his eating more than usual and the absence of the nervousness that he'd carried in his stomach for the past three days, Ray was still Ray despite having just won the biggest tournament in his relatively short career as a chess player. He wasn't dancing or bragging; he was simply eating dinner with his parents and talking little at the table, as usual. So normal was Ray behaving that, after dinner, he retired to the bedroom to study positions in one of the chess books he'd brought with him. I suppose that some people after having competed in such a high-pressure event would do anything but study chess a few hours after the last round, but not Ray. He loved the game, and I suppose that he couldn't think of a better way to end the most triumphant day of the year than by studying chess. He was simply indefatigable in his efforts to master the game of chess. Indefatigable: never getting tired or giving up. For an example, see Ray Robson.

And how was the chess dad holding up? I was in a kind of funk. Yes, I was drained by the lack of sleep and the worry (worry that had begun weeks before the event), but I was mostly drained by the conclusion of it all. It had a deflating effect on me. I liken my feeling and reaction to what is sometimes suffered by women who have just given birth. They've carried this growing thing within them for so long that they've become emotionally (in addition to physically) attached to it, and so when it's removed from them, they feel the emptiness and it saddens them. That's how I was feeling: empty and sad. The place that held the dream of a national title for Ray became empty when the dream was no longer a dream.

I felt the sadness for about a week, and then kicked in the euphoria: "Hey, my son's the national champ!" The empty space left by a dream-come-true was filled up with pride and a general happiness for my son. He really had done it. He started the story, he carried it along, and, in the end, he gave it a happy ending.

15

There are some advantages to being a perfectionist and in not wanting to make any mistakes. In my case, I have sat on the above story for years. I didn't want the story told unless it could be told correctly. I also worried about how Ray would come across. I did not want anyone to like Ray any less because of anything that I had written in my profile of him. I'm sensitive to the fact that I may have said too often and with too much conviction that Ray is smarter than the average bear, that he works harder than an ant, and that everything he got, he deserved. Also, I didn't want to write anything that would embarrass Ray, myself, or anyone else. Parents are sensitive, and chess tutors are infinitely more delicate when it comes to ego. So I've sat on all of this and stewed, and in the years that have passed, I find that even though Ray's becoming the 2003 Grade Three National Champion would have been an appropriate climactic finish to the story of a boy, his dream, and his meteoric climb to the top as he pursued his dream, it wasn't the end of the story; in fact, I thought that what remained to tell was at least as important as what I'd already said. And so there's more.

* * *

Ray's rating, by the time that he had won the national title, put him in the Class A category. He was just beginning the long trek through a new level in order to reach that which came next: expert. We'd found over the past few months that rating points were harder and harder to come by. At the level that he was at, Ray would have to have a number of wins over much stronger players in order to have any kind of a big upward movement in his rating. Gone were the days when a single strong showing in an event could garner him 60 or 70 rating points. It looked like he'd have to nickel-and-dime his way up one tournament at a time. And while it was getting more and more difficult to bring in the rating points, it was becoming easier to drop them. As a player solidly in the 1800s, Ray was now becoming the one to beat. He represented a huge burst in rating to every player ranked below him who could defeat him in tournament play.

The pressure on Ray was beginning to increase. He'd set himself goals, worked towards them, and then accomplished them. He was a national champion. He was a member of the All-American team. Partly because of the accomplishments themselves and partly because of what he had to do to earn his accolades (i.e., win-win-win), he was on nearly everyone's blacklist. The crowds that used to gather in admiration of the 7-year-old wonder-boy now gathered around the 9-year-old and prayed for him to lose. We were both learning that no one likes a perpetual winner. I was more sensitive to this than Ray, but he was aware of it too. It seemed that when he lost, there was relief on some of the faces in the crowd. If the expression could speak, it would have said, "Okay! He's human after all." And when Ray continued his upward surge by winning a Class A championship in January of 2004 and shooting his rating up yet again, it was clear that he was in for more antagonism.

The antagonism took a variety of forms. There were the middle-aged men – usually around master level – who were threatened by the presence of a child in their section. These were the men who had been playing chess for twenty or more years, had reached their limit over a lifetime's effort, and were now seated across the board from a nine-year-old who was beating on their door and who wasn't taking "No" for an answer. Some of these "adults" simply didn't want Ray – or any kid – in their section, for the presence of the youngsters served to remind them that not only had they reached their peak rating but that they were on the decline, losing memory, growing fatigued more easily, and losing a little of their ability to concentrate with the passing of each day, while across from them sat a boy who was quick, tireless, sharp . . . and who was just nine years old. It was only a matter of time before the inevitable happened, and none of the masters wanted to be the first one downed by this kid.

Sometimes the better players were simply rude, regardless of who they were facing. Dragoslav Bragkovic – a 2100 expert from Europe – was one such player that Ray had to contend with. Dragoslav hadn't been in this country long, and he struggled with the English language. Aside from being unable to talk with most people, he tended to alienate or outright annoy other players by his behavior. In one event, he loudly announced checkmate in two (certainly within the rules but considered rude nonetheless). Dragoslav sometimes talked at odd times and, when he did talk, it was in a voice so loud that he was promptly shushed by a half-dozen players. Once, just moments after a victory, he said in his all-hear-this voice, "Three down; one to go." He was also very antsy – darting to his feet and dashing to another part of the room, standing for a moment, then, squirrel-like, darting off in another direction. He was up and down like that dozens of times during a game. Another annoying habit had to do with the speed with which he played his moves. He seemed to not need to study the board, and he had often made his move and hit the clock before his opponent had fully retracted his hand after making his own move. Again, it may have been style, but most interpreted his actions as yet another way to look down upon his opponent.

When the two of them played, Dragoslav said to Ray, "What I play for first move? You pick." Dragoslav's meaning was not lost on nine-year-old Ray, for when I asked him about it afterward, he immediately told me that his words meant that Dragoslav thought that he could crush Ray with any opening. That was how their game began. Ray maintained his composure and in spite of, or perhaps because of, Dragoslav's disrespect, he held his higher-rated opponent to a draw.

Another time Ray was paired with another strong player – one who was even more rude and aggressive than Dragoslav. From the start I could see that the man was odd. He was physically twitching and turning and moving like one who'd just had three straight Cuban coffees or an extra potent snort of cocaine. When Ray asked if it'd be all right to use his clock (which was digital and preferred by the TD over his opponent's analog clock due to its accuracy), he shot back in rapid-fire English, "I-know-about-the-clocks!-You-don't-have-to-tell-me-about-the-clocks!-I've-been-playing-chess-for-many-years!-I-know-the-rules!" He spoke as if his words were bullets, and he looked as if he were shooting them into Ray's heart.

When the round started, Osshulio, Ray's opponent, made a series of half-second moves, which reminded me immediately of Dragoslav. I wondered if all of the rude players of the chess world tried to intimidate their opponents in this same way. The ones I'd seen firsthand certainly relied on it. But Ray was a composed player. He took his time and made his moves when he was ready. When I saw that he was up the exchange and had the advantage, I left the game to jot a few notes in my journal. Perhaps twenty minutes later, when I looked up from a seated position in the back of the hall, I saw a crowd around Ray and Osshulio. I quickly walked up to see what had happened and learned that, in a flurry of moves, Ray had miscalculated a combination involving a Rook sacrifice and so lost a piece with only a Pawn in return. It didn't look good, but things were not yet over, so Osshulio was out of line when he leaned forward and asked Ray if he would resign. In chess, you can offer a draw, you can announce checkmate, or you can resign yourself, but you don't ask your opponent if he's ready to resign. When Ray continued to play on, Osshulio gathered up the captured pieces from both sides of the board and began putting them away. Any piece that Ray captured until the conclusion of the game was scooped up by Osshulio and placed in his chess-bag. This is just the kind of player that I like to see Ray crush – the rude and arrogant types who often bully better than they play – but Ray's miscalculation was big enough to cost him the game in the end. Osshulio was leaving the table without the customary handshake, but Ray reached his arm so far across the table that Osshulio reluctantly took it, though I saw that he looked away when he gave his half-second handshake.

There were plenty of others, too – the expert who chastised Ray for fighting on instead of resigning in a difficult position; the master who shot Ray evil glances across the board and who stood beside the board criticizing Ray's play with his middle-aged cronies while the game was still in progress; and a host of others who through condescending speech and childlike behavior made it difficult for someone like Ray to fit into the upper levels of the chess world. It sometimes took an hour's worth of playing catch with the football to shake off the Osshulios of the chess world, and that's what we usually did to clear Ray's mind for the next round and to calm his dad who was the one who was always the most upset of all.

Besides the bullies and the adult children, I witnessed at one event yet another obstacle that Ray would have to face as he matured from child to young adult. Seated beside Ray was a strong player, a teenager whom we had seen at several events. He was a nice kid with good manners – clean-cut and a good sport. Seated across from him was a pretty young woman. Her face was made up perfectly, her hair was combed back into a cute style, and she wore tight jeans and a tube-top. I saw the teenaged boy's father take him aside seconds before the start of the match, and he later shared with me that he'd told his son to place his focus on the board. When they were seated at the table, the teen turned to the side. I mean he physically turned his body so that he sat side-saddle in his chair and would have had to seriously strain his neck to look across the board at his pretty opponent. His stratagem worked, and he won the game, though what a price for a young man to have to pay!

This kind of distraction didn't exist for my son. When he looked to the left, the only place his nine-year-old eyes rested was on the position of the pieces on the board. I was relieved to know that I had another few years to work out a strategy against what might prove to be the most dangerous obstacle of all: a lovely young woman.

16

Partly because of the Osshulios, the Dragoslavs, the frightened masters, and the folks who now rooted against him, and partly because of the pressure of being the one to beat, Ray stopped having fun. In addition to having to face the ugly, he was also struggling with time. He was thinking so deeply, seeing more and more patterns, and calculating to such depths that it was becoming difficult for him to make his own moves in less than the two hours that he was allotted for each game.

All of these pressures came to a head at a K-12 state event where third-grade Ray was playing against the state's best high school players in an abbreviated time control. In the middle of one game, I saw Ray emerge from the playing hall, on his way to the bathroom, with tears streaming down his face. Parents had been asked to keep away from their kids during games in order to prevent cheating, but I broke all rules by approaching him and asking what had happened – "Did someone say something?" "Did someone do something?" But I got no answers. Forty minutes later Ray emerged again, having won the game, and – because of the win – I was even more confused (I'd assumed that he was upset because he had made a beginner's error or something similar and so had blown the game). Much later I was finally able to wrench from him that he had been overtaken by a sudden feeling of dread and worthlessness; he doubted himself and his ability. "I just started thinking that I wasn't any good." It was then perfectly clear that he wasn't having fun and that it was time to re-think our program.

The first change in the plan was to cut down on the tournaments. Our three to four events per month became one event per month. We cut out the small-fry events – the one-day Tornados that used a relatively accelerated time control and that included players of all ratings. Ray gained nothing from these events. As one of the top-rated players, he'd have four of five games with extremely lower-rated players before he'd get one shot at another player with a decent rating. Oftentimes, he would put in a full day's work and get in return a single rating point. And the games he played weren't very useful because they were all completed under accelerated conditions. These events that used to be Ray's bread-and-butter had now grown stale and unpalatable.

The second step in the plan was to make the study time at home less onerous – at least for the time being. He had spent hours each day for one entire year preparing himself for the December Nationals. Now that it was over, he seemed reluctant to study. My first thought was that he had grown lazy, but I said nothing because he had worked hard and had achieved his goal; if he wanted to slack off for a while, well, he had earned that right. But when I saw later how the fun was disappearing, I realized that chess had ceased to become a labor of love; it was instead, pure labor. Consequently, we spent more time at the Ping-Pong table and on the basketball court than we did at the chessboard.

The third step in the plan was to look for a teacher for Ray. This step sounds contradictory to the second; however, I wasn't looking for a slave driver. I was looking for someone with whom Ray could share ideas, more of a mentor. From time to time over the past year, the question of whether or not there even was a teacher for Ray would cross my mind. I saw that Ray had done remarkably well on his own for nearly a year, and I was pleased that my nine-year-old son had the focus and the ability to improve himself, but still I wondered if there was someone who could facilitate his growth.

For a while, I had hoped that some grandmaster somewhere would have heard about Ray or seen his rise on the Top-100 list and thought to himself, "Here is a boy who seems deserving. He's worked hard, and he's one of the best in the country. This is someone that I would like to work with and help." I had hoped that maybe there was a grandmaster like that who was looking at Ray not as an hour's wage but as an apprentice. I understood, of course, that everyone needed to make a living, but perhaps there was someone out there who was willing to donate an hour or more a month to discuss chess with someone whose goal was to become a champion and who would work his heart out to achieve that goal. If such a grandmaster existed, surely he would see the benefit of being associated with a rising star; the connection alone would bring in a myriad of chess students.

Well before January, I thought that I might have found the right teacher for Ray. It was during the summer chess camp in Gainesville that I met a grandmaster who had given up chess as a profession in order to pursue the more lucrative life of a full-time tutor. Of the lessons presented at the camp, his, I thought, were the best prepared and the most useful. But the man himself impressed me as much as his method in the classroom. Others who had worked with Ray, or who had wanted to work with Ray, had given a similar pitch: "He needs a teacher (Pick me! Pick me!) to improve. Let me work with him, and in no time he'll be a master." When I talked with the grandmaster about lessons, his immediate response was, "I don't think that Ray needs to work with anyone. He's doing all of the right things by himself. However, if you want me to, of course I would be happy to work with him." Here, I thought, is the right person for Ray.

I didn't contact the grandmaster for a good six months after our initial meeting. When we had first talked at the chess camp, the 2003 Nationals were not too far off. I wanted Ray to go into that event without a teacher. He'd been working on his own for several months up to the event, and he wanted to win it on his own. But when the event was over and Ray was National Champ, it was time for me to call the grandmaster.

Beginning in January of 2004, Ray had lessons with the grandmaster, who lived in a distant state. They talked on the telephone and discussed theory and strategy while looking at an Internet chessboard that each could access. Ray had just one or two lessons per month – all that I could afford based on my teacher's salary. He loved the lessons, though. It was just as I had hoped it would be (sans the apprenticeship component): Ray had someone who could not only consistently challenge him at the board, but who could also discuss the most difficult aspects of chess theory quite fluently. In addition, Ray had contact with someone who had had similar developmental experiences as Ray had. This new arrangement with a tutor, along with the other steps above, served to build up the fire that had never really gone out; the fire was always burning in Ray, and he was beginning to have fun again.

* * *

Ray responded positively to the new plan. He was playing well and studying hard: the perfect combination to have when going into the 2004 National Elementary Championship in Pittsburgh, Pennsylvania. Our theme for this, the second of the two main national events of the academic year, was simple: have fun. I wanted to keep things light and enjoyable in order to avoid the heaviness of spirit that Ray had experienced a few months earlier. To this end, we did a crossword puzzle together on the plane instead of the usual chess puzzles. We watched sports on TV, played a paper football game, and threw a Nerf football around the hotel room instead of studying the few chess books that we'd brought with us. Before every round, I told Ray not to worry, that he didn't have anything to prove, that he was already a national champ and Florida's Player of the Year (an honor he'd been given a month earlier) – that all he needed to do was to try to play a beautiful game one move at a time and have fun in the process. I ended every pre-game talk with these words: Have fun, Bud.

And he did. It was clear by his face, by his looseness, by his ranging around the room to watch and enjoy others' games. Despite the change in approach from that taken at the Illinois national event, Ray played just as well – if not better – and was the only participant in his section to finish with 7 wins and 0 losses: a second national championship! Success and fun together: things couldn't have been better.

PART IV

17

How nice it is to be wrong. Things did get better – much better, in fact. After Ray won his second consecutive national tournament in April, and as he made the transition from third grade to fourth, he began playing in the Open sections of tournaments. It was in the Open section where he would have the chance to play most of the master-level players in the state. Having beaten scores of sub-masters up to this time, Ray had really no place left to go but the Open. In his debut event, and for the first time in his life, Ray drew a master. By July he had drawn four more – three in a row in one tournament. The fire that seemed to be dying a few months back was now an inferno.

Over the few years that Ray had played chess, I noticed some patterns. Although he always managed to increase in rating month by month, there were individual tournaments where he would slide backward. This seemed natural to me, for no one wins all of the time. Life would actually be pretty boring if one was always the winner. It's the unexpected element of any enterprise that makes it exciting, that makes it fun to do.

Along with Ray's cycles of poor performance, there were also cycles of advancement. He seemed to have his greatest surges between July and December. This happened in 2002 and in 2003, and it appeared to be occurring again as we moved into the same period for 2004. The timing was perfect because Florida was chosen for the site of that year's United States Open. Other than a few national events, Ray played all of his chess in Florida, so having a big event like the US Open in our home state was a big deal for us.

School in Florida starts early, so I would have to use my four personal days to miss work (I didn't have a fifth day, so we would just have to skip the last day of the tournament), and Ray would have to miss his first week of fourth grade in order to attend the Open on the other side of the state. Ray could always make up the schoolwork, and it was easy to get permission for Ray to miss school. The leaders of the Montessori program were supportive of Ray and his goals. They would occasionally post his achievements – for example, his national victories – on the big sign outside of the school. This was good for Ray, and his achievements may have helped to add to the enrollment at the school (not everyone could boast that a national chess champion was studying math and science in their school!).

Permission for me, however, was not so easy. I was still at the high school, working under one of the weakest principals in the county. My style with the students was to be supportive, encouraging, and enthusiastic. This contrasted with the boss' authoritarian/disciplinary nature. He would make long morning announcements in which he scolded the students, laid down – yet again – his long list of rules, and reminded the students that he was the boss. When any of my students, all of whom were non-native speakers of English, asked what the man with the deep boring voice was talking about, I would always answer, "Nothing important," and we would go back to whatever we were doing as a class.

In terms of work, the timing of my request couldn't have been worse. Mr. Gierke, the principal, had announced to all of the teachers at the very last faculty meeting that the new superintendent was coming to our school because of concerns over high teacher absenteeism. We had the worst record of all of the schools, and so now the principal decided that he was going to clamp down on absenteeism. I remember hearing from a coworker that several teachers had taken advantage of having a new principal the previous year by calling in sick every other Friday or Monday. And so now – because of their actions and a lax response from Mr. Gierke which allowed those actions to escalate – I might be penalized.

Public school teachers do not have vacation days that they can take during the regular school year. Instead, we have four personal days (which we are supposed to be able to take for any reason at any time), and we have sick days (which require a medical note if we're out for more than a day). Outside of that, the only thing one could do to get time off would be to make a special request for unpaid leave. I submitted my request for all four of my personal days. The principal did not immediately approve and instead asked to talk with me.

When we met, I apologized for the timing (which I had no control over), and reminded Mr. Gierke that aside from a couple of days off for two national chess events, I had a good attendance record. His response was to talk of his "surprise" and "dismay" when he learned last spring that one of his teachers had been looking for another job. (I had applied the previous year for an evening adjunct position at the local college in order to bring in more money for the chess expenses.) He was questioning my loyalty. He then asked about other events that I would need days off for, and I told him honestly that Ray had just been invited to the World Youth in Greece as the Under-10 representative of the United States and that it looked as though I would need to take two weeks of unpaid leave during the beginning of November. I explained the significance of the event and the importance of supporting my son while at the same time reminding Mr. Gierke of my teaching record and of my commitment to my students.

His cryptic response was that he would do what he had to do and that I would do what I had to do. And then he said that he would have to think more about the present request before he would make a decision. So, late that night, unable to sleep, I found myself calculating on paper whether or not we could survive economically if I became a substitute teacher by day and a pizza delivery guy by night. It would not be easy, but I felt that I needed to prepare myself for a change. As much as I loved my students, the job was less important to me than my son and his development. If Mr. Gierke rejected my request, then I decided that I would call in sick those four days. If he wanted to replace me as a result of that (plus the two weeks' leave in November that I also decided to take), then I would need to find work. I figured that it would work out; things always worked themselves out.

For several years – ever since we left Asia – I'd wanted to shift from full time to one or two part time jobs, but the problem, of course, was income. I needed money to take Ray to these events and to also pay our mortgage and bills. It would work out somehow. All I knew was that I urgently felt the need to start searching for other employment. I also thought it might be smart to take on additional work (such as adjunct teaching) now just so I could have it for next year (or sooner!) should it become necessary. However it played out, it looked like it was going to be an interesting year.

I often don't know what I really want, but life has an interesting way of telling me. I went to the Peace Corps thinking that I could change lives, but I was the one whose life was changed. I made what I thought would be no more than a brief stop in Taiwan en route to losing myself in the jungles of Sumatra, and I ended up a married man who never got closer to Sumatra's jungles than the southern tip of Taiwan. I thought I would never have a child before the age of 40, but it was with 29-year-old arms that I first held my son. I thought that I would never own a home, but I was 3 1/2 years into a 15-year mortgage in the fall of 2004. Things always work out the way they are supposed to work out; at least that's how it seems to me. Although I had all but put the pizza delivery sign atop my car, I was, at the very last minute, granted the use of my four personal days to take Ray to the US Open. While we were at the event, Hurricane Charlie blew through Florida, closing all of the schools in its wake, which allowed us to stay for all five days of the tournament without my having to miss another day of work.

We knew going into the Open that Ray wasn't going to win the tournament – there were, after all, numerous masters and a dozen or so grandmasters in attendance – but we also knew that with all of those masters around, Ray might get a shot at one. That's all that he was there for: some good games against some high-rated opponents along with the experience of playing in what for us was a major event. One game alone made everything worthwhile.

* * *

While Ray played the middle-aged master, I sat at a table looking around at the other players at the US Open, wondering if this would be the one. He had come close very recently to defeating a master, but to date the best he had managed was a draw. Before his game began, I told him that he could do it. I said that he was on the verge of a breakthrough and that he was ready to start taking out the masters. When his game began, I was left hoping and trusting.

After sitting and thinking by myself for about an hour, I returned to Ray's board to check on his game. I watched Ray sitting at the board. I liked his style. Although he had his quirks (for example, he often adjusted the chess pieces so they were precisely in the center of the squares on the board), for the most part, he was quite normal-looking at the board. Some of the other top youths were very twitchy and nervous, jerking their limbs and moving in and out of their seats. Ray moved around too, but he simply climbed down off of his chair (he still sat on his knees so that he could see the board better), put his hands in the pockets of his jeans, and casually walked to another board to view a game. At his own board, he sat with a posture that I envied – board-straight back (thanks to his Asian genes) and an expression that conveyed focus, determination, and confidence and that masked confusion or uncertainty.

I've had adults he's played come up to me after the game to tell me how frightening it is to play him. He does things (of which he is unaware) that unnerve his opponents. For example, he'll sometimes in the middle of his contemplations look up from the board and stare into his opponent's eyes. When I see that gaze (I've been on the receiving end of it many a time), I feel as if he's looking beyond the surface and that he's gauging my character – asking and answering the question of whether this person before him has what it will take to meet the move he's contemplating. One older man that he played, in describing how hard it was to play against him, said, "Oh! And when he looks up at you with those eyes, you just shudder!"

Another unnerving movement comes when he's about to make a good move. If it's an ordinary move, he simply moves the piece, but if it's a good move – a clever move, a trapping move, a winning move – then he creates a discernible aura of tension around his upper body. It starts with the clenching of the fist of his right hand – the hand that rests on his right cheek when he's thinking. The hand closes into a tight fist. Some minutes later – it's a very slow process, which mirrors his lengthy thought process – the clenched fist is moved a few inches away from the cheek with elbow suspended just a hair above the tabletop. The fist is then extended in ultra slow motion, punching fashion, until his arm is fully extended across and above the board. It's like watching a slow motion tape of a cobra moving from a coil to a full strike but with the camera pausing just before the actual strike. Ray keeps that pose for upwards of a full minute if it's a really big move, and all of the tension surrounding the cobra's strike is equally apparent in Ray's strike. You're just watching that fist motionless in midair over the board – full of deadly tension – and all you can do is wonder which piece he'll strike and how many minutes after the strike you'll have left to live.

I ended my visit to Ray's board and drifted off again to write in my journal at a nearby table. I wrote, looked around, thought about the future, and from time to time returned to check out Ray's game. There was nothing that I could tell from the position. His games were getting too complicated; there were too many variables involved for me to make any kind of sense out of with just a passing glance, or, truth be told, even with an unlimited amount of time for analysis. But Ray himself looked confident at the table, so I left it as I always did: in his capable hands. And at 3:30 p.m. on August 12, 2004, Ray's opponent resigned. Nine-year-old Ray Robson had defeated his first master. On our walk out, I told him how I knew that he could do it (my words to him before the game started) and that I was proud of him for working so hard to make this happen. "Nine-year-old Ray Robson defeats master!" I cheered as soon as we were outside and away from the crowd.

* * *

Soon after defeating the master, Ray reached another milestone when he achieved expert level. He did this shortly before his 10th birthday, and it meant that the next step up was master. After he had earned his latest title, whenever Ray asked me a question, I answered, "I don't know. You tell me. *You're* the expert." He smiled whenever I said this.

For Ray's tenth birthday, Yee-chen took him shopping after school, and he came home wearing a new pair of Nike tennis shoes. And after he found and unwrapped the football that I had placed on his bed, we played catch. The Harry Chapin song about the father who doesn't have time for his son was in my head throughout the day. I was glad that when my son turned 10, I made the time to play catch with him . . . and to play three games of Ping-Pong . . . and to help him with his homework . . . and to talk about the Chess Olympiad that was taking place in Europe . . . and to help him pick out his next book (Animal Farm) from my bookshelf . . . and to watch a few series of downs of Monday Night Football with him. Ray was in a good mood all afternoon and evening. It was a good day for him. I could tell. So Ray was now in the double digits. I hoped that in another 10 years' time I would still have something to offer him.

* * *

When I said at the start of this chapter that things got better, I wasn't just thinking about Ray's success at the board. In the summer of 2004, we received a letter from the United States Chess Federation informing Ray that he qualified to participate in the World Youth Championship in Crete, Greece. For this event, the best players in the world would gather and – by age group – battle it out to see who was the best among the best. The tournament was scheduled for November of 2004, and the eleven rounds would take place over two weeks.

There were many reasons not to go. Ray would have to miss another two weeks of school. I would have to miss another two weeks of work, and it would have to be unpaid leave, for I had already used up all of my available days for Ray. The trip would be expensive: the airplane tickets, the meals, and the $150 per night hotel room that we were required to stay in for two weeks all added up to a chunk of cash – $8500 was the best of the many estimates I made. Yee-chen didn't want to stay home alone for two weeks and miss this experience, so all of my calculations were for three. But despite the reasons against going, there was just no way that I would let this opportunity for Ray pass by. He'd been working hard for nearly three years, developing his chess ability, rising in the ratings, winning national championships, and doing it all with a humbleness and an intelligence that made me proud to be his dad. He had earned the right to test himself against the world's best youths, and I was determined to see it happen.

I tried contacting persons well known in the chess world to ask how they got their funding, but I received no response. I asked for help from the directors of local chess clubs where Ray was a member and was told that they had no money to spare for such expenses. I contacted the USCF and asked if they could provide any kind of support and learned that they had nothing to spare either. I wrote dozens of letters to national and international organizations and companies, telling them about Ray and asking for sponsorship, all to no avail. I had no millionaire friends to turn to and no one else who both could, and would, assist us.

I have never felt comfortable asking anyone for anything. If I couldn't do it myself, then unless it was an emergency, it wasn't going to get done. Maybe I received so many "No's" because the person receiving the letter or the phone call could tell by my voice or my words that I was willing to accept "No." There are some people who can ask for outrageous things and get them. My own father is like that. He can take a trip and come back with free airline seats, a hotel voucher, and a winning lottery ticket. I'm just not that guy.

In September, when the tickets needed to be bought, I contemplated taking out a home-equity loan. I had put a lot of money into the house – our first home – over the past few years, making extra payments whenever I could squeeze one in, and so I had that to fall back on. Of course, I could have used that same money to repair our thirty-year-old home or to replace that same ailing auto that the deer attacked over a year before, but Ray was more important than those other things. But before I had to add to my mortgage, and after I'd exhausted all ideas for getting funds for the trip, a sponsor appeared.

A friend had talked with another friend who had both the means and the interest to help someone like Ray. Suddenly, we had money for Ray's flight to Greece and for his share of the hotel expenses. More than that, we now had funds for chess lessons. Up to that point, Ray had been having lessons with the grandmaster just once or twice each month; the rest of the time, as usual, Ray worked on his own. Now Ray could study with a grandmaster over the Internet once a week. He would even have the chance to get in several lessons prior to the World Youth, immeasurably improving his chances of finishing strong in the tournament.

And so some luck had come our way. If anyone would make good use of such an opportunity, it was Ray Robson: devout student of the game of chess, intensely focused competitor, good son.

18

I taught Ray to play chess because I was looking for another activity – one more interesting to me – that he and I could do together. By the time that Ray qualified for the World Youth, we rarely played chess; I was too easy a target and hadn't seriously challenged him since the middle of the summer when I was studying daily along with Ray. In the privacy of my journal, I continued to wonder about my role:

Am I now the executed? In a way, yes, for the son has bested the father, and to such an extent that were I to devote the rest of my life to the study of the game, I would still be walking in my son's footsteps. But that is life, and that is how it should be. I am just happy to be here at all – happy to be my son's number one fan, happy to be his companion on his weekend chess adventures. I am enjoying it all now because there will be a day that will come far too soon when Ray will be on his own. He's ten now, soon he'll be eleven, then it's high school before you know it, and then it's college and all that lies beyond. Time does not fly; it rockets past me. So I've taken a page from my own coach's manual and devised a mantra for myself. It's one that I silently repeat at the start of each day: Enjoy your time with Ray while you are here now and while he is here now, for this is the only time that you have.

I intended to make the most of my time with Ray by continuing to be his punching-bag at the chess board, by giving him a coach's advice along the way, and by improving my own game of chess so that I could in some way grow alongside of him. What more could a parent do for a child that he loves?

As for Ray, he had moved into his fall groove. His record against the last six masters that he faced was one win and five draws. The older crowd still balked at the thought of a child in their midst, but if one thing was clear, it was that Ray was there to stay. By the fall of 2004, Ray was the youngest expert in the country. He was already playing at a master level, and it was only a matter of time before he would earn the actual title. But we both knew that it didn't end there, for international master and grandmaster came after master, and then there would be other goals. Where to? What next? Wherever Ray wanted to go, and whatever he wanted to do. If he saw a path, I would gladly accompany him along its straight-ways and over its rises and around its every twist and turn. I would walk with my son until it was time for him to walk without me.

19

I thought that I had ended this book (for the second time, that is) in the autumn of 2004. The importance of events is, of course, relative. The first draft of this book consisted of 150 pages of Ray's battles with the local scholastic kids. A short time later, after he had won a few nationals, the scholastic battles seemed unimportant. The truth is that they were actually very important – as important as anything in Ray's chess life – for one cannot reach the top of the mountain without first taking steps at its base. And a stumble along the way is often all it takes to keep one from reaching the peak. Still, I could not write about everything. And, in truth, all of the detailed move-by-move descriptions taken from hundreds and hundreds of pages of journal notes would probably be of interest only to me and perhaps a few local players. So in subsequent drafts, I tried to replace the minutia with the big experiences, the peaks. The difficulty has been that the peaks keep changing. I think we've reached a peak and soon after come to find that what I thought was a peak was just a bump in the floor of a canyon.

Of the tens of thousands of scholastic chess players, only a few of them ever win a national event. That seemed to be our peak. But fewer still beat masters at the age of nine. Every year I look back on what I have written and think about how funny it is that I have spent so much time focusing on such and such an experience when more recent events are so much more significant. That seems to be the way of things. Still, it's hard to imagine that there could be anything better than playing in a championship for the world's best chess players.

And that brings us back to October, when Ray was the only fourth-grade expert in the United States, and he was on his way to play in his first international tournament: the 2004 World Youth Championship in Crete, Greece. For a picture of the World Youth, just reflect back on my description of the K-3

National event in Illinois, except instead of the Sears Tower, it's the Parthenon; instead of English, it's Greek and dozens of other languages; instead of soup and crackers, it's baklava and various cheeses and olives; instead of snow, it's warm temps and sunshine; and instead of a half-dozen decent US players (out of a field of 200 or so), it's forty or more of the best players from around the world. But other than that, the scene is pretty much the same: a madhouse of bodies milling everywhere before the start of each round, hundreds of numbered tables in row upon row in a huge warehouse-like room, parents and coaches inching up to the closest possible spot beside their players, and a general nervous tension that permeates the room.

In this setting, Ray was a virtual unknown. He was a first-timer without a FIDE rating. FIDE is the World Chess Federation, the organization that governs international chess competition. Just as players get a rating in the United States by playing in USCF events, players get a FIDE rating by playing in international events. FIDE titles are more prestigious than USCF titles: an FM (FIDE Master) is considered stronger than its US counterpart, an NM (National Master). In addition, one can only earn the final two titles - IM (International Master) and GM (Grandmaster) by performing at a high level and achieving norms in FIDE-rated events. So this trip to Greece made us rethink our path to both the short-term and long-term goals. Now NM – what we had been focusing on all along – was replaced by FM and followed by IM and, finally, GM. And in order to reach the goals, Ray would have to start competing in FIDE events, most all of which occurred outside of the US. Just where was this "chess thing" taking us? Where would it all end?

In Greece, Ray had an advantage that he hadn't enjoyed since his first year of competitive chess: no one knew who he was. At that time, his games weren't posted online anywhere, nor could they be found in any chess database. In other words, no one could prepare for Ray through research; they would have to meet him over the board and battle it out.

One thing that I like best about the World Youth is that it is one of the few tournaments where Ray can face strong competitors around his own age. Since his win at the Nationals, Ray had mainly faced adults or the occasional teenager. It was important to see how he fared against the world's best in his age group, but it was also good for him to just interact with such kids. These were his peers, some of whom he would face in the years to come in other international events, and he had the chance to talk with them after the games. Granted, language got in the way, but Ray could communicate with any of the other kids through the movement of the pieces. Through moves and gestures and the occasional word, he was able to analyze positions and look at possibilities with his opponents at the end of each game. And after the rounds, the children continued the competition at the Ping-Pong tables in the hotel. To be a child surrounded by others like you, interacting, discussing, playing . . . this was a worthwhile experience.

In such an environment, Ray thrived. Just as at the chess camp that he attended with the grandmasters, Ray was inspired by the level of players around him. He played well enough to finish in the Top Ten in the world at his first international event. This was in spite of a last round loss. For the final round, Ray was on one of the top boards playing for a medal (medals are only given to the top three finishers). His opponent, Hou Yi-fan of China, was not only one of the strongest players in the world, but she was also the only girl in the boys' section. Having won the gold medal in the girls' section the previous year, she wanted to do the same in the boys' section this year. After beating Ray, and tying for first place, she went on to represent China at even more prestigious adult events, and today she is one of the top juniors in the world.

Ray's own top-ten performance at his first World Youth was also success. It seemed that nothing would ever top this experience, and I began to fear that Ray would experience what I had experienced in my twenties when, as a Peace Corps Volunteer, I had such a powerfully interesting and exciting experience that nothing for the next several years could compare and life became ordinary and dull. At that time, I drifted from place to place and job to job without enthusiasm, yearning for the experiences I'd had in my early twenties. What happens to a person who reaches the zenith at the tender age of ten? What does life hold for such a child?

I decided that I was asking the wrong question. Who was to say that Ray had hit his highest point? True, everyone has his limit – that level of ability that is the absolute maximum – but Ray hadn't shown any degree of leveling off, of finding a final plateau. If anything, his experience at the World Youth motivated him to work harder and achieve more. He came back from the experience fired up about chess and about the seemingly unlimited possibilities for improvement. He hit the books, was attentive in his lessons with the grandmaster, and then, six months later, revealed other peaks that lay waiting for Ray, the climber.

* * *

Autumn turned to winter; winter turned to spring. Between the time that I thought I might have to deliver pizzas in order to be with Ray and the time we returned from Greece, I found another job as a testing coordinator/teacher within the school system. This job, through the generosity of my new boss, allowed for more flexibility of time, and more flexibility of time meant more high-stakes events outside of our home state.

I tested this new flexibility by taking Ray to Tennessee in April of 2005 for the biggest scholastic event of the year. It was the Supernationals, and Ray, a fourth-grader, had jumped into an older age group, K-6, in order to compete for the top prize: a full tuition-and-fees scholarship to the University of Texas. This one was important to us because, as a public school teacher, I had all but taken a vow of poverty. Ray was keenly aware of the family's financial situation in relation to other chess kids' families. He knew that a mortgage (over $60,000 at that time) still hung over our heads. He knew that we couldn't afford to have two coaches and several lessons a week (as some of the top players had); he knew that most of his chess books were outdated and came from used bookstores; he knew that we couldn't pay for a trainer's personal expenses so that he could have the best coach available at his side, instead of his dad, at tournaments such as the World Youth and Supernationals; in sum, he knew that every chess outing involved some sort of sacrifice.

Ray shared in the sacrifice. You might wonder what he gave up. You might think that he was a privileged, almost spoiled, child to have such doting parents chaperoning him around the world to play chess. But that's not the case. Ray gave up his time. He couldn't talk to his friends about Saturday morning cartoons because he didn't watch cartoons. On Saturday mornings, we drove to chess events in neighboring counties. And the absence of an event was not a reason to lie on the couch and watch TV; instead, it was an opportunity to study. Ray's chess goals didn't leave any time for goofing off, for just hanging around doing nothing. When he came home from school, he finished his homework. Any remaining time – and sometimes there was none – was devoted to chess. When we could, we worked in Ping-Pong matches, and he sometimes broke up his studies to play football with the kids in the street, but that was pretty much Ray's day by the spring of 2005: school, homework, chess studies, and small breaks for recreation.

When we were at events and needed to get something to eat, Ray would invariably choose the cheapest item on the menu. When I heard him say on a few occasions, "I'll have whatever costs the least," I realized that my own concerns over finances had transferred to Ray. But I was proud of my son for responding as he did. Other kids might have complained about not getting the most expensive thing on the menu, or even that which they most desired, but Ray was looking for ways to contribute. He knew the sacrifices were for him, and he wanted to be worthy of them. Mostly he showed that he was deserving of the trips by dedicating himself to his studies. I think that he was the hardest working chess player in the country at that time.

And so when we came to Tennessee for the K-6 Supernationals, it was with a precise goal in mind: win the college scholarship. Two hundred fifteen others, mostly sixth-graders, had the same goal. Round after round, for seven rounds in total, Ray ground down the competition, including the favorite, a sixth-grade master from New York, until he emerged undefeated and the recipient of the college scholarship. Was fourth-grade Ray Robson going to run off to Texas to begin studies? No, that was still several years away, and who was to say where Ray wanted to study. It was important, though, to have the scholarship. It was security in case something happened to me, and it was a potential bargaining chip in case Ray wanted to study somewhere else. And a full four-year tuition-and-fees scholarship to a university was also a nice payback after the tens of thousands of dollars that I put into our chess life since the very first event back in 2001. It is easy for me not to care about money for myself, but I sure appreciated the college scholarship for my son. If anything happened to me, I knew that Ray was at least set through college. Isn't that every poor man's dream?

Just as Ray, perched on his Grecian mountaintop following the World Youth, was able to discern a still higher peak in Tennessee, so too from his perch atop Supernationals was he able to see yet another peak, this one in far off Brazil.

* * *

Every year that the event is not held in Colombia, the United States sends its top boys and girls to compete in the Pan American Youth Championship in South America. There were no invitations to the 2004 event, so you can guess where it was held. Ray didn’t get his invitation to the 2005 event until late in May. By that time he was consistently knocking off masters in tournament play, and his rating was 2112 – just 88 points shy of the magic master mark. As the competition would be limited only to the Americas – North, Central, and South – we knew that there wouldn’t be many good games for Ray in Brazil, the site of that year’s June event. And then there was the expense, especially when coupled with the costs for the 2005 World Youth that was to be held in July in France! Even with a portion of Ray’s expenses covered by a sponsor, I had barely managed to pay for the trip to Greece and had, in fact, burned my checking account down to zero. I had no money for a savings account – a far off luxury item at that time – and was just beginning to repopulate my cobwebbed checking account by five dollars at a time when the invitation to Brazil arrived.

I was able to meet the expenses of the trip in three ways: I scraped what I could from my own account and paid not a penny extra into the mortgage; I used Ray's contributions – nearly a thousand dollars – from his winnings in the adult tournaments over the past few years; and I took on extra work during my summer vacation. Why the scramble for an event that didn't offer the strongest competition? One reason and one alone: the FIDE Master (FM) title. The winner of the Pan Am was awarded this prestigious title, and from FM one could begin the journey towards IM (International Master) and then GM (Grandmaster). As that was Ray's path, I thought that we had to follow it, and so we did.

In Brazil, we found that there was only one opponent, a very strong player from Argentina, who could give Ray a challenge. All of the others were easy, or at least they should have been easy had Ray not hurt his own chances with time trouble. In every round that he played, he got so low on time that he forced himself to play the bulk of each game on just a dozen, or fewer, minutes. He would sometimes spend one-third of his entire time on just one or two moves, and he finished his games with just seconds remaining on his clock.

Time trouble was something that Ray had struggled with since early in his chess career. When I first noticed it, I gave him as many strategies as I could that would help him to manage his time better, but, when my suggestions didn't change his behavior, I thought that the time scramble was something that he would eventually develop out of on his own. I thought that maybe it was like the time that his chess rating seemed stuck between 1500 and 1600 – that it was a developmental thing that would pass as Ray matured, grew more confident, and improved in general.

The exact opposite occurred. The more that Ray learned, and the more time that passed, the bigger the problem became. He just had too many things to consider – too many variables that his mind was able to see – in order for him to make "the right" decision in a reasonable period of time. The perfectionist does not like to make mistakes, but Ray took this to an extreme. He was going over multiple lines in great depth (rechecking his analysis up to three times for each line of thought!) to ensure that he had the best move for every move. If he only had one or two lines to choose from, it wouldn't be so bad, but his mind was a jumble of possibilities. I'd been through a similar experience and wondered if I had learned anything that could help Ray.

It was not long after I had come back from the Peace Corps, and I was looking for a direction in life. I turned to philosophy and religion. I did nothing but study texts and fill my mind with possibilities. *The Tibetan Book of the Dead* and Russell's *History of Western Philosophy* butted heads with the *Koran*, the *Tao de Ching*, the *I-Ching*, and the writings of the Transcendentalists. I had spent weeks and then months focusing every waking moment on the study of these, and other, texts with the result that I had a head full of thoughts and no idea how to proceed.

In an effort to sort out the jumble of thoughts, I ended up in Central America, where I walked and hitched from Guatemala to Costa Rica along the main highway which ran from one end of Central America to the other. I would rise early, stretch my back, arms, and legs a little, wash my face, gather up the clothes I'd rinsed out the night before and hung out to dry, pack them in a plastic bag in my pack, and then hoist up the pack and head toward the highway. Whether it was sunny or rainy, I would walk.

While I walked along, alone, all I could do was think, but my goal at that time was to slow down the mad procession of thoughts that I had so that I could make some sense of the patterns and find the right one to follow: the right move. I tried focusing on one thought only – one line of reasoning – repeating it over and over in my mind, but before I knew it, the one thought would branch into ten others, which would branch in the same way, and I would find myself back in a muddled state with too many variables to consider while my own clock spun from one hour to the next.

After several weeks of these six hour per day walk-thinks, I did manage to succeed in finding a temporary release from the confusion built up in my mind. The release came about in this way: after realizing the futility of trying to block out certain thoughts by focusing on just one thought, I decided to give myself up to the crazy rush of thoughts – only rather than try and think through any of them, I would merely watch them all just as if I were watching TV. Thus, I began to detach myself from the thoughts and, in this way, I was able to act as an observer. The thoughts would come, I would "watch" them, or be aware of them, and then they would go. And over time, the thoughts would begin to thin themselves out, so that eventually they would form a long line, following one after another, rather than converging on my mind all at once. After hours of watching thoughts come and go, there would come a moment – a second or two at the most – when a thought would float by and there would be nothing on its trail, and for just a moment, my mind would be a blank. It was this momentary "Blank State," as I called it, that satisfied me. It was in that instant that I no longer doubted myself or questioned which path to take. It was a liberation of sorts from the variables.

So it was a release from all thoughts that ultimately provided me with a brief lucid interval. But this solution – if indeed it was a solution – came only after hours of working through my own thoughts. In addition, I had no control over when the lucid interval would appear. How could I take this experience and turn it into a plan for my son as he struggled with his own never-ending procession of thoughts while seated at a chessboard with the clock at his side ticking-ticking-ticking? I had to take the most important elements from what for me was a four-month experience and turn it into something that would fit within the parameters of a single chess game. I decided that trust in oneself was the key. The lucid interval was always there. It was my own self-doubt, my own fear of making the wrong decision, that allowed for the paralyzing parade of thoughts in the first place.

So it was at about this time that I started working out a plan for Ray that centered on him trusting himself, trusting his instincts. He had done all of the thinking and studying that he needed to do; when it was time to play a tournament game, he needed to trust himself and the lucid intervals would appear. This was just the beginning of an idea that wouldn't develop into a more structured plan for another four years. I was still working it out in my own mind while Ray was involved in the Pan Am event, and, even if I had come up with the complete plan, it wasn’t something that I would spring on Ray in the middle of a tournament. We had a routine, and it wasn’t the time or place for a big change.

At the end of it all, Ray and Sebastian Iermito, the Argentine prodigy, ended up undefeated, each having drawn two games (including one against each other) and tied for first place. Consequently, they were both awarded the FM title. Iermito went on to greater successes at more challenging events, eventually earning the International Master title. He remains today one of South America's strongest junior players. Ray had more ahead of him as well, and the result of this event left me wondering, "Where's the next apex?"

* * *

From Brazil, we stopped in the US just in time to catch our breath, wash our clothes, and pack our bags for France. This was Ray's second World Youth event, and this year he was moving up in age group to the Under-12 section. But the chess would come after the tourism. In Greece, I could only squeeze four extra days into the trip to see the ruins in Athens; in Brazil it was even worse, because I worked right up to the day of our departure – doing extra work as a teacher trainer during my summer vacation in order to bring in cash for all of our travels – and Yee-chen ran a Chinese summer camp that started the day after our return.

This time, however, I decided to do it right. If I was going to deplete my checking account getting us over there, we might as well stay for as long as possible. We spent two weeks in Paris filled by outings to the Louvre, the Eiffel Tower, the Rodin Museum, Notre Dame Cathedral, and everything else we could take in. We managed this by using a homestay network and thus saving 100% of the hotel expense. We did the same thing in Thun, Switzerland, trekking through the mountains in the daytime and sleeping in the home of a local family at night. I had purposefully planned the trip in that order, Paris then Thun, thinking that Ray would tire from the museums (he did) and energize from the mountains (he did, though he did struggle through mild acrophobia – something impossible to be aware of in Florida, where a six-inch bump in the yard was the highest point above sea level for miles around).

When we returned to France for the World Youth, Ray was healthy, rested, and definitely ready for some chess. He hadn't had time to crack a chess book over the past four weeks, so he was particularly hungry for the game. His competition this time was much stronger than in Greece, where he finished in the top ten. This time the field included six youths who would, in just a short time, be among the youngest grandmasters of the decade: Wesley So of the Philippines, Parimarjan Negi of India, Sanan Sjugirov of Russia, Hou Yi-fan of China, Samvel Ter Shahakyan of Armenia, and Dariusz Swiercz of Poland.

Ray, by playing well and staying on the top boards the entire tournament, faced four of these six at the event, beating Swiercz and drawing So, Negi, and Sjugirov. The last two meetings resulted in multiple heart-pounding moments. Negi came first in what, at the time, seemed like a marathon game: a 105-move draw. This was the longest game of the tournament until Ray faced Sjugirov in the final round. A win for Sjugirov would have given him yet another title; a win for Ray would have put him in a tie for first place. Ray, with the Black pieces, battled Sjugirov for nearly six hours. The 30-second time increment (30 seconds were added to a player's clock after each move) allowed for a game to go on indefinitely, provided that a player could make each move within 30 seconds. Ray, who characteristically was low on time from the beginning of the game, ended up playing the majority of the game on the 30-second increment alone. While each player tried to out-think the other, the rest of the games ended one by one, the other players' tables and chairs were folded up and moved out of the playing arena, and even the artificial flooring (which covered an ice rink below) was taken up and moved to a storehouse – all but the part beneath the chairs of the two remaining players. One hundred and eighty moves! A one hundred and eighty move game that ended in a draw. No clear first for Sjugirov, and no first place at all for Ray, who finished one-half point behind the leaders. But he did have another Top Ten finish, and it was done in style.

What do you say to a kid, to your child, who can go head to head with the very best in the world for his age? I found that words wouldn't do it; Ray got a hug instead. Outside of the hall, the words came, and I told him how great I thought he'd played and how proud everyone was of him – me and Yee-chen, the Kempers and his grandparents, his USA teammates and coaches, and everyone at his school. I told him that this was his greatest tournament ever and that he had a big heart to hang in there for six hours against Sjugirov (just as with Negi), and I recounted all of his accomplishments: his draw with the two highest rated players; his having drawn three of the four players who finished tied for first (he didn't play one of the four); his having gone undefeated (5 wins, 6 draws) while having played nearly all of the top players, including big draws on boards one and two in the final two rounds; his having improved his performance over last year's by half a point despite having played against stronger opponents and as one of the youngest players in the group (most were a year older); and, of course, his having finished in the top ten once again.

The World Youth in France was the highlight of his career to date. He'd done so much; he'd done so well. And all of this provided him with experiences and lessons – opportunities to grow stronger not just as a player, but, more importantly, as a person. He'd learned things in France that would flavor the rest of his years. Here is how I summed up the experience in my journal:

How can I go home after this and resume my life? How can Ray settle back into the drudgery of school next week? We should be on our way to an IM tournament in Spain or a jungle trek in the Amazon or a mountain hike in the Himalayas! How are we going to gear ourselves DOWN to the level of normal daily existence with work and school and home?

* * *

In the six months between the successful showing at the World Youth in France and the start of the new year, Ray had moved his rating to within five points of master level. True, he already held the more prestigious FM title from his first-place tie in Brazil in the summer, but in this country, he wouldn't be considered a master unless he crossed the 2200 rating mark.

Most chess players never even reach expert (2000 – 2199), and for those who do get there, they find that it's nearly impossible to get any kind of a sizeable ratings jump. Once you achieve a certain rating, you have to have a series of strong performances to move up, and even then the leaps are 5 or 10 points instead of the 30 or 40-point leaps that are possible for lower-rated players. For example, in the six months since his tournament in France, Ray had faced seventeen masters. His record against the masters was 5 wins, 7 draws, and 5 losses. He was playing at master level and had been doing so for some time; however, his rating didn't reflect that.

With strong play over several months, Ray edged as close as he could to the magic mark: 2195. Five more points! We never talked about it directly. This was mainly due to superstition. If my father had been a voodoo doctor, I'm not sure that he would have brought more superstition into my life. If we watched a sports event on TV or in person, my father had a special whammy that he employed to hex the opposing team. His hands would come up to chest level and his fingers would wiggle as he directed the whammy at the opposing team's free-throw shooter. If the ball bounced off the rim, it was attributed to the whammy. My father, in his mind, had just earned an assist for his team. If I didn't do the whammy with him, and the ball went through the hoop, I was solely responsible for the player making that shot. And if, sitting in front of the TV screen 2000 miles away from the actual game, I said something disparaging like, "There's no way we're going to win this game," then I had just jinxed the team which, though 10 points down with 20 seconds remaining, would still have won according to my father.

Over the course of a few decades – and without any therapy whatsoever – I was able to eliminate most of the superstition from my life. But when Ray started to play chess, my father brought the voodoo back into my life. If Ray wore a hat and had a good tournament, then the hat, to Grandpa, became "the lucky hat," and the wins were attributed to the hat, not to the wearer of the hat. That's not what I wanted Ray to believe. I wanted Ray to understand that his results were due to Ray alone, a reflection of the amount of hard work that he put into whatever he did. Likewise, I made it clear to Ray as early in his career as possible that I was not responsible for his success, that the mantra that I whispered in his ears was not a magic spell that allowed him to win his games, that my belief in him was not what made him excel; instead, he was told that he earned everything he got through his own hard work: Edison's "Genius is one per cent inspiration and ninety-nine per cent perspiration." That's what I believed, and that's what I told my son. He didn't need a crutch, and he didn't have a crutch. But still, we both kept silent about those five points.

On a whim, I bought plane tickets to Georgia for a January event that we would never have gone to ordinarily: a relatively small event – just a few masters – that didn't justify the expense. The five points lay like a monkey on Ray's back, and the trip to Georgia was a sort of desperate attempt to knock that monkey off before it became an orangutan and then a gorilla. I'd witnessed a number of top players who got so close to the mark and then froze, or, even worse, who had crossed the magic mark and then fallen right back behind it, dropping dozens of points in one event after another. Although there was nothing in Ray's history that indicated that he would freeze or choke, I just didn't want to take any chances, so we went to Georgia for the next available event that was closest to our home state.

Going into the penultimate round, it looked like my decision was going to pay off. Ray was paired with Kazim Gulamali, a solid teenage master who, with a loss, could give Ray his own master title. This was the game we were there for. I thought that all of the pressure should be on Kazim: he was a hundred rating points above Ray, he was much older, and he was playing in front of his home crowd. I hoped that it would work out to Ray's advantage.

Ray's game went nearly the distance. After they'd made time control, I told the two other dads, who were waiting with their kids to eat with us, to go ahead without us – that Ray would be playing for a while. Shortly after the opening, Ray looked to be in a better position. He was the one mounting the attack; he was the aggressor. At time control, things looked different (time control is when more time is added to the players' clocks – for example, thirty minutes or one hour – after they have completed a certain number of moves). Kazim – who had characteristically arrived 20 minutes late – made his 30th move with two minutes and twenty seconds on his clock. Ray got his move in with twenty-seven seconds remaining. He almost played a move that would have dropped a pawn; however, he caught it just in time and so had to move the piece he'd touched (his Queen) to another square. With just those few seconds left, he seemed to pick a square almost at random and then immediately hung his head in seeming defeat. A moment later, he left his seat and shook his head in front of me in what looked like great despair and resignation. And then when Kazim – after a forty-minute think, using most of the time he gained after reaching time control – took a pawn with his Knight, I thought that it was over; the whole board suddenly looked like a trap for Ray. Even though Kazim had two pieces attacked by Ray's pieces, it looked like Kazim had all of the threats to Ray's King, whereas Ray's originally threatening attack looked completely diffused.

And Ray was sneezing so much! Twenty, thirty, forty sneezes, and he was continually sniffing his nose or physically plugging his nostrils to keep from sniffing. I thought for certain that he was allergic to the room itself. It was at that time that I thought, "Win, lose, or draw, we should go home." If he lost, a last round win wouldn't make him a master. If he drew, a last round win might not do it either, and he would go into that round psychologically down and feeling the pressure to win. And if he won, which didn't look likely, then we should go anyway. He'd have his title, and he'd have his health. A win in the last round would only add a few more rating points.

After Kazim's 40-minute think (leaving him just 20 minutes for the rest of the game), Ray had an extended think of his own. The result of it all was that, a half-dozen moves later, the Queens and other pieces were off the board and the position now looked more like a draw. The main differences were that Ray had 20 minutes to Kazim's 5 and that Ray looked alive and dangerous. And it might have been a draw had Ray not played so well in the endgame and had Kazim played a little better.

A win! From looking good to looking bad to looking equal to a win. People were shaking my hand and Ray's. He'd just beaten their best local player – the 2300 teen who'd won this event the last two years. I let Ray analyze with Kazim for a while and then

I talked with him about withdrawing. At first he wanted to play, but since he didn't look so good and was still sneezing away, I convinced him that it was best to just head to the airport early. Everyone was amazed that he would withdraw when he would surely win sole first and the prize money, and I nearly let myself be convinced to stay, but in the end I made the right decision.

And so the whim paid off: with three-and-a-half points out of four rounds, including a win over the highest rated player in the event, Ray became a National Master, the youngest in the history of Florida, and one of the youngest ever in the United States. He was eleven years old. There was no problem with slipping backwards either; Ray soon left 2200 so far behind that it became difficult to even imagine that he was once "only" 2200.

* * *

By this time we had it figured out: there were peaks in all directions and as far as the eye could see. It was simply a matter of choosing the peak, doing the important preparation work, and then throwing one's self full force – both head and heart – into the climb. That's what Ray did in April of 2006 as a fifth-grader when he entered and won the National Junior High School Championship (both the regular tournament and the speed chess event), finishing ahead of some of this country's strongest 9th graders. His performance was remarkable, considering that we slept on a hard floor in an unkempt room where cats wrestled over us and chewed our hair each night and where cat dander was so heavy that Ray had mump-like bumps on his face by the last day of the event.

One of the drawbacks to couchsurfing (the homestay network that allowed us to save $400 or more in hotel costs per trip) was that we could never be 100% certain of the condition of our host's couch (or floor). The obvious benefit besides the savings, though, was that we got to hang out with some really cool local people. Most couchsurfers are green friendly, left-leaning thinkers – kindred spirits. Over the years, we broke bread with folks in France, Switzerland, Ecuador, Russia, and over half a dozen states here in the US. We often slept on floors, but our hosts made up in personality for any domestic shortcomings.

Besides sleeping on floors in local homes, these trips were manageable because I was holding down three jobs. In addition to my full-time job as testing coordinator for the county's non-native speaking population, I was managing mandatory online trainings for the school district's teachers on a part-time basis. My third job was as an adjunct instructor in the College of Education at a local college. During the 2005/2006 academic year, I taught three sections of upper-division courses at night after finishing my day job in the county.

During that year, I fantasized often about selling our home – which had ballooned in value to nearly twice what it was really worth – so that we could pay off the remainder of our mortgage and use what was left over to buy ourselves a home in another state where our money would go much further. I imagined that we should be able to buy some big country home with an acre or two in, say, rural Idaho with the money left over from the sale of our Florida home. But our home had become the symbol of security that Yee-chen had long desired and that she deserved for putting up with me and my Peace Corps-itis for so many years. She had no reason to give up what I had already taken too long to give her for some unlikely future in an unknown place, and I resolved to work harder to pay off the home faster. If it was the mortgage that was tying me down, then the goal became to pay off the mortgage as soon as possible.

In the meantime, I had the income from my extra work to help pay for everything that was important to us. That's how we were able to spend a month in Ecuador in the summer of 2006 where, after swimming with penguins and sea lions in the Galapagos, Ray went on to tie for first place with the Peruvian prodigy and international star, Jorge Cori, at a Pan Am event. We had long since lost the sponsor who chipped in for portions of Ray's expenses on certain events, so I ended up spending all of the $10,000+ that I had managed to scrape together for the trip. But it was worth it: another interesting international experience for Ray, coupled with time to see another culture. When you are doing something that you care about for someone you care about, and when there are myriad lessons to be learned from the experience, dollars don't mean a thing. You need them to take a trip, but you don't waste energy mourning over their loss.

PART V

20

The fall of 2006 was a new chapter in many ways. First, we took Ray out of school. Three years before, when Ray started to become known in the chess world, the parents who would talk to "Ray's dad" invariably got around to asking about his home-schooling. Most assumed that, in order to get as good as he was, he never attended school and instead devoted his days to chess alone. I suspect that some parents didn't believe me when I said that he not only attended school, but had so much homework at night that sometimes he didn't study chess at all. Everything that I have described thus far, aside from the international trips where we took time off from school, occurred around Ray's busy school schedule.

I haven't really talked much about Ray's education apart from chess. Ray was reading and calculating before most kids started preschool. When Ray was four, during our last year in Flagstaff, Arizona, he attended kindergarten at a Waldorf academy. As an educator with an interest in progressive schools, I knew about the Waldorf philosophy and decided that, if Ray had to attend school, this would be a good place to start.

In the early grades in a Waldorf school, academics do not appear. The focus is not on reading, writing, arithmetic, etc. Instead, the focus is on becoming responsible for one's self and others, being culturally sensitive on an international scale, and connecting to the visible world through direct contact – by tending a garden, caring for farm animals, etc. Parents were advised to eliminate television from their children's lives, and a life based on nature and simplicity was emphasized. Yee-chen loved the idea of Ray going to any school, so she was happy about the Waldorf program. Her main concern has always been to get Ray involved with other children. I thought that that was fine, but, knowing myself, and knowing Ray to be a lot like me, I figured in any environment that involved a room full of people,

Ray would try to go as unnoticed as possible and would probably connect with just one person in the room. This is just what happened; he became friends with another shy and gentle boy named Winston, and Winston remained his lone buddy for that year.

Outside of the human connections – which were indeed important, even if on a small scale – I had mixed feelings about the program. I'd grown up watching four or more hours of television every day. As an adult, I realized how much of my life I'd wasted and for many of my adult years I did not own a television. I soon found that what I did not have, I did not miss. That said, when Ray was young, one of my favorite activities was to watch Batman cartoons with him. Batman is a character who puts his entire focus and all of his energies into achieving his goals; I saw value in that. So even though Ray attended a Waldorf school, we still watched TV. I made sure, however, that Ray never wore his Batman T-shirt to school.

Aside from a focus on caring for plants and animals, the curriculum seemed to consist of singing songs and learning about myths and stories from around the world. This, too, was okay with me because I was working with Ray at home on the academics. It wasn't that I was actively working against the school's philosophy; instead, this was just something that Ray wanted. It was at this time that Ray grew interested in numbers and letters – when he was in his counting phase and spelling phase. He seemed so hungry for this academic side that this is what we focused on at home: impromptu math lessons and spelling quizzes.

The best thing that I liked about the Waldorf school was that it genuinely seemed like a family. I trusted and liked the people at the school, and I felt that it was a safe place for my son. My first preference was always to have Ray study at home and learn from his mom and dad, but this was a reasonable second option. If we hadn't left Flagstaff to return to Florida, I am sure that we would have kept Ray in the Waldorf program, and I would have continued to supplement Ray's academics at home for as long as he showed interest in math, science, language, etc.

Florida, however, was another story. Even though Ray had already had one year of kindergarten and was years ahead of his peers academically, the school officials in our area focused solely on rules. The rules said that a student had to be a certain age by a certain date in order to attend a certain grade. Ray's age at the start of school placed him in kindergarten, and we were faced with either having Ray repeat a grade or keeping him at home. I, of course, was for keeping him at home. I had attended public schools my entire life and could hardly bring myself to put Ray in any grade, let alone a grade that he had already completed. For me, gym class was the only good part of school. The rest of it was boring, embarrassing, or frightening. However, Yee-chen was always more sensitive to the social component of school. So we compromised: Ray went to school until noon – when the students were doing spelling and math, even though it was at what seemed to me a remedial level – and Ray left home at lunchtime. He really missed nothing because the after-lunch sessions consisted mainly of naps. Ray didn't nap.

Even though his kindergarten teacher was only seeing him for a few hours each day, she saw certain characteristics in Ray and suggested that he be screened for gifted services. The counselor at the school who was in charge of the screenings spent a few minutes with Ray and decided that he had failed the screening. I could've told her that before she even began the process. In a room full of people who were familiar to Ray, he still would remain quiet, focusing quietly on whatever task he was asked to do instead of socially interacting with others. Faced with a complete stranger in an isolated setting, he was lucky to produce one-word utterances in response to any question. Ray was, and to some extent still is, the kind of kid who would stand by and watch silently. Even if something was going on that he really wanted to be a part of, his natural shyness would keep him on the sidelines. Someone would have to go up to him and directly invite him into the activity for Ray to become a part of it. Only with those who he was extraordinarily comfortable with – his parents and his cousins – did he take the role of initiator or leader. I knew this, but I also knew that Ray was gifted, so we tried the second route: an IQ test. As the test was based mainly on a series of tasks and puzzles that Ray was asked to solve on his own – independent of conversation skills and degree of extroversion – he did well on the test and qualified. This meant that for grade one, Ray could attend the one full-time center for gifted studies in the county.

To me, the only thing about the gifted program that was accelerated was the number of worksheets that the students had to complete each day in the classroom and each night at home for homework. Give Ray something to do, and he will do it well, but I didn't think that he was getting anything from a worksheet-based curriculum. His scores put him at the top of his class, and, as usual, he had one close friend, but it just didn't seem to be the right environment. So when Yee-chen completed the Montessori teacher training program that she had been working through for the past year and had secured a position in a local school, we moved Ray from the Center for Gifted Studies the following year.

Ray spent grades two through five in a Montessori school where Yee-chen worked as a pre-K/Kindergarten teacher. I had studied Maria Montessori's writings years before when we were living in Guam, and I had found many connections between Waldorf and Montessori. The main difference was that academics came into play much sooner in the Montessori method. The similarities included the use of natural, wooden, objects as educational tools; a focus on community and respect for others; and the opportunity for the students to direct their own studies and, in the process, to grow responsible and independent. The environment was family like, and that was what I liked best about it. In just a short time, everybody knew who Ray was and called him by name. Every day Ray was greeted by friendly faces. I felt that people looked out for one another there and that it was a safe environment. And of course having Yee-chen on campus was an added bonus. I liked the extra security of knowing that family was on the scene in case of an emergency.

As in the other educational settings, Ray didn't gain much academically, but he was around others his age in a family environment, and he was able to play sports. Cross country/triathlon team, flag football, soccer: Ray participated in them all. Afterschool sports and free time to play during PE were the only parts of school that Ray liked. The sports were the upside; the downside was the useless homework that absorbed hours of his time each day. When I was a kid, I used to be able to come home from school and do what I liked best, which usually meant watch TV or play sports. Ray, who was at the top of his class in all academic subjects (art was his bane), labored for hours over boring worksheets that were arduous and, most times, meaningless. His personality forced him to do even the most meaningless worksheet with the utmost care; he felt that he had to do everything he was told to do by a teacher and that he had to do it without error. The result of this was that Ray grew to hate school.

This was the environment that Ray was in during the entire time that he was making his mark in chess. He had to work his chess studies around his school schedule, the afterschool sports, and the wasted hours he spent each night on worksheets. All of the progress that he made in chess – when he got good and, later, when he got better – resulted from his efforts on the weekends and from whatever time he could squeeze out of each weekday for chess. It's surprising how much time a child can find when he gives up television, video games (Ray had none to give up), and do-nothing moments. The last is the only thing I had any regret about. I am a big believer in having time to do nothing. It's important to have such downtime to reflect on one's experiences. Do-nothing time can be extraordinarily stimulating. But Ray had little of this, and the reason was that he cared so much about chess that that is how he wanted to spend any spare moment he had. This is why he had chess books beside him at meals, so that he could read a passage or analyze a position in the short time that he had to finish breakfast. This is why chess books were on the back seat of Yee-chen's car, so that he could read during the 15-minute drive to and from school each day. It was obvious to me how Ray wanted to spend his time, and I often complained about the wasted time spent doing homework that just didn't seem very important. So it was actually a relief to me when Yee-chen, who had been enjoying her own position less and less each year, decided that it was time for her to leave the school. When she left, Ray left with her, and this is when I finally – after years of wanting to do so – was able to create a homeschool program for Ray.

Homeschooling is actually the wrong word. It's more appropriate to call what we did *un-schooling*. In homeschooling, children usually follow a set curricula developed by outsiders. Such curricula are often developed by far right Christian educators. As a left-leaning independent thinker who was more comfortable and familiar with the philosophies and religions of the East, I decided to avoid those curricula. Also, by that time I had been an educator for just about 20 years, had a doctorate in education, had a wife who was an educator, and had a son who was intelligent, self-disciplined, and focused. To me, un-schooling seemed the way to go.

Essentially, I gave Ray control over the direction of his studies. The first book he chose for free reading was Orwell's *1984*. Soon he moved on to other challenging pieces, but he also read several books that were just good literature (Ray Bradbury, for example) or just fun reads (such as the *Series of Unfortunate Events* collection and all of the Harry Potter books, among others). In addition, the chess publications that we subscribed to, *New in Chess* and *The Yearbook*, were written at an adult level, yet he understood what he read better than many of the adult college students that I was working with.

For science, Ray occasionally listened to Professor Michio Kaku lectures on the radio. For both history and current events, he learned about what was happening in the world from me (and I got my news by reading Noam Chomsky, Howard Zinn, and Arundhati Roy and by listening to Alternative Radio and Amy Goodman's *Democracy Now*). He studied math at his own pace through a virtual school. Also, there was a connection between the deep analysis that Ray engaged in when he studied chess – what I called the geometry of the board – and basic concepts found in mathematics. And as for grammar, Ray already wrote better than most college-level students, but he still improved in this area by editing his mom's graduate school papers and by learning from the few corrections that I made to his corrections.

In addition to the core subjects outlined above, Ray also studied Chinese (Mandarin) with his mother each week. It was our goal for him to become as proficient as was possible for one who studied a language outside of the country where it was spoken. It was also important to both Yee-chen and me that Ray embrace his Asian ancestry along with his American roots.

And, of course, in addition to all of the rest, Ray had his chess studies. I'll be honest: with the new arrangement, Ray spent the bulk of his time studying chess. He finally had the time to devote hours each week researching opening theory and analyzing important games. He had more time for chess lessons, too, and he corresponded more regularly with his grandmaster tutor, asking questions and getting quick responses through e-mail, Skype, or telephone. Did Ray ever once ask about going back to school? Did he ever show any regret for leaving school? No. He was happy.

My only area of concern was not in keeping Ray intellectually stimulated – he had taken care of that for himself – it was in finding physical activities for him to do. Our neighborhood used to house a population of kids who played street football or basketball regularly, and Ray was an active part of that group. Over the years, that group disappeared. To offset the loss, we at first took Ray almost daily to a local recreation center, but later we made our home recreation-friendly. The cars were parked out in the driveway, leaving room for a brand new full-sized Ping-Pong table in the garage. I dug up the backyard and installed an in-ground regulation basketball hoop. Soon after, I added nearly 250 large pavers that made up the playing court. As a family, we played net-less badminton in the street (no boundaries, which made for a great workout), and Ray and I tossed the football around. While the other kids around our neighborhood became in-dwellers, spending their time playing video games or watching TV perhaps, we remained an active family.

Ray maintained friendships with other children mainly through family (the Kemper kids), through weekend Chinese classes at the local school, and through chess. His circle of chess friends was ever broadening and extended well beyond the United States. True, he had to settle for monthly in-person interaction (at chess events) and infrequent electronic correspondence, but the friends he met through chess were intelligent, kind, and interesting people (both kids and adults), so the trade-offs were worthwhile.

* * *

Just as Ray had a new chapter in his educational life, so too did he enter a new phase with his grandmaster tutor. I sang the grandmaster's praises to anyone who asked me about Ray's most recent tutor. He was not just a great chess player and a great tutor; he seemed to be a genuinely kind and caring person who I suspected would have a positive effect on Ray, both in chess and in life.

The grandmaster started working with Ray around the time that he had won his second national tournament. Since the grandmaster lived far away, Ray had to call him on the phone (which, later, was replaced by calls from Skype). The two used the Internet Chess Club, an online site that allowed them to access an electronic chessboard on which they could analyze Ray's recent games. They moved the pieces on the board with their respective computer mice, and they discussed the moves and their ideas over the phone. It was not the best way to have a lesson, but it was the best that we could manage. For the first couple of years, they had lessons only once or twice a month, but even with this infrequent tutelage, Ray improved his chess, and he grew closer to the grandmaster.

Later in this same period, Ray had much more time with the grandmaster. In April of 2006, for example, he was one of the few invitees to a special chess training, a program designed to help promising young chess stars continue to progress. The grandmaster was involved in the program, and the first session was held near his home. I trusted his tutor enough to let Ray stay at the grandmaster's house on his own. This might not seem like a big deal to some, but in his eleven years, Ray had never stayed a week with anyone besides his parents. We're a close-knit family, and we've arranged our lives around this family of three. So it means something when I say that I trusted the grandmaster to treat Ray like a parent treats his child.

After the positive training experience, we were able, in conjunction with another family that the grandmaster worked with, to bring him to Florida. For five days in the early fall of 2006, we drove Ray to Tampa where the two worked together for six hours a day in a small library. For Ray, it was a perfect week. Here he had someone who could not only understand his own thinking and lines of inquiry, but who could guide him even further, showing him areas previously unexplored (by Ray) that served to stimulate his mind and – something I didn't think possible – motivate him even more to devote himself to the study of chess. I liken it to a young music prodigy who gets to spend a week in conversation and performance with Mozart, or a talented young artist who gets to paint with Picasso.

The wonderful thing about the grandmaster, that which made him so special, was the seeming absence of ego. Whereas some masters would, through words and actions, attempt to belittle or discourage young players like Ray out of fear and self-preservation, the grandmasster said, and meant, things like, "I cannot wait until the time – and it is very soon – when we can share ideas and work together as equals, not as teacher and student." I had not found this attitude, this kind of personality, anywhere else in the chess world. Even some of the kindest people we've met – and there are many kind folks in the chess world – were secretive when it came to chess; they didn't want to reveal anything that might lessen their own advantage. With the grandmaster, it was all generosity and good will.

I had to give up some of my own ground to let the grandmaster into Ray's life, because he was sharing a spot that I alone used to occupy: teacher, mentor, confidant. Truth, however, always outweighs other factors in the long run, and the truth was that I hadn't been able to advise Ray on the practical part of chess – the nuts and bolts of the game itself – for a few years. Ray needed another caring, well intentioned adult who could guide him to greater levels of complexity and understanding. The grandmaster was that person for Ray, and I considered him to be a friend of the family – a well-intentioned distant neighbor who had something to share with my son.

* * *

Ray's relationship with the grandmaster seemed to be strengthening daily through increased contact, and Ray was more focused and serious about his chess studies than at any other time in his career. This, along with the absence of serious financial support to help cover Ray's rising chess costs (soon to reach $25,000 per year), forced me to reevaluate my own role. The result was a new chapter in my own life – a chapter that would allow me to continue to help Ray, though one that would take me further out of the chess scene.

I stated earlier in this book that I once worked at a university and left because it wasn't the right setting for me. I preferred the classroom to administrative duties, and I preferred the public school teacher's schedule that allowed for extended holidays and free summers. What it all amounted to was time, and all free moments were devoted to Ray. He needed me then to help him along with his interest in chess; to pump him up before tournaments; to bring him books and to read and discuss them with him; to play game after game of chess; to chauffer him to all of the local events; and to help him manage the experience whenever things grew confusing or difficult. However, by the time that Ray was eleven, he was both the current youngest National Master and the current youngest FIDE Master in the country. He was directing his own studies with the assistance of his grandmaster tutor, and he had mastered all of the chess demons, save the one that he had created for himself: time management. He had also outgrown all of the local events and the local players. What he needed was to attend the strongest events in the country. He needed a situation that would allow him to travel to the biggest event that we could find each month so that he could play the country's best – the international masters and the grandmasters – and find lessons to improve imbedded in the subsequent draws and losses. In other words, what he needed was a plan and the money to see the plan through.

My Peace Corps-itis helped to get things rolling. I had completed just over two years at the high school, and, directly afterwards, I put in two years as testing coordinator/teacher for the county. Clearly it was time for me to move on to another job! I had had a doctorate sitting on a shelf for several years, so I dusted it off and left the low pay but abundant time of a public school teacher to accept a 12-month professorship at a local college. My income nearly doubled; my free time nearly vanished. Consequently, I was able to pay for Ray and Yee-chen's fall trip to the 2006 World Youth in Georgia (the country), but I was unable to accompany them. Likewise, I could pay for the hotels and send them to the big events of November and December – the Chess Congress in Philadelphia and the North American Open in Las Vegas – but I had to get the game reports from long distance, from calls home after the events. I was home alone during the weeklong training at the US Chess School in Arizona in the winter, and I did my coaching before and after rounds via telephone and Skype when Ray was with Yee-chen for events in North Carolina and New Hampshire in the spring.

Back when Ray was a fourth grader, playing for the college scholarship at Supernationals, I penned a line in my journal as Ray went into his last round:

I am the hand on the back of the chair before the start of each round.

That was my role. I was the support person; the familiar physical presence projecting every ounce of positive energy I could muster towards Ray. I could no longer explain anything about tactics or strategy, but I was there with Ray. And that was something. But in the 2006/2007 year, I wasn't there at all. It was my first year at the college, and I needed to make a good impression on my new boss. I wanted to keep this job that paid for all of our expenses and that dramatically shrunk the mortgage with the passing of each month. In order to do this, I needed to be at my desk each day, and I needed to be in my classes without absence. But I missed my time with Ray. These chess trips had become our special time together. Yes, we played basketball and Ping-Pong at home, and we watched sports games together, and we did a myriad of other things together, but chess was always the main event. I spent a lot of time that first year at the college thinking about what I could do to get back into the chess scene.

Did my absence make a difference in Ray's play? I didn't think it would. For five years – five years – I had been Ray's companion at every one of his over 100 chess tournaments, but when I sent him to the 2006 World Youth with his mother, who knew little more than how the pieces moved and even then got that confused most of the time, I knew that Ray would still do well. I was a supportive coach and his emotional manager, yes, but Ray was the one doing all of the work. One relative frequently said to me – and also to Ray – that we were a great team, always overemphasizing my own role and making it seem as if Ray's successes would have been impossible without me. Nothing could make me feel angrier, short of a direct insult to Ray. The minute we were alone, I would tell Ray that what he heard was all wrong. I told him that he was the one who was spending 4 to 6 hours every day in concentrated study and that he was the one who was sitting at the board playing out the moves for every game. I did not want my son to grow up thinking that he could only make it through difficult experiences on the back of another – that he couldn't do it on his own. I said, just as I believed, that Ray's success was due to Ray and that he should fully own all of these things that he had earned himself.

So when Ray traveled without me, I had no doubts that he would continue to do well. In fact, I reminded Ray before each trip that I knew that he would do well – that he knew what he needed to do and that he just needed to trust himself. And Ray proved me right by finishing in the top ten at the World Youth, just as he had done the two previous years when I was standing on the sidelines. Later that year, Ray finished in the top ten in November in Philadelphia, just one point behind the winner. His only loss in that event was to a top grandmaster, and his 4.5 points included wins over two masters, one international master, and a draw with another international master.

To prove that this wasn't a fluke, he had the same top ten finish in December in Las Vegas, once again finishing one point behind the winner. With three rounds to go, Ray had two points. He told me over the phone that he had to win the next three rounds. He did just as he said, with wins over two international masters in a row followed by a final round victory, with the Black pieces, over GM Melikset Khachiyan: Ray's first tournament victory over a grandmaster, and he was just 12 years old! The game was broadcast live over the Internet, so I was able to watch every move from my computer at home late at night. Within minutes of winning the game, Ray called me on the phone. He didn't need me there to secure the win, but he did need me to share the experience with, and that was enough.

But not really. That was just the rationalization of a man who could not be where he desperately wanted to be: right at Ray's side, or, more exactly, right behind Ray. It wasn't enough to watch the game in this way; I should have been there. I knew that I would have to come up with some plan to get things back to the way they were.

* * *

Ray had a performance rating of over 2500 in each of his last two tournaments. In other words, although his actual rating was in the 2300s by the end of the year, he was already playing like a grandmaster. That seemed to be the path that Ray was on – the one that led to becoming a grandmaster. It would take time, study, dedication, heart, and money, but it would happen. I could usually tell about such things. I knew that Ray was a special child from the time that he was three years old. I knew by his third tournament, when he was eight years old and rated 677, that he would be a master, and, four years later, when he was a master, I knew that he would one day be Grandmaster Ray Robson. He would see to it. And when it happened, I would give him a hug and tell him that I knew all along that he could do it.

21

Ray's outstanding performance at the chessboard earned him a spot in the 2007 United States Closed Championship. At 12 years of age, he was the youngest person to ever qualify for this, the biggest chess event in the country. Such an accomplishment did not go unnoticed by the media.

Actually, Ray had received quite a bit of attention over the past few years. I had mixed feelings about this. In the early years, Ray received almost no attention at all from the chess community. Even after he had become the number one youth for his age group, it seemed that his accomplishments were grossly underreported – at least by the USCF. I figured that this was because Ray was outside of the main chess circles. He was this kid from SW Florida where not a single grandmaster resided. Or maybe, I thought, it was because people were waiting to see if Ray's success would last – that is, if he were the real thing. Very few young prodigies continue to improve year after year, and most young superstars never even reach master level. The few who do rarely make it beyond international master level. We have only a handful of homegrown grandmasters in the United States. One look at the list of top players in this country will reveal that the vast majority were born elsewhere: Russia, Ukraine, Armenia, etc.

Over time, when Ray's accomplishments could not possibly go unmentioned, reports that included him began to appear in USCF articles. This is when my mixed feelings kicked in. It is very difficult for a parent, who for years has watched and supported his child as he works so hard toward his goals, to read a stranger's report about a disappointing loss, a crucial blunder, etc. as opposed to a report about the nice tactic or beautiful win. I wondered how such persons who wrote about the failures of the young prodigies could so easily ignore the fact that they were writing about children and that what their subjects really deserved was support for their efforts. This idea, of course, goes well beyond reporting. I've found that, in general, most people who interact with Ray on the chess scene think of him as a mini-adult. Because he is able to play against 40-year-old grandmasters, they forget that he is, in fact, a child. Their language, their topics, their actions, etc. reveal that they are entirely unaware that the person standing before them is a 12-year-old boy.

Outside of the main chess news scene, Ray's name showed up in a myriad of blog discussions, international chess sites, twitters, etc. A Google search in 2007 would bring up 8,000 or more hits. Poorly policed Internet sites such as Wikipedia have resulted in erroneous information (e.g., wrong grade, incorrect norm info, etc.) appearing throughout the cyber world. What I once thought we were missing – media attention – I later wished we'd missed entirely.

The newspaper reports were another matter altogether. Nearly every newspaper article on Ray – and there have been dozens over the past several years – has been written by someone who knew nothing, or next to nothing, about chess. Many of the reporters apparently knew little about facts as well. These pieces differ from the articles written by the chess reporters because they are easy to laugh about. These are the reports that exaggerate his study habits (reading a book a day!) or that fictionalize his tournament performances (dominating a field of grandmasters!). Nearly every fact about Ray Robson – save his gender – has been misreported in one article or another.

For Ray's part, he didn't seem to take anything said about him too seriously. A comment from one reporter, which I would interpret as a jab, Ray would ignore and soon forget about altogether. This was the healthy response that I could only hope for. Instead of what was said about him, Ray was always more focused on the task at hand: his studies that would prepare him for the next big event. And at this time, the next big event was the United States Chess Championship.

* * *

The Championship was one event that I simply refused to miss. The tournament took place at the start of the summer semester. By that time, I had received two semesters' worth of student evaluations. For the past year, I had put all of my own focus and energy into my classes when I was in front of my students, and this was reflected in the overwhelmingly positive evaluations I received at the end of each semester. With the evaluations in hand, I met with my boss, and, by the time I left, I had the two weeks that I needed to accompany Ray to Stillwater, Oklahoma, for his first US Championship.

* * *

There wasn't much of a ceremony. I was expecting something spectacular (this was, after all, a US Championship); however, it turned out to be just like any other event. In fact, the scene reminded me of the local club where Ray first started playing. We were in a room where at least one a/c unit was dripping onto the table (Ray's table). The organizers didn't have enough chess clocks that could run with the correct time control. There was a big argument as to what replacement time should be used for the first round (while the necessary clocks were being ordered for the second day). And, in general, it was unorganized and very ordinary. In a way, this was good for Ray. I knew he was both pumped up and nervous about the event, and maybe a big production with a lot of people in suits would have added to his nervousness. As it was, he seemed fine and ready to play. It was touching that Ray's tutor (dressed in a nice suit, appropriate to the occasion), sat beside Ray at his board and talked with him before the start of Ray's first round of his first US Championship. I remember thinking that the grandmaster was a good man and a good friend to Ray.

* * *

After losing round one to a grandmaster, Ray's opponent for round two was a friend of his, Josh Friedel – a soon-to-be grandmaster who was the latest recipient of the Samford Fellowship. The Samford is the premier scholarship in the

United States. While other top young players, like Hou Yi-fan of China and Negi Parimarjan of India, have the support of their respective nations, here in the United States any meaningful chess support comes from private sources – almost always wealthy individuals who have an interest in chess. The brief support that Ray had earlier in his career was by one such individual, and some of this country's top players are mainly supported by chess aficionados with large pocketbooks.

The Samford, however, was the jackpot in terms of chess support in the United States. Players received approximately $36,000 each year (for two years) in order to support them in their chess studies. Extensive training with grandmasters – usually costing around $100 per hour – was made affordable by the Fellowship. Overseas tournaments – the ones that were necessary in order to secure grandmaster norms – were now possible to attend. The winner of the Samford was supposed to be the most promising player in the country, one who was thoroughly devoted to chess. Josh, who had forgone college in order to focus on chess and who was an active player working hard to achieve grandmaster status, was an obvious choice for the Fellowship.

Ray had applied for the same award for the past two years, but we knew that other players, like Josh, were probably ahead of him on the list of those who were seriously being considered. Also, all of the awards thus far had been given to players who were around twenty years of age, so it wasn't a total surprise when 12-year-old Ray did not get that year's award. He did, however, get a junior version which helped, on a much smaller scale, with the expense of lessons and some events.

Ray's preparation for his game against Josh paid off, and, after playing a solid game, he secured a draw. Playing such a young and up-and-coming person evenly was, in my opinion, better than beating one of the down-and-out aging grandmasters, and this included Ray's tutor. In their training games together over the past few months, Ray had beaten or drawn his tutor several times. Ray's grandmaster tutor, who was once a professional player near the top of the rating list in this country, had evolved from top player to top tutor. While the grandmaster moved down the top 100 list, Ray, in the same period, went from nowhere on the list to 39th. Ray was rapidly climbing up the list that the grandmaster was slowly slipping down.

* * *

After a second loss followed by his first win, Ray was hoping for a good game to get him back on track. His fifth-round opponent, Michael Mulyar, was a contemporary of Josh Waitzkin, a young prodigy who, in the late 1980s, received a tremendous amount of media attention. At that time, some were saying that Josh would be the next Bobby Fischer. He never made it beyond international master, however, perhaps having gone as far as he could. In any event, Michael Mulyar, Ray's opponent, was a part of that long-ago scene, and this tournament was a sort of comeback for him. He was then like Ray is now: rated 2400 as a young player, representing the US at the World Youth events, and knocking off top players while still young.

I thought that this should be a tough game for Ray. This guy, who was now around 30, was good. I wondered if perhaps Ray would remind him of himself (or of Waitzkin). This would be their first game together; before that day, however, I'd never heard of Michael Mulyar. I think, like Waitzkin, Mulyar couldn't break the grandmaster barrier, drifted away from chess (while his rating dipped into the low 2400s), and is just now (unlike Waitzkin) returning to chess. While he may not have been playing at his best, he had played well enough at the North American Open (tying in score with Ray) to qualify for the US Championship. This, I thought, would be a good win for Ray.

While Ray and Michael were engaged in battle, I read one of the books that I had brought: Bertrand Russell's autobiography. Perhaps he lived as long as he did – 98 years! – because he had a purpose in life and because he was needed by others his entire life. He was doing many important things all the way until the end of his days. I knew that some people who retired died off rather suddenly and that a feeling of uselessness brought one closer to death. As for me, I'd always wanted to retire – ever since I started working. Russell's book had me thinking about my own plans. Unlike him or Noam Chomsky, my modern-day hero, I was not a leading intellectual (hardly an intellectual at all) who must address the larger issues on behalf of all mankind. I was not that person – neither in ability nor in desire.

I thought that what I would like to do with my remaining time (and who knows how many years one has left?) was much more personal and on a much smaller scale. What I wanted to do was to write about the most important experiences in my life, to continue to support and be with Ray until he moves on (and afterwards to support him in whatever way is necessary, in addition to supporting his children, my grandchildren), to continue to maintain my relationship with Yee-chen, and to maybe do a few other things, such as finally mastering Mandarin, improving my own chess game, reading more good books, maintaining a weight and shape that I was proud of, maybe keeping a vegetable garden of tomatoes and peppers, and going through the thousands of pages from journals kept off and on over the past 20 years to sort, save, and destroy as necessary.

I thought that I would try to keep my job for as long as I could (or at least for a while longer), but I no longer intended to let my life revolve around my job as I did in my first year, owing to the fact that it *was* my first year and that was what people did who wanted to have a second year. Instead, I would try to do my work around my life (like missing classes to be with Ray for the US Championship, which was just where I should be). I planned to accompany Ray to Turkey, too, for the next World Youth, which would mean more time off. If I had the days, I'd take them. If I didn't get asked back after year two, that would be okay. Barring tragedy, I figured that I would have the mortgage paid off and might even have a few thousand in the bank come next summer. And if Yee-chen did indeed get the full-time job that she'd been talking about for the fall of 2008, then all I'd need would be a part-time position that paid for Ray's chess needs and also for the normal expenses (which, sans mortgage, would be more easily manageable). I thought that my plan might have me returning to work as an old man, but maybe at that time I'd be in need of filling my days with something like work anyway.

One of the benefits of accompanying Ray to these events is that I had lots of time – often six hours at a stretch – to think about things like life, where I'm at in it, and where I would like to be. But I also had plenty of time to look around and to observe what was happening in the immediate scene. Chess players are some of the oddest people I have ever encountered, and the US Championship had its share of characters, the king of which was an old-timer whom I'll call Grandmaster Cocoa.

He was the jumpiest, twitchiest, most nervous person I have seen in a chess hall. He made me nervous just watching him. I watched as he raced over to the snack table, purposefully kicked the garbage can a foot to his right, started pouring the coffee while the cup was still on its way to receiving it, snatched a cream, ripped at the top, threw it back in the bin when the top didn't release easily, snatched another one, ripped off the top, tried to throw the contents into his cup – tried to override gravity, I guess – then hurled the cream container into the trash, snatched a pack of sugar, violently ripped it open, forced the contents into his cup, threw the pack away while sugar was still dropping from it (apparently, he had a time limit of 0.2 seconds for how long he would wait for sugar to fall out of the packet), repeated this with a second packet, repeated this with a third packet, grabbed a stirrer like a starving man snatches a fish out of the water, gave a .025-second stir, hurled the stirrer into the garbage can, tasted the cup (his lips were moving towards it between the time that he stirred it and tossed the stirrer), snatched yet another packet of sugar, did the sugar drill, and then raced to his seat. The preceding scene took all of 12 seconds. Grandmaster Cocoa was obviously a madman. I think it was a combination of too much caffeine and way too much sugar that had so super-charged him and led to his insanity. Later in the event, I would watch him bark at a young man for being too close to his board.

I shifted my attention, as I always do eventually, back to Ray's board. Michael, Ray's international master opponent, seemed to be traveling with his dad. There was a smaller and much older version of himself who had been hovering over his board throughout the game. I wondered if that would be me in 16 years. If that really was his father – and I think that it was – I figured that there must be something right in their relationship for them to still be traveling together to a chess event. Perhaps they had the kind of strong relationship that I hoped to continue to have with Ray.

I then turned my attention back to Grandmaster Cocoa who had yet another cup of coffee, complemented by a pack of M&Ms and a chocolate-chip cookie (couldn't seem to get enough sugar or caffeine!). I watched as he, red-faced, pulled at his hair with both hands and literally punched himself in the head. It looked as if he was furious at himself for not being able to focus or think properly.

Later I saw him leap out of his seat, violently wrestle off his jacket, twisting it horribly in the process, and then bunch it up like a wad of paper and throw it down onto the empty table behind him. For a moment, it looked like he was going to hurl the jacket at his grandmaster opponent, or at any other nearby human, but he was able to control his madness and so took out his anger on the nearby table. With such a red face, he looked certain to have a heart attack. I don't know how he didn't. He was a madman.

* * *

Ray lost his game with Michael. Time was definitely a factor. He played the last hour or so mainly on the time increment, keeping only a minute or two on his clock. With too little time to think over a critical move, he made the wrong choice (taking a pawn that should have been left alone), which led to his being checkmated in what was before that time a slightly better position for Ray. This was tough. The loss put Ray near the very bottom of the pack.

* * *

Ray's opponent for round six was 20-year-old WFM (Woman FIDE Master) Iryna Zenyuk. I could never understand why there was a separate rating category for women players. For every man's title, there is a woman's title, and the requirements for the women's titles are much lower. For example, it is easier to become a women's grandmaster than it is to become a regular international master. What is the message? Are the international chess authorities saying that women cannot compete equally with men on an intellectual frontier? Why do we have separate men's championships and women's championships when there are players like Hou Yi-fan, along with her predecessors (Judit Polgar, for example), who play as well as men and who earn the grandmaster title? Ray once asked me why, at World Youth events, girls could play in the boys' section but boys could not play in the girls' section. I did not have an answer for him.

The game between Ray and Iryna was an exciting one to watch. It went all the way down to the end time-wise. Iryna had an imposing attack going, with three connected pawns zeroing in on the back rank. Ray, having nothing to do in the way of defense, turned to the attack. I think Iryna could have won this game if she'd played the ending differently. As it was, she took one long think on a move that depleted most of her time, and then when she really needed a few minutes to think about her moves, she didn't have it, allowing Ray to get a better position and the final win. Maybe this – seeing a time-related loss from the other side of the board – would help Ray to realize the importance of managing one's time. I hoped so. In any event, he won his game. I really liked Iryna's attitude (graceful smile and a genuine desire to go over the game because it was quite interesting); this is the best way to lose a game if one must lose.

* * *

Ray picked up another win the next round, but he did so under extreme time pressure. His final two games – both losses – were also influenced by time. His time management problem had become more important than his results. Why couldn't he play faster? He had nothing to lose in any of the games. His rating placed him near the bottom of the list of participants, so losses against higher-rated opponents would have little effect on his overall rating. Why didn't he give himself at least a chance by moving in a timely manner? I was not the one playing, so I didn't have the right to judge. Still, it was very frustrating for me to watch, and I knew it was the same for Ray's tutor who, just a few days before, had said to Ray, "It's inexcusable," in reference to the amount of time he used in one of his games. Just how were we to fix this time problem? My thought from long ago – that this was a developmental phase that Ray would simply grow out of – was obviously wrong. I needed to come up with a plan, and Ray needed to buy into the plan. This was one of the things that we took away from the event.

* * *

After Ray's last game, we took a long walk to town. On the way, we talked about time. It wasn't until the walk back – when I was revisiting the topic (and even then, it was at the *end* of the walk back) – that Ray finally said some revealing things. He said that he went over the move he was considering sometimes as many as five times because he was afraid he might miss something – either something good or something bad. I said, "But after you look at something five times, even if it's a bad move, you still play it if you haven't found something else, right?" He admitted that that was true. He also said that *maybe* he didn't have as much confidence as other players but that he didn't want to play with too much confidence because he might make a mistake. But all in all, he still didn't "own" this as a problem. He thought that if he wasn't this careful, then he would make a mistake and lose a game (it didn't matter to him that if he played the perfect moves that came from using all of his clock's time he would lose anyway). He also thought that he always had the chance to eventually catch up to his opponent on time.

Over the years, I had tried to approach this time problem from different angles, and I was never able to get through to Ray. He didn't see the issue as something that was impeding his development – a bad habit, for example, that might stay with him for years or longer – and I didn't know what else to do to help Ray to see that the situation was more serious than he'd imagined. His attitude was frustrating for me. I thought that it was pure foolishness on his part. Still, I wasn't ready to give up. Part of the plan that I'd come up with was to work with Ray's tutor as a team to address this problem with Ray.

Shortly after my own talk with Ray, right on cue, we had a visit from the tutor who had spent most of the event with his grandmaster friends. He came over to our room to look over games with Ray. In the middle of this, he started talking about Ray's problem with time, and then he proceeded to cover the *exact same items* that I had covered earlier that night with Ray. I chipped in when necessary to make sure that the grandmaster got the full picture (sharing some of what came out of my own talk with Ray). In effect, we teamed up on Ray in what turned out to be a kind of intervention. At the end of it all, with both of us having said the same things within such a short time of one another, the person who Ray probably trusted the most in this world along with the grandmaster he had worked so closely with . . . because of this, I thought that maybe Ray would finally come around and face his time trouble problem.

We even talked about a plan. To me there were two main issues that connected with one another: time management and confidence. For time, we talked about a number of strategies that Ray could use that would save him time. Most of these I had already pointed out to Ray over the past few years, but maybe now he would be ready to listen and act on them. For confidence, we talked about how Ray was the best player in the country (playing like a grandmaster already, according to the tutor) and that it was important for him to realize this. The tutor added that Ray should come to an event and play as if he were the king.

This last idea was actually something that I had tried to get Ray to *avoid* throughout his chess career. I had good reasons for this. First, the exceptional players that I had observed who seemed to bring an arrogant, overconfident bearing to the board were, with few or no exceptions, jerks. Partly because Ray was so exceptionally talented, I took extra care early on to ensure that he was also humble, kind, and polite; it was too easy to cross the line that separated the humble from the braggart, and I wanted to act in ways that would benefit Ray in the long run.

Second, Ray was just not the kind of person to have the cocky swagger that the grandmaster was suggesting. Yes, he could trash-talk with the best of them if he was on intimate terms with everyone in the group and if others were doing the same. But Ray was too inherently shy to behave in any way that would draw undue attention to himself. In the end, however, I agreed that, at the very least, *acting* more confident was something that Ray could try at an event. I decided that Ray had a solid enough base by that time that he could have a little attitude at the chess table and still remain who he was: a nice kid.

* * *

On Thursday, after only three or four hours of sleep (for Ray and I stayed up past midnight talking about our new plan of action), we drove back to the airport with the grandmaster. The two played a number of blindfold games as we walked down the airport corridors. We separated in Georgia, not one of us knowing that those would be our last positive moments together.

22

Every decision we make in some way supports someone in the family. Sometimes we cannot support everyone at the same time. In such cases, the one who needs the most support gets the attention. When I grew unhappy and so antsy at the prospect of doing any job for longer than two years, Yee-chen gave in to my restless feet and walked with me, ending up in a dozen homes in different states and in different countries. When Yee-chen absolutely needed to have a child, we had a child. When I wanted to leave my job in sunny Florida for graduate school in another state, that is what we did. When Yee-chen wanted a house and more security, we got a house and I got a more secure position with medical and dental benefits – luxuries we had only known sporadically during our life together. When Ray showed talent in chess, we put our time and money towards his development. When Yee-chen was lonely on weekends, we skipped events to spend more time with her. When Yee-chen found her career path, we supported her through her Montessori teacher training and, later, through her graduate studies. In our family, someone always has to give something up for someone else, but, at the same time, someone always gets to do something for someone else – someone they love. Don't get me wrong. The decisions over who gets what and when sometimes involve hurt feelings and even arguments. Nevertheless, we are a family, and we operate as a family.

From time to time, situations arise that require us to change our plans – to shift the focus as necessary. For example, our plans for the summer of 2007 included a scholarship-based trip for Yee-chen and Ray to Hungary, where Ray would work with a grandmaster and perhaps participate in one or more events in the area. However, when Yee-chen was offered a job as a Chinese teacher at a local middle school – a chance for her to begin a career as a public school teacher – it was an easy decision to make: we canceled the Hungary trip, which coincided with the start of the school year.

The grandmaster had been instrumental in setting up the plans with the independent foundation – a chess-related agency through which Ray was offered $10,000 in funds for training. I was uncomfortable with the deal from the start because the director of the award insisted that the agency wanted to operate independent of the parents. They had tried to give this same award in the past to another young prodigy. The deal fell apart when the boy's father, who was extremely involved in his son's chess career, had views that differed from those of the agency. I knew the other prodigy and his father – had met them at international events on a few occasions – and I knew that they were a father-son team similar to what we had: a father who managed the details and who was the constant traveling companion, and the son who was extremely gifted at chess and who put in all of the hard work. If the agency had trouble with these folks, I was sure that they would have trouble with us. I should have trusted my instincts and passed on the scholarship. Still, things happen for a reason.

It was actually the grandmaster who convinced me to accept the offer. He was staying in our home for an expensive week of one-on-one training shortly before the US Championship and, after I shared with him my misgivings, he argued strongly for accepting the award. This, he said, was something that Ray *absolutely had to do*. He needed to get to international events, he needed to do the summer training, and we needed to maintain this relationship with an organization that included some persons who were important in the chess world. I did not care about the last point in his argument; I simply could not – cannot – be driven by such things. But I did care about Ray's development, and if the grandmaster thought that Ray would benefit from this deal, then we would do it. I decided to trust another, but I worried that I would have immediate regrets. As far as the grandmaster was concerned, I had made the best decision for Ray, and he insisted that he would work out all of the details himself.

The arrangement that was finally settled on included a trip to Hungary and lessons with a grandmaster there, more lessons with our own grandmaster tutor, and lessons with another who, in my opinion, had very little to offer Ray in terms of training. In a 10-game match between Ray and this other trainer, I would have bet my house on Ray. The best part of the plan, I thought, was more lessons from the grandmaster that would be paid for.

The plans had been made prior to the US championship. Shortly after our return, we learned the news about Yee-chen's position, and immediately after we had made our family decision, I contacted the agency to tell them that we had to cancel the Hungary part of the plan – at least for now. The response I received, which I interpreted as, "We will have to consider your request and let you know what we decide," was more than a warning sign to me. I could see that the arrangement wasn't going to work. When I learned in a separate message from the grandmaster that the agency personnel were angry about the changes, it just made it easier for me to do what I knew I should have done in the first place: cancel the deal. And that's just what I did. This in turn angered the grandmaster, who had worked so hard to make the arrangements in the first place. The end of our own relationship was near.

The situation turned crazy when the grandmaster, already upset with me over the canceled plans, ran into us at an event a few weeks after the cancellation ordeal. Ray was in the middle of a game and, while lost in thought about the position and mentally calculating his lines as he walked to the bathroom, passed by the grandmaster without noticing him. When Ray is deep in concentration, he is practically in a fugue-like state, going through actions – like walking to the bathroom and using the toilet – without really being conscious of what he's doing, focusing instead on his calculations on his invisible mental chess board. The grandmaster, however, was so agitated with me that he immediately assumed that Ray had purposely ignored him and then later, in a very angry e-mail, accused me of setting the whole thing up.

A day later, the situation got even crazier. Twice the grandmaster snubbed me in front of my son, and once, as we were leaving the tournament, the grandmaster spoke to Ray (not to me). When I told the grandmaster that we were going, he again spoke directly to Ray, telling him to come over to him so that he could analyze a game with him. Ray left with me, of course, but how awkward – almost like two soon-to-be-divorced parents calling to a child from opposite sides of the room; only the grandmaster was not Ray's parent.

It took a long time for me to work through my own anger, but, ultimately, I came to the realization that the grandmaster had simply gotten too close to Ray. His words in his angry e-mails and his actions at the chess event belonged more to a slighted loved one than to a paid tutor. The bottom line for me was that, when I had made my final decision about our family's plans, the grandmaster should have respected my decision. He had become too close, too involved, and he was assuming rights that did not belong to him. The end result of this awful situation was that he quit, and I fired him. No tutor – no matter how good he is – is indispensable. The grandmaster was no different. So now my job was to soften this as much as possible for Ray. What I felt worst about was that I was forced to do something that I knew would hurt Ray, and that was always the very last thing that I ever wanted to happen anytime.

* * *

For most of my life, but especially after I turned 40, I viewed time as an enemy. But nothing is ever entirely bad, just as nothing is ever entirely good. The good part about time is that it helps to soften emotionally charged experiences. After some time had passed, I began to feel pretty good about things. I had talked with Ray about what had transpired between me and the grandmaster, shared with him the correspondence between us, explained things as best as I could, and got his thoughts. In no time, we were brainstorming plans.

We were soon able to come up with several options for the future. The nicest thing Ray said – the one that meant the most to me – was that I could be his coach again, that he could wait for me to study and catch up and work with him. That moment ranks at the top of my list of all-time best moments. The truth, of course, and he must have known this too, was that I would forever follow him in chess. Still, it was true that I was a good teacher in general. The thought occurred to me that if I could just get my basic knowledge of chess (openings, end game, etc.) up to a certain level – even a level well below Ray's – then perhaps I could still be an effective coach. In any event, I was just happy that he added that as a possibility – that it even occurred to him. One of the best periods of my life was when he and I were working together after we'd left his second tutor. That time was also productive, and I wondered if we could work out a plan to move forward in spite of my limited understanding of chess.

I don't use the word *pride* very often. There is something about it that makes me uncomfortable – something negative. Others who know about Ray always ask me how proud I am of my son. I usually move away from pride and tell them how pleased I am that someone who genuinely works hard at something is rewarded the way that Ray has been rewarded for his work. I only bring out *pride* on exceptional occasions. The grandmaster affair made me think about how proud I was of my son. The grandmaster had been a major part of Ray's chess life for about two years, and, after a string of events that occurred over just a few days, he was gone. It was a major event in his life, but Ray understood. And now he was looking towards the future. Ray's own response made we want to come up with the best plan possible.

Ultimately, I decided that the "independent student" option might be best for Ray. For a while, he had only been using the grandmaster as a sounding board: when he wasn't sure what move to play in a certain position, he would Skype or email the grandmaster and get a quick response. I thought it would serve Ray better if *he* had to figure out what to play – even if it took him a week to do it. And I also thought that this might connect with his problem of time management at the board. It could be that he was so used to calling on the grandmaster for help in confusing positions that when one occurred at the board, he didn't feel confident to find the solution on his own or else he used much more time to find a move than would someone who was used to finding these answers totally on his own. The other reason why I leaned towards independent Ray was that some of the greatest grandmasters (Bobby Fischer, for example) were essentially solo and did just fine over the board. Ray knew how to study, he had the equipment (programs, texts, etc.), he had the time and the will, and he had the support of his family.

* * *

I still had the "grandmaster affair" on my mind for several weeks. Eventually, I realized that I had thought about the situation too much already and helped myself to move on by recalling a favorite Zen story. *Two monks, one older and one younger, were walking along when they encountered a beautiful young woman who needed assistance crossing a river. After just a moment's hesitation, the old monk picked the beautiful woman up in his arms, held her tightly, and carried her to the other side of the river. Then the two monks resumed their own journey. Hours later, after miles of walking, the younger monk, who had obviously been extremely agitated since the river crossing, finally blurted out, "How can you, a venerable monk, have held that young woman in your arms?" The older monk replied, "I left that woman by the side of the river. Why are you still carrying her?"* It was time to leave the grandmaster by the side of the river and continue on our journey in peace.

* * *

By July of 2007, I had the new plan for us in final form. The plan consisted of advice and directions based on everything that, at that time, I believed Ray needed to work on. This is the plan that I shared with Ray:

Attitude: Be open to others. Let them help you. If you play a bad game, don't take your frustrations out on others. You must own your mistakes and then learn from them. Sometimes when you play badly or lose, it increases your negativity and deepens bad habits. You must be aware of this. You must also believe that you can beat the grandmasters.

Time: Part of the game of chess is managing your time wisely. If you found the perfect move after using all of your time to think and so lost the game, then you have made a mistake. There are many good moves in a given position. Pick one and save yourself time to pick others. In order to learn from your mistakes, you have to know what your mistakes are.

Psychology: Play with confidence! It is important for you to come in and – like a champion – play to win.

The Plan:

1. Keep track of your time.

2. Study Openings. Much of your time trouble comes when you encounter an opening that is unfamiliar to you. You need to do a thorough examination of possibilities that arise from opening positions.

3. Increase your repertoire. Start with one new line but, eventually, expand into other areas.

4. Prepare a d4 line that you can use as a surprise for an important game.

5. Do an in-depth computer-based *and* Ray Robson-based analysis of each of your tournament games after each event.

6. Do detailed annotations to determine where you could have improved.

7. Play practice games on the Internet to work on your time (give yourself 10-15 seconds to make your moves and then later analyze the games to see if your instincts were correct). When you confirm that your instincts are good, you will have more confidence to play your moves more quickly in real games. If you learn that your instincts are bad, then you can study more games and work on improving your memory so that you can recall the best moves to make in games.

8. It is best to solve your chess problems on your own (i.e., answer your own questions with or without the computer).

However, there may be times when you'd like to share ideas with another to get input. At such times, you should send messages to the chess friends who are currently available to you.

9. Review *The Week in Chess* each week in order to get ideas for your own games.

10. Continue to set goals for yourself for each tournament that you play in. The goals can be about performance (number of wins), time, attitude, or related to openings.

Final Word: I am now your trainer once again. I gave up that position (to the expert, the master, and the grandmaster) when I realized that you needed the kind of technical knowledge that I couldn't provide. Now, however, by others' accounts (everyone who has worked with you and many others in the chess community in general) you have the technical ability to become a grandmaster. You also know both what you need to study and how to study. All that you need now is an intelligent, supportive person who can help to guide you as you progress towards your goal of becoming a grandmaster. I have the intelligence (not chess intelligence, but intelligence in general); I have supported, and always will support, you in all that you do; and, best of all, I love you too. I think that you will have a lot of success working with me. Welcome to my training program!

23

One of the main highlights for us before the start of the 2007/2008 academic year was the arrival of the final Harry Potter book. Our copy was pre-ordered and in the mail on the first possible day. I read the first 200 pages before giving it up to Ray. The Potter books had a part in our life together. I started reading the books to Ray; then, as Ray's reading improved, we read them aloud together; and finally we would each read them silently and talk about them as we went along. And now the last one was out. We had read dozens of other books together, but we never shared in a series over such a long period of time. Now that the series had ended, I wondered what our next book would be. It was not the same with chess; we knew exactly where next to turn. The next step for Ray was to achieve the international master title, and so we began our norm hunt.

It is extremely difficult to become an international master; there are, in fact, less than 50 active international masters in all of the United States. One has to have a FIDE rating of 2400 or above. FIDE (international) ratings are not on the same scale as USCF (United States) ratings. A USCF rating of 2200, for example, could roughly be considered 2100 on the international scale. In other words, a 2200 FIDE-rated player would be considered stronger than a 2200 USCF-rated player. Aside from the required rating, one had to earn three international master norms; this is when things get tricky.

A norm is achieved at a tournament when several conditions have been met, including international time control for each game (different from what is usually used in the United States), number of rounds (nine rounds compared with the five or six that are usually played in this country), number of international opponents faced (playing the required number of foreign nationals in a typical United States event is nearly impossible), number of titled opponents faced (a certain number of one's opponents had to be grandmasters, international masters, and FIDE masters), and having a performance rating from the tournament that was equivalent to an international master (in other words, in order to become an international master, one had to play like one).

Tournaments in this country that met the norm requirements were really rare at the time that Ray began his hunt. The few that were organized were usually private invitational events where you had to know someone to have a shot at one of the few spots. Even with Ray's success and his growing popularity, we were still very much outside of the chess loop because of our geographical isolation from the main chess centers in New York and California. In addition, the norm events that were put together in this country were few and far between. This is one of the reasons why we had earlier considered going to Europe, where there was no dearth of titled international players at events conforming to FIDE specifications.

In August, we thought we'd have a chance when an open norm event was set up in Massachusetts. We made the trip, only to find that no one would have norm chances since a number of foreign nationals had dropped out of the event at the very last minute. It wasn't until October that another event appeared. Here we thought we were even luckier because it was just on the other side of the state. The timing for this event, however, posed a problem.

Yee-chen, who was now working every day at a public middle school, was no longer available to take Ray to events as she had during the past year. Throughout the semester, while Yee-chen was at her school, Ray was with me at the college. While I taught my classes, Ray studied chess in the college library. We met in the middle of the day to have lunch together on a bench, and then we both returned to our respective duties until the end of my workday at which time we would drive home together and play some Ping-Pong or shoot some baskets.

I had already used the last of my vacation days to take Ray to Massachusetts. I would've asked for leave without pay to accompany him to the Miami event in October except for the fact that my formal performance review was scheduled in the middle of the event. But since there were so few norm chances, I had to figure out some way to get Ray to the tournament. The plan that I came up with left me with some worries, but it seemed the only way.

I decided to fly out with Ray for the first round, leave him in the charge of another chess player, and then fly back at 5:00 a.m. the next morning to make my review that same day. As it turned out, the Scottish poet, Robert Burns, summed up our experience best with his lyrical line, “The best laid schemes o’ mice an’ men / Gang aft a-gley”; in other words, things don’t always work out as we had planned. Ray got sick on the first day of the event, filling up the back of the taxi on the way to the hotel after the first round. He stayed sick while he was there, played poorly, and ended up losing 25 rating points in a tournament where it turned out there was only a tiny chance anyway that he would get the exact pairings he would need in order to meet the strict requirements for a norm.

Ray's adult caregiver, too, turned out to need as much attention as Ray, for he did not handle common sense type situations very well. His airline had lost his luggage, and he said he had no idea what to do about clothing, toothbrush, etc. And after Ray threw up in the cab, it was all I could do to keep his companion from dropping out of the tournament and leaving the state. About their time together, Ray complained that he had to make all of the decisions for himself and his companion – from asking directions, to getting the cab, to talking to the driver, etc. He could not believe how someone could have so much trouble over the simplest tasks. Ray couldn’t believe it, but I could.

I have thus far been silent about Ray's greatest weakness – that which has caused his mother no end of frustration. Yee-chen, who was chopping vegetables with a razor-sharp cleaver and cooking rice over an open fire by age 3, could not understand how her 12-year-old son could fail at picking tomatoes from our garden. Ray would walk outside without thinking to bring any kind of container with which to carry the tomatoes; then Yee-chen would watch in absolute disbelief through the kitchen window as her brilliant son wandered in a circle, eventually walking all the way around the house, in search of tomatoes that could only be in the garden – the same garden where not long before Ray had handed the baby tomato plants to his father as he planted them. This was a fairly typical scene all through Ray's life, and I could only laugh.

Throughout my childhood, I thought that I had a hyphenated first name – Dammit-Gary – because that was what my father said during all of the years that I was his helper for various tasks inside and outside of the house. As a 12-year-old, I stood by puzzling out the simplest things that an infant could do. From my own experience, though, I knew that there was hope for Ray. I had my breakthrough in my early 30s, when I started fixing my own car. TK, my extraordinarily patient brother-in-law, started me off by showing me how to change the oil and do simple repairs. I eventually reached the point where I could change out a carburetor, and I made several on-the-road repairs with minimal equipment and no guidance. And once we got our old and decrepit home, I learned how to fix, patch, repair, and replace just about anything that a home contains – and to do so by often using tools that were intended for other purposes. If I was able to develop in this way, then Ray would do the same.

For the Miami trip, I thought that it was good for Ray to see what it was like to have to travel with someone who seemed to need as much assistance as he himself did. I thought that if the two ever roomed together for a longer period, Ray would grow tremendously, for he would be forced to handle the majority of the practical matters. Maybe, I thought, there was even a connection between common sense in terms of practical actions and the use of time in a chess game. This, anyway, was something to reflect on.

Although the tournament ended without a norm for Ray, there was a bright spot. During my performance review for work, my boss gave such a positive report that I felt that I could finally bring Ray's chess into the picture, and we discussed ways that I could accompany Ray to more events while still meeting work expectations.

The downside to such a positive evaluation was that the boss now wanted me to play an even greater role outside of the classroom – to take on a leadership role both at meetings and in projects. As a consequence, I now had to work on developing online versions of the courses I was teaching, and I was asked to take the lead in the program we were designing for a nearby county. I have never had an interest in leadership or administrative roles in any job that I have had. I have always preferred to focus on the one thing that I liked to do best: teaching. But I could hardly pass up additional tasks and responsibilities when chess trips with Ray were the reward. So I ended up working much harder while also accompanying Ray to more events.

It wasn't long, however, before I felt that we were doing something wrong. We would soon be going to Turkey for another World Youth event, and our lives were so busy and complicated that neither Yee-chen nor I could squeeze out even one extra day to explore the country. Each of us had to "find" a week and take shifts to be with Ray on the trip. In a saner version of the trip, we would all travel together and then spend an extra two or three weeks afterwards exploring Turkey. I felt that I was deep in what the Buddhists call Samsara: an overly busy lifestyle with too great an emphasis on work and money and the other daily distractions that occupy most people in the world. I was missing out on a more beautiful and intelligent way to spend my time.

Earlier in the year, I had moved almost all of my books to my office, leaving at home only the books that I cared most about along with those books that I really wanted to read. However, I didn't read even one of them. They sat on the shelves collecting dust. I stole a few minutes each day to record some of my thoughts in a journal, but that was it in terms of self-reflection and "free" time. Months passed and the moments were lost. I still spent time with Ray, but it seemed far less than usual, and always surrounding our time were a host of other things that I had to get done. Yee-chen's life was her classes (both the ones she taught and the ones she took at the university). That was it.

I would not have allowed myself to live like this at another time. I approached this type of life – this Samsara – during my two years at the university job upon our return from Flagstaff, but I was never this busy, and, when I came home, I was home. There were no up-until-3:00 a.m. nights grading papers. I came home, and we went to a basketball court, or the beach, or we played chess. That was it. I watched cartoons on TV. I developed a friendship with a co-worker. There was time, even then, to live.

Soon I began to think that I should get out of my job at the end of the year. I could work as an adjunct and then devote my life to other pursuits. But would I still have the time I needed as an adjunct? I would still need to teach three or four classes each semester, and it was the teaching and the grading of papers that took up all of my time. Maybe I could squeeze out a few more hours from each day; however, I would be sacrificing so much income to do that. It seemed that if I had to give up my salary (a salary that I was certain I would never match), then I should do it for more than a few hours per day of extra time. But I didn't think I could arrange that. I might have to go back to the classroom. I thought that maybe I should do something that I had often thought about before: teach math in a public school. I would give up about half my salary, but I would have easier assignments to grade, I would be free in the afternoons, and I would have all summer off. Maybe that was the best thing to do. This was something that I really needed to consider. In the meantime, I had both my work duties and Ray's norm hunt to focus on.

* * *

Just before the World Youth event in Turkey, Ray was lucky enough to secure a spot in a private norm event in Chicago. The event was set up so that the requisite number of foreign and titled players would be available, which meant that anyone could earn a norm provided that he played well. This was exactly what we were looking for! I had no doubt that Ray could manage the performance side; it was meeting all of the logistical requirements for the norm that caused the biggest problems. With those gone, I knew that this was our chance.

After four rounds, Ray had 3 1/2 points and was on track for his first international master norm. In round five, however, he lost to FM Tsyganov. Afterwards, Tsyganov came up to me and simply said, "Sorry," figuring that he had just dashed Ray's norm chances. He sincerely meant what he said; it was not a sarcastic apology. He saw how well Ray was playing, and he just felt bad for him. At the same time, Tsyganov was working on his own IM norm, and I congratulated him on his win. After this last game, Ray would need three out of four wins to get the norm, and all I could say to Ray was that he could do it. He would have to do it one game at a time. He started with a win over the lone Canadian participant.

Ray played a solid game against the Canadian, and, when it was over, the 39-year-old was in tears. He knocked his King over (Ray saved it from hitting the floor) and then stared up at the ceiling blinking and muttering to himself while Ray set the board back up and prepared to leave. Even as we headed out the door some minutes later, his opponent was still in his chair in the same position. No handshake for Ray. No words to Ray or to anyone else.

Two out of three sounded a lot better than three out of four; however, Ray still had to face the two strongest players in the event – both international masters. Perhaps ninety minutes into the next round, the alarm on the cell phone of Ray's international master opponent went off and beeped for perhaps 15 or 20 seconds. The tournament director left the room immediately and about 30 minutes later – after having consulted with others to learn the FIDE rules – declared a win for Ray. This was *not* the way that Ray wanted to get the point, but he had no say. It was the rule. In fact, Ray never even made a claim after the alarm had gone off; instead, it was the director who made the call. As in tennis and other sports, I found that luck in chess often went to the best players.

Luck, in another form, helped Ray in the next round against his international master opponent. At our first norm event in Massachusetts earlier in the year, Ray learned about a chess site that contained lectures by various strong players. One of the players at the Massachusetts event gave Ray access to the site, and it was there, in preparation for his next round in Chicago, that he found a lecture by his upcoming opponent. Ray studied the lecture carefully and then used his computer to find improvements in the line that the lecturer was discussing. During the game the next day, his opponent, as Ray predicted, played into the line that he knew well enough to lecture about; however, he was unprepared for the improvements that Ray had found. With the help of his own preparation, Ray played a beautiful game and beat the international master, who played on until the very end, making sure Ray earned the win – and that, I thought, was just as it should be. With that win, Ray had secured his first IM norm with one round to spare! Afterwards, Tsyganov – the one player who had beaten Ray – approached me and shook my hand in congratulations. And later he would say, in reference to his win, "That's probably the last time I'll beat him."

A last round draw gave Ray clear first place in the tournament. This, of course, was simply gravy, for we had come for the norm alone. I figured, though, that if one played well enough to earn an international master norm, he probably would end up finishing near the top. All in all, the Chicago norm tournament was a tremendous success for Ray, and I expected more good things to come.

* * *

Next up for us was the World Youth in Turkey. Between the Chicago event and our departure for Turkey, Ray was able to raise some money on his own for the expensive trip. Some kind folks at the Clermont Chess Club, one of our weekend destinations when Ray was still working his way up in the chess world, contacted us and asked if Ray would be interested in doing a simul (simultaneous exhibition). Such an exhibition involves one player playing several people at the same time. In Clermont, Ray played over a dozen opponents from the chess club, moving in a circle from one board to the next, making move after move, and keeping track of each game as he went along. He played a variety of openings, won every game, and enjoyed every second of it. I had the distinction of being the last opponent to fall; it was the first time in quite a while that Ray and I had played a game of chess together. All of the money that was collected from the participants went directly to Ray for his trip to Turkey. During that same period, Ray conducted a few more simuls, one at the Orlando Chess and Games Center and another at the St. Petersburg Chess Club; the latter club was where Ray had played his first tournament games, losing two out of two and earning his first rating at the very bottom of the chart.

I felt good about the outpouring of support from the folks at the local chess clubs in our home state. I once thought that early support for Ray had been displaced by disgruntled chess players who were tired of seeing Ray win all of the time, but this was ultimately overshadowed by an overwhelmingly supportive community. The people we met at these simuls were all very proud of Ray and were happy to be able to contribute in some way to his progress. I have never been much of a community person (just ask any of my neighbors who secretly thank their gods every time I bring out the lawnmower or – miracle of miracles! – the edger for the lawn). The support I saw for Ray, however, made me want to open the door to our very private world and let some of these kind people in.

* * *

The World Youth in Turkey was another success for Ray. Although the elusive first-place gold medal still escaped him, he did, for a fourth consecutive year, finish in the Top 10 in the world. A bonus from this event – something that took us completely by surprise – was a second IM norm. The norm certificate came in the mail some weeks after we arrived home. Neither Ray nor I could believe that he had earned a norm, considering that there were so few titled players out of the 150 who were in Ray's section. However, the Turkish Chess Federation, in answer to my message, assured us that Ray had in fact earned a norm. This meant that there was just one to go!

* * *

Ray's shot at a third, and final, norm was waiting for us back home in the United States. The University of Texas, the school that offered Ray a full scholarship after he had won his section of Supernationals back in fourth grade, was the location of a December norm event, and Ray was one of 12 invitees. With a strong performance at this event, Ray could wrap up the international master title, having earned a norm in three consecutive tournaments in just three months: October, November, and December.

As with Turkey, Yee-chen and I covered the Texas event in shifts (for both events, she stayed for the first half, we were all together for a day, and then I stayed for the second half). On Saturday, December 8, I put everything in order at home, watered the vegetable garden (which by that time consisted mainly of tomatoes, the very same tomatoes that were somehow invisible to Ray), started up the car, and then drove to the airport to catch my morning plane. I chose as reading material for the flight the philosopher Bertrand Russell's *Why I Am Not A Christian*, and I ended up in a seat next to a young man who had as his reader the *Holy Bible*.

The University of Texas event, held at the Dallas campus, was an 11-round tournament. By the end of the fifth round, Ray had defeated two international masters and two grandmasters. For his round six game against a young grandmaster from Costa Rica, all that Ray needed was a draw, and that's just what he got. With five rounds to spare, my 13-year-old son had become an international master at chess!

I used to tell Ray that he would be a master (said with the utmost certainty), but I never knew about "beyond that." After he became a master, I was certain that he would become an international master, but, once again, I never knew about "beyond that," especially after I learned how many talented players became international masters but never made it to grandmaster. At the moment that Ray earned his third norm, I was absolutely convinced that Ray would become a grandmaster; it was just a matter of when.

Bobby Fischer, the greatest modern chess talent to come out of the United States, became a master at the age of 12; Ray was 11. Similarly, Bobby became an international master at age 14, while Ray had just earned his title at age 13. Bobby earned his final title, grandmaster, at age fifteen-and-a-half. I was not one of those persons who cared about who did what first, but if I could gauge Ray's progress based on how he compared with Fischer, then I would predict that Ray would be a grandmaster no later than his 15th year. This seemed reasonable, and it was something to shoot for.

* * *

We ended 2007 with two items of note. First, Ray received an invitation to play in a strong event in Reykjavík, Iceland. This invitation was different from any other we had received, and it was a hint at what the future held for Ray if only he could continue to improve and become an even greater player. The invitation was a package deal: a flight for Ray and one accompanying person from the USA to Iceland; a double room at a hotel in downtown Reykjavík; breakfast at the hotel along with one additional meal for two persons each day; and a stipend for Ray.

This was too good to pass up. Even though I had asked for days off to accompany Ray to Chicago, Turkey, and Texas, I thought no more than a minute before requesting two weeks off to take Ray to Iceland. We would not leave until March, and I would put in all of the time necessary in order to fulfill my work responsibilities. In addition, I had helped myself out the previous semester by designing online versions of the courses that I taught. This trip, I thought, would be a good opportunity to test how well the courses would hold up in an online format.

The upcoming trip to Iceland gave me an idea. Bobby Fischer, who had been hunted down for playing chess in Yugoslavia against the wishes of the US Government, had forsaken his citizenship in order to become an Icelandic citizen. Iceland was where Fischer became World Champion in the 1970s, and he was revered by the chess playing population there. I had read that he was living somewhere in Reykjavík, and so we sent him a letter, asking if he would be willing to meet with Ray – if not for a few games of blitz, then perhaps for some Ping-Pong. We had read that he was ferociously competitive about all sports, and we figured we would probably have a better chance of meeting him over the Ping-Pong table than over the chessboard. It was a long shot, of course, but there was no harm in asking.

* * *

The second important event pertained to the house. By the end of the year, I had made our last mortgage payment. The house was ours! 6 1/2 years in one home was longer than I had lived in any home, including during my childhood years, and I wasn't sure which was the greater accomplishment: owning the house or managing to stay in it for as long as we had.

Yee-chen and Ray were now financially secure. If I should die, Yee-chen had a home that was paid off, and Ray had a four-year scholarship to the University of Texas. Yee-chen would soon have her master's degree, and she was already in the public school system with a secure job. I intended to be alive for as long as I should be, but it was nice to know that if I went at any time, they wouldn't be burdened with debt.

We got the home as quickly as we did in the same way that Ray earned everything he earned in chess: through focus on the goal, determination, and sacrifice. Regarding the latter, we took the cheapest flights available to our destinations, even though that often meant multiple stops with long layovers. We couch-surfed when we traveled, sleeping on friendly strangers' floors and walking or taking buses to get to chess events instead of sleeping in the hotels where the games were held. Our home in sunny Florida had been without a working A/C unit for the past two years, and we endured the summers with windows and doors open, fans running in each room, and shorts and T-shirts as our daily attire. Yee-chen's newer car had a working A/C; my 160,000-mile Toyota did not. I wore a crew cut most of the time and drove with the windows down. Nobody complained; everybody understood. The goal was to pay off the house first. Now that that was accomplished, we could focus on other goals, starting with the A/C for the home. 79° never felt better!

Owning the home meant even more in terms of Ray's chess. We could fly directly to our destination, making trips less exhausting. We could stay in hotels and sleep in beds. We could attend more expensive events and in more locations, including international sites. I had had a really bad year in terms of work – extra responsibilities and an overload of classes each semester – but it was the money from all of that work that made other parts of life easier. Still, I couldn't help but start the wheels turning, focusing on how much I would need to put away in the bank in order to give me what I valued more than anything: even more time with the family.

* * *

Ray's life paralleled mine in many ways, one of which was that we both spent much of our youth in front of a screen. When I was a kid, I built my day around the schedule in the TV guide, taking breaks only to go outside for sports and to do – very reluctantly – any schoolwork that I had. It was the same with Ray, except swap TV screen for laptop monitor. Another difference, of course, was what one got out of the time spent. I learned how to predict what would happen in most movies within five minutes of the beginning (not a particularly useful ability and more annoying than anything as far as Yee-chen was concerned). Ray was learning how to think deeply, research, study, prepare, see patterns, etc. One of us had gotten it right.

Ray used his time in front of the monitor to prepare for the event in Iceland. The event had become more important than we originally thought because, shortly before leaving for Reykjavik, we learned that the norm from Turkey was invalid. The Turkish Chess Federation had made a mistake after all, and Ray was still one norm short for the international master title. Ray was not upset. Instead, he and I both looked to Iceland as an opportunity to earn the title once and for all.

I loved Iceland. We arrived in the middle of a snowstorm and left on a snowy and windy day. In between we had days of snow, days of rain, and days of sunshine. The air was fantastic, and I breathed easily. Most days the temperature was around -2 degrees Celsius – quite a change for a couple of Floridians!

The Icelandic Chess Federation was a class act, fully devoted to making the participants feel that they were important and that chess itself was important. Reporters covered the event daily, there were grand opening and closing ceremonies, and several important people in the world of chess were there. Among the various VIPs, former world champion Boris Spassky stood out. Spassky was there to mark the passing of Bobby Fischer (who had died not long after our letter had been sent out), and the president of the Icelandic Chess Federation introduced us to Boris shortly after his arrival. Ray would have preferred to have met Mr. Spassky from the other side of a chessboard, but this was something too.

There was something about Iceland itself that made it a special place. I felt good – physically and mentally – every day that we were there. The Icelandic people were incredibly friendly, especially the chess folks like the organizer of the event, Bjorn Thorfinnson, and the president of the chess association, Lilja Gretarsdottir. Both of these people were excellent representatives of their country, and they made Ray and I feel as if we were at home.

Aside from the people, the location itself was fantastic: an ice mountain surrounded by ocean. We took long, very cold, walks every night from the chess hall back to our hotel, and there was something about walking in subfreezing temperatures that was invigorating. I know that we arrived at the hotel feeling more alive than when we left the warm playing hall.

Part of the general feel-good atmosphere of Iceland had to do with me watching Ray connect with other young superstars from around the world like GM Fabiano Caruana of Italy, IM Illya Nyzhnyk of Ukraine, IM Nils Grandelius of Sweden, and IM Sahaj Grover of India. Ray talked with, or played blitz with, these young prodigies during the event. These were the kinds of kids who Ray could learn from and have fun with, challenging one another in speed chess and knowing that they shared a similar path.

In this ultra-positive atmosphere, while crowds gathered around Ray's board each round to watch him play, I sat nearby taking in the experience, talking with kindred spirits from among the spectators, and finishing the one book that I had brought from home: *War and Peace*. I'd long since given up standing for the duration of Ray's games and had learned to enjoy the six-hour blocks of time by hiking, writing, reading, and meeting others who were drawn to the events. I spent plenty of my own time with the crowd around Ray's board, of course. We were there for the norm performance, and I was hoping to see it happen.

Part of the reason for the crowds around Ray's board had to do with his results. After the first eight rounds, Ray had three wins and four draws, each of the draws coming against grandmasters. With one round to spare, in what was a very strong tournament, Ray had earned his final IM norm (again!).

Part of our celebration included a two-hour "bath" in the Blue Lagoon – a gigantic heated pool the size of our neighborhood back home and surrounded by ice and snow and mountains. Fantastic!

More good news greeted us upon our return home. While we were gone, Ray had become the first top recipient of the Schein-Friedman Scholastic Recognition Project. In effect, he was awarded a $6000 scholarship to assist him with his chess. The cycle in life is usually good news followed by bad news followed by good news, etc., but I was willing to take an extra helping of good news if that was how things were meant to be.

* * *

Every step is followed by another. International master was always an intermediary goal. The larger goal – grandmaster – never lay hidden, but instead always stood out clearly somewhere off in the distance. It was a mountain to climb, and it was important to be rested and prepared before the attempt to reach the top was made. After returning from Iceland, we took it relatively easy. I caught up with my work at the college, while Ray caught up with his math homework. His online studies in math had been put on hold during our overseas adventure, and he needed to get back on track. It was the same with his reading, his Chinese, and the rest of his studies. And when spring rolled into summer, we continued to tend to other matters.

Instead of taking the path to a norm, Ray spent a month in China with his mom, with me joining them for the last few weeks of the trip. Aside from Yee-chen's mother, who had lived with us for a year in Flagstaff, no one in her family had seen Ray since he was 10 months old. Although Yee-chen had traveled back herself to visit the family, we were long overdue for a full family trip. We had the money, we had the time, and Yee-chen's family would finally all be in one place at the same time rather than scattered about in Thailand, Myanmar, and China. The time was right for the visit. Family always comes first; the grandmaster norms could wait.

PART VI

24

Ray started the fall of 2008 with an international rating in the high 2400s. Having worked the entire year on his own, he managed to increase his rating by 100 points and had become an international master. I could have let things stand as is, but I decided that Ray would benefit from the guidance of another during the next stage of his development. This was not a new thought, for Ray and I had talked off and on over the past year about who might be a good person to work with. An earlier response to this question yielded Garry Kasparov and Bobby Fischer as Ray's only choices. The latter was now no longer an option and probably would not have been a possibility in any event. Garry Kasparov, considered by many to be the greatest chess player of all time, was, on a small scale, already accessible to Ray.

We had first met Kasparov in the summer of 2005. Ray had been invited to join a few dozen top scholastic players for a two-day training session in New York City. Each participant was expected to present two or three of his games before Kasparov and the group. Kasparov would then critique the games, soliciting ideas from the participants. Ray presented first. He was nervous to the point of being terrified. He looked away from the master of grandmasters, staring instead at the overhead screen that displayed his game, and only turned to face him when Kasparov called him by name or asked an obviously direct question. Still, Ray couldn't even respond to some of the direct questions; he just silently kept himself turned away whenever he could.

Most of Ray's responses – when he did speak – were one-word utterances. Anyone watching would think that Ray was rude or dull; however, I knew that he was in an emotionally charged state. He was embarrassed and frightened, and after each critical remark (no matter how gently put), after each unanswered question, he became more ashamed of his games, of how poorly he had played, of how he had represented himself at the board. By the end he was close to tears and so flustered that he couldn't even answer such simple questions as "How long have you been playing?" "What section did you play in?"

At my request, Ray had seated himself beside Kasparov at the start of the training, so when Ray returned to his seat after presenting, he was still right beside the grandmaster whose presence had just about crushed him. Kasparov kindly put his left arm around Ray's shoulders and spoke some quiet, friendly words to him in a very gentle tone. He thought that Ray may have been upset by his comments about his having lost the last presented game (a game in which Ray walked around and wasted precious clock time), and so he told a story about how he had gotten into the same kind of trouble in the past. A few minutes later, Kasparov asked for the next game and quickly began his analysis, taking the focus off of Ray. He kept his arm around Ray's shoulder though.

The group broke for lunch around 1:00 p.m. Kasparov and I met one another in the hallway, and I introduced myself as the father of the little boy who was sitting on his left. As we walked down the hallway together, I explained about Ray's pre-seminar jitters and how he didn't feel worthy enough and how embarrassed he felt about presenting an error-laden game to the world's best player. I also let him know how grateful I was for his post-incident kindness. Kasparov said in his Obi-Wan Kenobi voice that his comments were intended to teach and that he wanted Ray to learn from the experience. I told him that I thought that Ray would never forget the kindness he showed him. Then I thanked him again, shook hands, and let him continue on his way to lunch.

One of my own long-standing fears was that I would do something to publicly embarrass myself – to draw attention to myself. I had this fear as a shy child, as a shy teen, as an introverted young adult, and, to some extent, I have the fear today. Ray had some of that in him too – that stage fright, that feeling of not wanting to do something "wrong." Who are the kids who can go into potentially embarrassing situations and just enjoy the experience – the kids who can just enjoy the excitement of being on stage in front of everyone? I wished that Ray had this courage; I wished that I had it for myself.

Other than the bonding that resulted from the incident with Kasparov, I did not think much of the training. There were too many players present who didn't follow the discussions, and several of the youngest kids goofed around and made noise instead of paying attention and contributing. The training itself was not the reason for our return later in the year. The main reason was so that I could give Ray another opportunity to make the same kind of presentation under the same circumstances. The easiest thing in the world would have been to never return. Ray had had an embarrassing shut-down in front of a room full of some of the top players in the country at the time – all of them Ray's peers. What could be more embarrassing? I knew, however, that the best thing for him to do would be to face this fear, this embarrassment, and to do well in the process.

The next session did indeed go much better – smoothly, in fact. With that accomplished, I thought that we had gotten all that we needed from the sessions; however, when they changed the format so that there would be a much smaller group, comprised of the most promising young people, I decided to send Ray back for additional trainings. By the fall of 2008, under these new conditions, Ray had attended a winter and a summer session with Kasparov for the past few years. Each year, Kasparov seemed to grow more interested in Ray and his progress, and he always included Ray's name in his answers to interviewers' questions about who the next great American chess players would be.

As far as being a trainer for Ray, although he would certainly be the best choice imaginable, I couldn't see how it would work beyond the two-day training sessions twice a year that we were already attending. Kasparov was probably the busiest ex-World Champion on the planet, and, in any event, we could never afford to pay him the kingly salary he would surely demand. It seemed ridiculous to even consider asking. We were lucky enough to have three or four days a year with him. If he was beyond consideration, then who was left?

Well before Ray and Yee-chen left for China – perhaps even as much as a year before that trip – I had taken a walk with Ray and, somewhere along the way, asked him again who he would like to work with, limiting his response to persons in this country and excluding Kasparov. Ray came up with three names, in this order: Gata Kamsky, Hikaru Nakamura, and Alexander Onischuk.

Kamsky, originally from Russia, was at that time the strongest player in the United States, someone who had come closer than anyone since Bobby Fischer to claiming a World Championship title for the US. Nakamura, originally from Japan, was often described in his youth as an *enfant terrible*; he was an emotional and aggressive young chess player who, early in his career, had been called the next Bobby Fischer. Onischuk, originally from Ukraine, was third in rating and was one of the top 100 grandmasters in the world. All three had strengths, and, of course, they would also have weaknesses.

While Ray was working alone during the 2007/2008 year, I was working on getting one of these three to train with Ray. Actually, it was Ray who contacted Kamsky directly through the Internet. Kamsky was interested, but he had months of preparation ahead of him for his next shot at a World Championship match and would not be free until after that time. A mutual acquaintance contacted Nakamura for us, but he reported back to me that Nakamura was not interested in teaching anyone at that time and that, besides, he thought that one of Ray's tutors had already "screwed up" his chess openings.

While we were working on the first two, I received more feedback on the third possibility, Alex Onischuk. Friends in the chess world were telling me that Alex was an emotionally stable man with a wife and a young son. I heard that he was kind and intelligent and a good role model. This sounded right to me. Consequently, I contacted Alex around the time of the China trip, and we were able to work out a plan for the fall of 2008.

Alex, who was a professional player and who didn't have students, agreed to work with Ray because, as he said, he knew that Ray had talent, and he thought that it would be interesting for them to work together. I thought that Ray would benefit from a mentor as he worked towards his next goal of becoming a grandmaster. I figured that if Ray continued to work hard on his own just as he always had, and if he had some extra support through Alex, then he would be able to earn his three grandmaster norms within the next two years.

When the first lessons began in the fall, I knew that we had made a good decision with Alex. He was very open with me in terms of telling me about his ideas for Ray, while also asking for my input. The plan that we came up with was for the two of them to work over the Internet whenever time permitted. Alex had a very demanding schedule, and Ray was leading almost the same lifestyle in terms of chess. It would be difficult for them to find much time to train together, but we decided to squeeze in sessions whenever we could. That was the best that we could do, and all parties, especially Ray, seemed happy with the plan.

25

The 2008/2009 school year was a busy one for Yee-chen. She was working full time at the middle school during the day, and she was a full-time graduate student at night. She had no time for anything chess related. My own work schedule was insane. The other professor in my area of expertise – ESOL (English for speakers of other languages) – took another position, leaving me with an overload of classes each semester and with a new position: ESOL Coordinator. While I was pleased to keep up my change-every-two-years plan, the new role gave me control over everything related to ESOL issues. As coordinator, I had already attended more meetings in the first 10 days of the semester than I had attended all of the previous summer.

Despite the overload and the additional responsibilities, I did not want to give up any of my chess time with Ray. I managed to be where I wanted to be by arranging a mostly online schedule. I just hoped that my boss would continue to support me in my requests for lengthy stretches off campus. I was beginning to do more and more of my job in the middle of the night in hotel bathrooms with the door tightly shut so as not to disturb my sleeping son who would be playing some grandmaster in the morning. The schedule was exhausting, but Ray's performance that fall made everything worthwhile.

Perhaps it was just my imagination, but Ray always seemed to do particularly well in the fall. I knew he had had good tournaments at every time of the year, but every fall, I always got the feeling that something big was going to happen. In September, Ray started the fall season by tying for first place in the Florida State Championship. This was a good event for Ray. He drew his co-champion, Grandmaster Julio Becerra, and overall played some good games. Because the Miami Open – a much bigger and more important event – was just a short time later, we considered skipping the State Championship. The only reason why we played was because it was literally in our backyard – a 10-minute drive from our home. Sometimes things just seem to work out.

The state event was a reminder of the crazies that I occasionally had to watch out for on Ray's behalf. A few years back, I made the mistake of sharing our e-mail address with an adult who had lost a game to Ray but who seemed normal enough. He later sent e-mail after e-mail and grew angry when I did not acknowledge his messages within a few minutes' time. Since then, I have kept an eye out for the crazies who grew too interested in Ray. One such person hovered around Ray at the state event, eating up his time and later criticizing me for taking my son away from him in order to ensure that Ray got regular meals and sleep during the event. I later learned that this middle-aged man used a picture of Ray as a screen saver on his computer. I hated to hear of such creepy things; they made me wonder if I had to add a stalker discussion to the list of things I needed to talk to Ray about as he grew older.

* * *

As nice as the first place finish was, the state event paled in comparison to the Miami Open, which was held later that month. This was the same tournament that we went to the year before, where I left Ray with a young international master after Ray vomited in a taxi. This was the event where Ray did so poorly that I had to go back to 2002 to find another event where he'd lost so many rating points. We were going back this year because there was the possibility of a grandmaster norm.

We started each day with a "flying squirrel" game which I devised as a means to help wake Ray up in a happy mood. I would run from across the large room and dive onto his bed while he tried to pelt me with pillows in defense. We had the room due to Ray's own efforts. A short time before, he had won an online speed chess event; the prize was a hotel room for three nights for the Miami Open. The room was fine, but the elevators were not secure (one ended up not working at all – almost broke down while we were in it – and the other one's door closed so slowly that I could step in and out five times before the door would finally close). It was sort of the nicest rundown hotel we'd ever stayed in – huge rooms with lots of potential but in a building that seemed to be falling apart. For this trip, we even ate breakfast in the hotel downstairs; I could finally afford to pay for hotel breakfasts!

Ray ended up winning everything but the norm. He started off with 5 straight wins (including wins over Grandmaster Friedel and some international masters). Later, he also beat Grandmaster Gonzalez, drew an Israeli grandmaster that we had met and walked with in Iceland in March, and ended up in a two-way tie with a grandmaster from Kazakhstan, the only player to have handed Ray a loss. Consequently, Ray and Grandmaster Sadvakasov had an Armageddon playoff to determine who would get the title.

An Armageddon in chess is a blitz game, where White has more time than Black and where Black has draw odds. That means that if the two players draw, then Black wins the game. In the game, Ray had the White pieces and so needed the win. Although it wasn't the prettiest of games, Ray prevailed, and, in doing so, had won his first major event (an event is considered major if it consists of a strong playing field and a large prize fund). It was important psychologically to have one's first major out of the way. This was akin to a tennis player winning his first big event or a basketball team winning its first playoff game.

This was the same event that dropped Ray's rating a year ago by some 25 points. This time, he earned 55 points, moving his rating solidly into the 2500s and putting thirteen-year-old Ray third on the list of the highest rated players in the country under the age of 21. Ray became a master (2200) after his 105th regular chess event. Seventeen events later, he reached 2300; twelve events later, he reached 2400; and nine events after that (his 143rd event), he broke 2500.

The only downside to the experience was that Ray did not earn a grandmaster norm. He had the required performance, but since two of his opponents were grandmaster-elects – that is, they had earned the grandmaster title, but it had not yet been officially bestowed on them – he didn't meet the norm requirements. For our part, although we of course wanted the norm, we still viewed the event as a success. I told Ray that this was more proof that he was playing at a grandmaster level already. The norms would come; he just needed to keep studying hard and improving.

26

The next big event for Ray was Essent in the Netherlands. Aviv Friedman, one of the regular coaches for the World Youth teams and a great supporter of Ray, put me in contact with the organizer. In this way, we were able to get an invitation, and so we spent Ray's 14th birthday in Holland. The highlights were Ray's wins over Grandmaster Romanishin of Ukraine and Grandmaster Ulibin of Russia.

Going into the last round, Ray had a chance to earn his first grandmaster norm. He was paired with Grandmaster Gupta of India. Ray played an aggressive game – playing all out for the win – but Gupta was able to find flaws in Ray's plan and so played the winning moves. Once again, Ray was so close to earning the norm – just one little game away. The problem was that the one little game was against a strong grandmaster. Ray would have to continue to work hard in order to make up the smallest of differences between himself and the grandmasters. The norms were within his reach; everything just had to fall into place for him to get them.

* * *

In December, Ray was once again invited to work with a small group of students under the tutelage of Garry Kasparov. Since that training coincided with our Christmas break, we decided to drive from the training in New York to a state park in Pennsylvania where we could have a week in a cabin in the woods surrounded by snow and a lot of small creatures – mostly outside, but some inside the cabin. On our way home from the park, we stopped off in Washington, DC. While Ray played in a local event, I arranged to talk in person for the first time with Alex Onischuk, Ray's new tutor.

Alex and Philip, his little boy, drove over from their home outside of DC. Alex peeked in to watch Ray's game against one of his grandmaster opponents, and then the two of us, with his son in tow, went to a nearby coffee shop to get to know one another and to talk about the future. While Philip concentrated on his cookie, I talked with Alex about how difficult it was to find strong norm events for Ray. It wasn't just the norms that we wanted. What we really wanted was for Ray to gain access to the strongest events possible, where norm chances would exist but also where he would simply get to play some of the best players in the world. The stronger his competition, the more he would learn. In the past, Ray always learned the most from his losses. Now, however, he needed to find stronger events and stronger competition so that he could continue to learn.

Over the next couple of weeks, Alex thought about what we had talked about and later contacted me with an idea. He asked me to let Ray travel with him to Russia for a month. They would spend two weeks in Moscow for the Moscow Open, take a break for one week in Ukraine at the home of Alex's parents, and then return to Moscow for two more weeks for the Aeroflot Open. In both events, Ray would be able to face strong masters and grandmasters in each round. Alex would arrange for the invitations to the events; I just needed to pay for the airfare and hotel/meal expenses for Ray. There were no tutoring expenses; Alex generously said that they would both be assisting one another.

How do you thank someone for such kindness? What do you say to someone who provides your child with exactly what he needs in order to move to the next stage of development in something he cares most about? I saw this arrangement as the next step in the Vygotskian program that I had developed for Ray.

Lev Vygotsky was a 20th-century Russian thinker who taught that the best way to approach learning is to find the student's zone of proximal development (essentially, where a learner is in terms of understanding a concept in relation to where he can reach with the guidance of another). This is what I had consciously done with Ray from the time that he was three until the time that he was beating me at chess. When he was beating me, I put him in the hands of an expert (someone above his own level who could help to move Ray up to the next level). From there, we moved to master, to instructional software, to grandmaster, to independent study (but with resources such as software programs, textbooks, and chess friends for support), and finally once more back to grandmaster – but to one who was performing at the highest level.

The plan that Alex came up with helped move Ray to the next level. He would get to live with, eat with, and discuss with someone who was a leader in the field. This was Ray's window into the life that he would soon be leading as an adult chess professional. This was the mentor/mentee relationship that I had always hoped for. I decided that the best way to thank Alex for such generosity was to say yes and to entrust him with the education and well-being of my son from January to February of 2009.

Although Ray's chess performance at the Moscow Open was nothing special, he was able to play against some strong players, and there were lessons to be learned. One interesting lesson was that a 2300-level player in Russia might be quite stronger than what one would expect elsewhere. I think the reason for this is that only the very best players received the kind of financial support that allowed them to play in international events, and some other players simply didn't get to play in the very strong events that could result in major rating changes. It was a mistake to assume that these players – with lower ratings, few FIDE events under their belts, and no games to look up – had little experience and were weaker players. Nothing was further from the truth. Ray played a number of strong players rated around 2200 and 2300, and he left with respect for the quality of play of the local masters.

With Ray in Russia for such a long trip, something happened to me that I hadn't experienced since childhood: time stopped. For the past few decades, when I thought of time, Bukowski's line always came to mind, "The days run away like wild horses." When Ray was in Russia, the days crept along like weighted-down turtles. We talked for 15 or 20 minutes each day, but I thought often about how I wasn't doing my job as emotional manager, health expert, and sleep monitor.

At the Aeroflot Open, Ray had a slow start and then had a great run in the middle, where he beat Grandmaster Van Wely of the Netherlands, Grandmaster Bocharov of Russia, and Grandmaster Akobian of the United States all in a row. As often happened, though, the amount of mental, physical, and emotional energy that Ray put out in such games resulted in a weaker performance for subsequent rounds, and Ray was not able to keep the streak going. Still, he was able to compete against some very strong players and learn just by being with them, eating with them, and talking with them.

I had asked Ray to keep a journal of his experience, but he was too much in the moment to do so. When he was home, I asked him to do the same – to write about all of the famous players he had interacted with and to note some of the things he had learned from them – but he was more interested in analyzing the games he had played than he was in recording conversations. He said that he remembered everything anyway and didn't see the point in recording the experience. I still felt like we had lost something by not having a journal.

Regarding the emotional part of a long trip shared together, though neither Ray nor Alex offered details, it was obvious from talking with both of them that there were some rough times between them during the trip. I could only guess what they were. Alex was used to experiencing these events without having to worry about a young companion who was away from home for the first time and who was quite green when it came to anything related to Russia. Also, Ray could be extremely challenging, drifting into the role of devil's advocate at just the wrong time and having little-to-no common sense about matters which Alex would have found simple. For Ray, he was probably expecting more attention, and he probably felt that he had to scramble for himself more than at any time in his life. For my part, I was grateful to Alex for giving Ray this opportunity. This was the first major trip for Ray with another companion, and I knew that he would never forget the experience.

* * *

After his return from Moscow in February, Ray spent the next several weeks catching up on his math and his Chinese. He managed to complete his work and still have time to prepare for a grandmaster norm event at Texas Tech University in March. The invitation had come from Susan Polgar herself while Ray was in Russia. Susan is one of the three famous Hungarian sisters who had become the superstars of women's chess in the 1980s and 1990s. She had been following Ray's progress and thought that he deserved a chance to earn a norm. Consequently, he received one of only three invitational spots that were given to international masters; the other three participants were all grandmasters. This was an excellent chance for Ray to earn his first norm.

Upon our arrival, Susan, who had picked us up herself, told me that she thought of Ray as the next Bobby Fischer, but without the bad parts (Fischer was a recluse who suffered from psychological disorders). She said the same thing to the group of spectators and reporters who had assembled to observe the start of the chess tournament. It was a generous statement made by one of the best known grandmasters in the country.

Ray’s time trouble appeared throughout the event, and I talked with Susan about this problem. She said pretty much what I had said to Ray and what Alex had said and what others had said: namely, that Ray needed to study more so that he was more familiar with different openings. In other words, he would not be surprised as he so often was by opponents' moves. Susan also said that his problem was a psychological one as well as one of confidence – something, of course, that I had already talked with Ray about. She said that by learning more opening theory, he would gain more confidence and that might help with this time trouble. She suggested that he set a certain amount of time per move and then simply follow that. That, of course, had been suggested many times before by others; however, Ray simply did not follow anyone’s advice in this instance. Instead, he just did what he always did: he went back to the familiar pattern of getting into time trouble and losing or drawing games in which he could have done better.

Novel situations also stopped Ray. I had known all along that Ray’s weakness pertained to surprises in the form of unusual situations or moves that he was not familiar with, along with complicated closed positions that required a lot of thought. In such circumstances, he just sat and spun his mental wheels, all the while eating up minute after minute on his clock.

I thought that Ray had to follow his instincts. After his opponent made his move, all Ray had to do was to think about initially what he would like to play in response. Then he could give himself five or ten minutes to think about a plan, and if he couldn't come up with anything better, just move based on his original instincts. That was it. Ray had enough chess knowledge now not to make a huge blunder; his instincts were developed enough for him to see decent moves upon his first glance at the position.

Ray's problem was that he doubted whether it was the best move or not. He was absolutely right. The first instinct may indeed not have been the best move; however, if he were down to a few minutes and had to move, then he really had no choice. He had to trust his instincts. If he had just done that, I was sure that he would've at the very least drawn most of the games that he lost in the event. Instead, because Ray didn't want to make a mistake, he over thought everything and doubted his instincts, questioned himself, ate up all of his clock, and ended up losing just enough points to miss the norm.

One thing that I decided at the Texas Tech event was that it was up to me to solve this problem of time. I had had many experiences where others could not provide me with what I needed. I'd had poor mechanics work on the car, and they'd returned it in such a state that I was forced to do the work myself anyway. I'd had the same types of experiences with repairs of other sorts too. For Ray's time problem, I'd asked for his old tutor's advice, for Alex's advice, and, most recently, for Susan's advice. I believed that now it was up to me. I decided to think out a plan for Ray, and we were going to follow it. He would simply have no other choice. Once he turned 18, or once he became a grandmaster, then he could choose another coach. Until then, however, I was in charge. Alex had become Ray's mentor and occasional training partner; I was his coach.

I decided to go still further with my plans for Ray and to talk to my boss about arrangements for the next academic year so that I could be free to travel with Ray and take him to all of the important events. I thought that if I did this, and if I came up with a plan, and if Ray followed the plan, then he would be a grandmaster before the age of sixteen. Of this I was certain.

So in thinking about the events of the Texas tournament, I realized that it had been a very good trip in spite of the missed norm. Even though I'd long known about Ray's weaknesses, I'd never felt so compelled to take a leading role in helping him to solve those problems and to become a grandmaster. I thought that we could do it. I had a history of solving problems on my own. Of course, in this instance I had to do this with Ray; he would have to work with me in order to achieve success. I started working out a plan before the Texas event was over, taking into account everything I knew about Ray, his strengths, and his weaknesses. This is what I came up with:

Coach Robson's notes for student Ray Robson:

– No preparation during tournaments; all work will be done prior to the tournament. Time before and after rounds will be spent relaxing and/or doing recreational activities.

– Preparation for events will include physical exercise on a regular basis to generally build Ray's stamina.

– We're going back to the basics: this means that Ray will identify immediately his first move based on his instincts. After this, he will have a limited amount of time to find another move or to confirm his move. Regardless of what he sees, he must then make a move. Exceptions will only be made in extraordinarily complicated or critical positions, and he will only be allowed two of these per game.

– Henceforth, part of Ray's training will include setting up chess positions on a daily basis and giving himself so many minutes to solve the problems. This is something that Ray did before with an earlier tutor, and it is something that he needs to do now.

– Ray must continue to study opening theory. For every tournament, I want him to play something new – either for White or for Black. Even though he will play something new, all the rules about time management listed above still apply.

On the flight home, with Ray crashed out in the seat next to me, I thought about everything that we had received from the event. Once again, we were short one grandmaster norm, but the trip was still a success. We had more positive publicity for Ray, including Susan's statement that Ray was the next Bobby Fischer. We had the possibility of another scholarship to college. We had another person who was willing to help Ray both with his preparation and with possible tournament invitations. Through Susan, we had an invitation to another Texas Tech event in September as well as an invitation to an event in Norway in August. We had the new plan that I had outlined for Ray, and, of course, we had more lessons to learn from the chess games themselves. Yes, this had been a successful trip.

Perhaps the most interesting part of the experience came when Susan had commented to me on how much Ray reminded her of her younger sister, Judit Polgar. In terms of chess, Judit was the most famous of the three sisters and was once, in fact, a Top 10 player in the world. Susan told me that Ray's g4 move in one of his games reminded her that Judit, at one time, loved to play g4 and thought that whenever she did, it would lead to a win. This was the exact same superstition that Ray had! On many occasions, he had told me that it was g4 that was the magical move that had helped him to win the game.

* * *

We were greeted with good news shortly after arriving home from Texas. Allen Kaufman, of the Samford Fellowship Committee, called to tell me that Ray was one of the finalists for the two-year ($36,000 per year) fellowship for chess. Allen said that there were four or five who were really close and that he needed more information. He asked me about my job and Yee-chen's job. He asked if Ray was still homeschooled, and he asked how we proved that he was homeschooled – whether or not he had to take an annual assessment. I told him about the FCAT (Florida Comprehensive Assessment Test) that Ray took each year to prove to the county school system that he was progressing academically.

He asked if we were receiving any money right now as financial support for Ray's chess. *No to that one.* He asked how many hours a day Ray spent studying chess. *Four to seven hours, depending on the day.* He asked how many hours he spent studying for school. *Three to four – and the school schedule was built around his chess schedule.* He asked me who was in charge of his homeschooling. *I was. Ray was taking online math classes. He was also studying Chinese with his mother and had recently taken Russian lessons with me. In addition, Ray read at a college level and so took books from my shelf which we discussed together. He always scored at the top of the percentage charts in terms of reading and math when he took the state's annual examination.*

Allen asked about our financial situation. *Although we could have fallen under the category of "financial needy" back when I was the sole breadwinner as a public school teacher, it was no longer the case since I now work as a professor, and my wife is now a full-time middle school teacher.*

Allen said that Ray had been described as quiet and shy and asked if that was an accurate description. *Ray is initially shy when he meets people, but he is more open once he gets to know someone. And if the talk is about chess, then often it's difficult to get Ray to stop talking. He's given public simuls and discussions that found their way onto YouTube and Google videos; you can learn from them how Ray conducts himself in public.*

Just as Allen was ready to end the conversation, I suggested that he say hello to Ray. I did this knowing that Ray was never the best person to talk to on the phone. All I heard from Ray was *Yes*, *Okay*, *Uh-huh*, *Oh*, etc. I wondered if I had made a mistake after all. The good news was that Allen told Ray that if he didn't get the fellowship this time, then he would probably get it next time.

I always figured that if the committee was very sensitive about age (in the past, they had given the award to older applicants who would soon be ineligible due to their age), then

Ray was at the bottom of their main list only because they knew that he could get the award at any time over the next six years. If Ray did not get the money this year, then it was reassuring to know that he had a very good shot at getting it the next year or, if that failed, one of the following years.

Later that same day, I spent a lot of time on a hiking trail thinking about who the other people were. I could think of two or three viable candidates. These others were strong players, but I thought Ray deserved the award more than they did. Ray put everything into chess, and he was someone who would probably continue on as a professional, whereas the others most likely would not be playing at Ray's level of chess just a few years down the road. Also, of course, Ray was 14, so he was much stronger than the others who were all around the same rating but who were three or four years older than Ray. It was important, I thought, to give the support to the youngest players at the time that they most needed it. Ray was on the verge of becoming a grandmaster; this was when he needed something "extra" to help him reach his goal.

After the call from Allen, I thought of a few more things to add, so I sent him a follow-up e-mail. I just wanted to make sure that he knew that my job would not interfere with Ray's training – that I could complete my work online in many cases. I also wanted to emphasize that the money for Ray would be for Ray: that I could financially support a chaperone, if one was even needed. After Allen's comment to Ray, I felt that someone else would get the award this year. However, this was all still very good news for us – if only for next year.

* * *

In April, after yet another unsuccessful try for a norm in Connecticut, we returned home to find good news waiting for us; Ray would be the 2009 recipient of the Samford Chess Fellowship. I wondered if this meant that the committee saw Ray as the future of American chess: the next young professional to follow in Fischer's footsteps. Ray wouldn't begin until July as the official Fellow; in the meantime, I needed to connect with the committee to work out all the details. My job would be to help decide how we should spend the money in order to support Ray in his chess development. Chess was on my brain, and I found myself wishing that I could be Ray's manager full-time. I also found myself wishing for more time to finally finish the chess book that I had been working on since before Ray won his first national event over five years earlier. I needed to find my own right moves.

My first act was to explain the fellowship situation to my boss and ask for more time to do my work off-site. If that wasn't acceptable, I offered to give up the professorship to become an adjunct. I was risking my high-salaried full-time job, but circumstances had developed over the past five years that put me in a position where I could teach part-time, if necessary, and still provide for our needs for two years. Yes, I would eat up every last penny of my savings, but I was more familiar with a zero bank balance than I was with an overflow of cash. We could get our health insurance through Yee-chen's employer, and I would take care of everything else, just as I had always done. As it turned out, this wasn't necessary – at least not for the moment.

The boss, who had been very understanding of my responsibility to Ray and his gift for the past three years, agreed to my plan. For me, this would mean even more hours spent grading papers and answering students' e-mails in hotel bathrooms, but, more importantly, it would mean that I could be with Ray. The next year would offer him more opportunities to play abroad. He needed a steady father-manager-coach to be his companion along the way. That was my role.

* * *

Ray had one more opportunity to earn his first grandmaster norm before he assumed his role as Samford Fellow. The event was the 2009 United States Closed Championship in St. Louis, Missouri, and, as an up-and-coming player with an exciting style, Ray had been given one of the few wildcard spots for the tournament.

He had already played a number of the other participants, and I believed that with best play Ray could give anyone at this event a good game. This would be an interesting event for us because it was possible for Ray to play both his old tutor, the grandmaster, whom we had not seen or communicated with since the breakup two years before, and his new, albeit infrequent, tutor, Alex Onischuk. I was hoping for the best.

* * *

The championship event marked the first time that I secured a rental car. This was such a big event, and I finally had the money, so I thought we should have everything to make this experience as easy to manage as possible. I also brought from home the GPS device that I had purchased in December. With the extra directional help, I was able to navigate to our hotel. I picked one with a full kitchen and refrigerator. We had just enough time to pick up some groceries and settle in before we had to get dressed for the opening ceremony. I ironed Ray's brand new suit for him – the first suit that he had ever owned – and then we drove to the chess center in downtown St. Louis for the players' meeting.

In the back of my mind, for the past several weeks, I held some anxiety related to meeting his grandmaster tutor. It was just about two years ago that we had our rotten end, and I figured that he still had hard feelings. It certainly wouldn't serve him well to have our situation ever present during his games, and I knew with equal certainty that it wouldn't be good for Ray to feel uncomfortable with the grandmaster in the room. Perhaps the grandmaster thought about this too, for when we saw him during the meeting, he came over and shook my hand and he later did the same with Ray. That was the best that we could expect, and I felt better from the beginning. I'm sure the grandmaster did too. Really, what other course was there to take?

After the meeting with the players, there was a photo shoot. They took some group photos and also some individual portraits of each player. The next day all of the pictures were in nice frames hung on the wall of the playing area, Ray looking very handsome and mature in his suit and tie.

From the photo session, we were driven to a university for the formal ceremony where the players were introduced, the colors were determined, and the refreshments were served to everyone present. It was a gathering with several interested onlookers and some special chess guests. I sat with one of them, Susan Polgar, during the opening ceremony at a table just to the side of where Ray and the others were seated.

There was a funny scene during the selection of colors. Each player, once his name was called, had to go up to a table and choose a cup of wine. It was all a formality after the first player chose, because his choice actually determined the colors for all of the rest of the players. However, they still wanted each player to come and grab a glass of wine as their name was called so that they could stand with the glass in front of the group and be recognized. When Ray was called, he hesitated at the wine table – afraid to grab a glass of alcohol – and ended up not taking a glass at all. The person who was sort of the emcee for the event made a comment about Ray being too young to drink wine, and the entire affair brought a laugh from the crowd.

From the first minute of the players' meeting, we realized that the tournament would be run in the way a National Championship should be run: there was a very elaborate opening ceremony; the chess center was beautiful, well kept, and well run; there was daily commentary covering all of the games in front of a live audience; and there was a tremendous amount of media covering this event. People knew about it, and the organizers had done an excellent job of taking care of everyone. The post-game talks were part of the whole package, and Ray actually had to sign a contract to the effect that he would participate in the sessions. After each game, he was also regularly interviewed by chess media or local media. The Sinquefield family – Rex and Jean – were the multimillionaires who had put up the money for this event. I'd talked with both of them briefly, and it appeared that they, along with the rest of the local crowd, were rooting for Ray.

Ray had some interesting pairings throughout the event. Out of 24 players in total, the only two from Florida – Ray and Grandmaster Julio Becerra –were paired together for the first round. For round two, Ray was White against Grandmaster Boris Gulko: the only person to have ever won both the Russian National Championship and the United States National Championship. Ray made the most of this pairing by playing solidly and winning convincingly. There was a lot of excitement by the media and the local chess commentators after Ray's win. Even before this time – but certainly after this win – Ray gained the support of the local crowd. I guess most people wanted to see the young person do well; at 14, Ray was certainly the youngest person in the room.

Later in the event, Ray took extra time to do some preparation at night for his next opponent: the grandmaster, his former tutor. Each one played solidly, and the game ended in a draw. What was interesting was that very early in the game, the grandmaster played into a repetition of moves, in essence playing into a draw. Ray, however, forced the grandmaster to play the game by refusing the repetition of moves. This was very important. It showed what the grandmaster thought about Ray and his abilities. More importantly, it said a lot about Ray Robson. I was pleased to see that my son was not afraid to play the grandmaster – that he was the one who wanted to try for the win even though he was the lower-rated player. Ray certainly learned a lot more playing the game as he did than if he had simply accepted the early draw.

At the end of five rounds, Ray had played five grandmasters. He had two wins, two losses, and one draw. It was interesting to note that, of the five players, not one of them was born in America: three were Russians, one was Cuban, and one was Armenian. Ray, in fact, was one of the few American-born players in the event.

Ray picked up two more points out of the next three rounds and found himself just one-half point short of a grandmaster norm with one round to go. If he could only draw his final-round opponent the next day, he would have it. His opponent for the ultimate round was Alex Onischuk.

It is every student's dream to face his tutor and win. I think that Ray wanted this game more than any other. This was his chance to show his tutor, who was one of the three strongest players in this country, that he could give him a good game. I knew of plenty of instances when prearranged draws would have decided such an encounter. That was not, however, the way that Ray wanted to earn a norm, and we were not expecting Alex to offer a draw. The best way for Ray to earn a draw would be through a hard-fought game over the board.

As it turned out, the draw was there, but Ray missed it. Instead of playing the move that would most likely have led to a draw, he chose another and, in a game that lasted six hours, the tutor ground down the student and won the game. Because he was so close to the draw, and because the loss came from Alex – the person he most wanted to impress and defeat – this game hurt. It would've been a nice way to get the first norm. Everything seemed to be pointing to it: the need for just a draw, the pairing with his own tutor . . . it looked to be a setup for a storybook ending. But the game ended as it should have ended.

After the game, I told Ray that this was just another lesson – another experience – to learn from and to grow from. It was important, I said, that Alex played the game to win and that that was how it should have been. The move which Ray missed was something else to learn from; however, I did not think that Ray would make that mistake again in a similar position in any future game. Ray could just as easily have had the draw and earned the norm, and that was another clear sign that he was playing like a grandmaster already – in this case, like one of the best grandmasters in the United States. He would put it all together in the future and get his norms.

On the flight home, I thought about how I liked seeing Ray in this new light as young adult – wearing nice pants, dress shoes, and a dress shirt each day. Although he was still as skinny as a stick, he looked much more mature in his dress clothes, and he comported himself well at the board. He'd done very well too with the media, answering questions intelligently and without much hesitation. I thought the entire experience had been a very positive one for Ray – just something else that he would grow from. This "chess thing" had more benefits than simply learning how to analyze positions.

PART VII

27

Ray was the 24th Samford Fellow, and, at age 14, he was the youngest recipient ever. Although two former Fellows – Gata Kamsky and Hikaru Nakamura – eventually became the top two players in the United States, some of the others never managed to go beyond international master or, if they did, had not become distinguished grandmasters. Ray's goal was to become the best. On a national level, he wanted to be up there with Kamsky and Nakamura – not just up there, but ahead of them. Before he could reach that goal, he needed to capture those elusive norms and become a grandmaster himself. Ray's first goal as Samford Fellow, then, was to earn the norms.

As early as June, the month before the official beginning of the fellowship, we dipped into the funds to spend a weekend at a seminar with Garry Kasparov in New York City. Ray was one of about a dozen promising young players who presented four games each. Kasparov started with the weaker players on the first day and ended with the strongest players on the second day. On both days, Kasparov seemed almost angry to have to go over what I suppose he considered poor quality games. He seemed short with some of the participants, making cutting comments such as, "Don't you have any games against good players?"

On day two, after coming back one full hour late from lunch – wasting valuable analysis time for the remaining three players, which included Ray – Kasparov continued his generally negative responses to the players' games. Ray was first up after the late return, and, in response to one of his losses, Kasparov said simply, "Terrible," with a note of finality in his voice and without any further discussion. He did throw Ray a bone with a "nice game" comment after Ray presented his final game – a recent win over GM Larry Christiansen.

At the end of the session, during the question-and-answer period, one of the participants asked a question about routine that led to a tangent on Kasparov's part. The tangent proved to be important in explaining Ray's former trouble with time. Kasparov said that people spend too much time on the computer using programs to analyze the positions. The problem, he said, is that computers calculate to find the best move for each position, and humans – who are not computers and who do not operate like computers – make the mistake during games of trying to find the best move for every move. The consequence is that they cannot find the best move, they doubt or constantly question their proposed moves, they get into time trouble, and they are under tremendous stress. Instead of trying to calculate like a computer, Kasparov said that players should look at positions over the board (a real board) and that they should strive to learn general chess principles. Knowledge of principles will serve one best. This tangent, which was no answer to the original question posed, was the most valuable part of the training.

Far more valuable than the Kasparov sessions was a Noam Chomsky lecture that Ray and I attended the night before the training began. The lecture, which took place at the historic Riverside Church in Harlem, covered myriad issues related to social justice and right actions on a global scale. These are the kinds of issues, I thought, that Ray needed to learn more about. Although I have focused mainly on chess in this book, I mention this lecture so that my readers know that there was more education going on than simply chess. My overall goal has always been to guide Ray towards becoming a good human being. Chomsky, his books, and his ideas – along with the ideas of Howard Zinn, Arundhati Roy, and other leading intellectuals – have for the past several years found their place in our discussions at home and during our chess trips together.

Actually, there is a link between Chomsky and chess. As the most accessible intellectual in the world, Chomsky accepts e-mails from anyone and responds to them himself. Thus, I have been able to correspond with him both on social issues and on linguistics for the past several years. On one occasion, I asked him about chess. Noam's response was most revealing:

Chess. Until age 16, I was obsessed. I remember clearly one day when I was thinking about the fact that I was actually spending time memorizing games of grandmasters, and asked myself why am I doing this when there are so many important things to do in the world. After that, never looked at a board, except to play with my grandchildren.

I think that there will come a day when I might need to discuss this message with Ray – maybe not for many years yet, but I think that there will come a time. Strange thoughts, perhaps, considering that my son had just received a $72,000 chess fellowship and was about to devote several months of his life to an accelerated training program and to an aggressive tournament schedule. But, as I have said, the goal is to be a good human being. Ten or twenty years from now, chess might be of peripheral significance to the larger life that Ray will be leading. If chess is still a central piece in his life, then I am sure that he will also have direct connections with matters of consequence and that he will not live in a bubble unaware of other human beings and world issues. It is part of my responsibility as a parent to see that this is so. As Thoreau said, “A man should not live without a purpose, and that purpose must surely be a grand one.” I am pretty sure that Henry did not have chess in mind when he wrote this sentence.

* * *

When July 1 rolled around – the official start of the fellowship – Ray was already playing in an event: the World Open in Philadelphia. Other than the Kasparov training, Ray had basically taken the month of June off. He spent time with his favorite people – the Kempers – and he played some tennis in a group camp at a nearby recreation center. He also watched a lot of tennis on TV, read some books for fun, and generally took it easy. Sometimes he would accompany me to a track at the local middle school. While I ran my laps, Ray shot baskets at the adjacent court. Of course, he still worked on his chess. I don't think that it would be possible for Ray not to study chess or follow chess tournaments on the Internet; that would be like a person not brushing his teeth in the morning before going into work: it probably wasn't going to happen. In general, though, I still considered this a month off, and I was expecting a well rested Ray to begin his first year as Samford Fellow with a strong showing.

If the World Open was any indication, then Ray was indeed off to a good start. On his very first day as the 2009 Samford Fellow, Ray defeated Grandmaster Bhat, the 2008 Fellow. On his second day, he defeated Grandmaster Friedel, the 2007 Fellow. And on day four, Ray drew Grandmaster Benjamin, the very first Samford Fellow (1987). Considering that there had only been 24 Fellows, including Ray, it seemed unlikely that three of his opponents out of nine would be former Fellows. Still more unlikely was the fact that his first two opponents on his first two days were the two previous Fellows. Overall, of the seven grandmasters that Ray faced at the World Open, he ended up with a 50% score: two wins, two losses, and three draws. Not a bad start for his fellowship.

We didn't return from Philadelphia alone. We brought Grandmaster Jaan Ehlvest of Estonia to our home so that he could work with Ray. Over the next four days, they worked together for about eight hours a day, taking late afternoon breaks to play tennis. Jaan had since changed his federation from Estonia to the United States, so he was considered one of America's 35 active grandmasters. It is interesting that, of a total population of approximately 300 million people, only a handful of them are grandmasters, and most of these players were born outside of the United States. There are some American grandmasters who feel threatened or "crowded" by the foreign players; however, I was grateful to have these professionals in this country, if only to improve the level of play in our own tournaments as well as to provide instructors such as Jaan for my son.

The arrangement with Jaan worked out beautifully. Ray thrives on engaging in challenging analytical discussions with capable partners, and Jaan kept Ray engaged for four days. The two looked at openings, discussed the middle game, talked about preparation, discussed the strengths and weaknesses of various players, and played a number of blitz games together. This was all part of a larger plan – developed with Alex's input and help – for the use of the Samford money. I decided that I would use most of the money at the beginning of the year for trainings such as this one, thinking that the extra assistance might make the difference in a norm for Ray.

Immediately after Ray's session with Jaan, he was scheduled to play in the Junior Invitational. Although he could not get a norm at this one, it was still an important event because the winner earned a seat at the next US Closed Championship. In addition, there would be some funding to participate in the World Junior event that we planned to attend in the fall. I had scheduled additional training sessions with other grandmasters interspersed with tournaments from July to October. I was hoping that this first session with Jaan would give me an indication of the kinds of results we could expect from the additional training. The Junior Invitational, then, would be the first test.

* * *

The Junior Invitational was held in the unlikely location of Milwaukee, Wisconsin. Important chess events in this country usually take place in cities like Chicago, Philadelphia, Las Vegas, etc. Milwaukee was the choice for the Invitational only because it was the hometown of the organizers of the event. I hadn't drunk an "Old Mill" (Old Milwaukee beer) since I was a poor college student, when we referred to it as "Old Swill" and drank it then only because it cost half as much as any other beer. But we were going to Milwaukee for the chess, not the beer, and I was looking forward to exploring the city and enjoying some good chess games by Ray.

There would be only seven rounds, and of the seven opponents, there were only a few that I felt were particularly dangerous. The highest rated participant, Alex Lenderman, had recently earned some grandmaster norms. Rated at 2650, he was a full 100 points ahead of the rest of the field. Ray had played him before and drawn him, so he certainly wasn't untouchable. I also thought that Ray had to be careful in his game with Sam Shankland, a young international master who had recently earned two grandmaster norms back to back and who had been tearing up the chess scene of late. Ray had played him before and beaten him; however, Sam had certainly improved a great deal since their last meeting. The third challenge, I thought, was the second youngest participant (only Ray was younger): Michael Lee of Washington. Michael had recently had a tremendous increase in rating by getting good results against strong players in his last five or six events.

The others, of course, were competent players; however, for various reasons, I didn't think they would be as dangerous. Sal Bercys, an international master, had beaten Ray before; however, he had been relatively inactive for the past six months. It is difficult to do well against someone like Ray if you are not working and playing regularly. Joel Banawa, formerly of the Philippines, was a solid player, but it was unlikely that he would take a game away from Ray. Elliott Liu, of California, liked to play very sharp, tactical, and aggressive lines, but one could pay dearly for playing like that. The only other player, Maxx Coleman, was rated well below everyone else. He was there because he had earned a qualifying spot by winning a much weaker event the year before. We didn't see him as a threat. Most folks in the chess community were probably viewing the favorites as Lenderman, Shankland, and Ray, possibly in that order. I figured that the same three would fill the top three spots; however, I reserved the number one spot for Ray Robson.

Other than the players, there were a few factors that I thought would work against Ray. The first was the two-game-a-day schedule – physically exhausting and a possible problem for Ray. We would have to keep an eye on his meals, sleep, and energy level in general. The other factor had to do with time. They would be using a relatively abbreviated – 90 minutes for each player – time control. Although Ray had been following my Texas directive and was pretty much out of time difficulties by this date, I still worried that the short time control would work against him. In addition to this, there were an odd number of rounds, and, as luck would have it, after they drew lots, Ray was given four blacks and only three whites: a disadvantage for sure. Also, the schedule was arranged so that Ray would play his three highest rated opponents one after another in the last three rounds of the tournament. This wasn't going to be an easy one to win! The only good news, I thought, was that Ray had white in his final round game. That might make a difference, for it's much harder to find wins with black when facing strong opponents.

In the first round, Ray was paired with Joel Banawa, the 19-year-old Filipino. Ray had the black pieces and could not find a way to proceed against the drawish line that Banawa played. Although this was one we were hoping would be a win, we had to settle for half a point and a less than promising start to the tournament. Ray was upset that he didn't start with a win, but there was really nothing he could do; sometimes draws are simply inevitable. Instead of looking backward, he needed to look ahead to the next round, and that is where I helped to focus his attention.

There was little that Ray could do to prepare for his game against 19-year-old Maxx Coleman, for Ray had few, or no, games in his database of strong players to refer to. He basically just went out and played his game. He had the white pieces, so I was confident that he would do well. Although the game looked even for a while, Ray made a nice sacrifice and opened the board up in his favor, which resulted in a victory. Since all of those who had scored one point in the first round drew in the second round, Ray found himself in a four-way tie at the end of the first day.

For the second day of the event, Ray had to play the black side for both of his games. His first game was against 15-year-old Michael Lee of Washington. While preparing for this game, Ray found that Lee only played one main opening with white; consequently, all of Ray's preparation was for that single opening. When the round started and it was Lee's turn to begin the game, he played a completely unexpected opening move. All of Ray's hours of preparation, all of his thought, were for naught. I was absolutely certain that Lee and his mentors thought to gain a psychological advantage against Ray by springing a surprise opening on him. Ray, however, after some thought at the board, came up with his own surprise: a response to Lee's opening that he had never before played in a game but which, unknown to the others, he had been working on by himself for the past few weeks. As the game played out, it was Lee who was most affected by Ray's surprise, and Ray ended up with the win.

For the second game with black on that same day, Ray played the sharp tactician, 19-year-old Elliott Liu of California. It was a long game, with both players getting low on time, and in the tension of the position, it was Elliott who made the mistake that turned the game from a probable draw into another win for Ray. After Ray's third-round win over Michael Lee, Ray was in a two-way tie with 17-year-old Sam Shankland. After his fourth-round win over Elliott, Ray was in sole first place with just three rounds to go. Of course, Ray still had the three highest rated opponents to play.

Sam had his destiny in his own hands for round five the next morning when he faced Ray with the black pieces. Although the game could have been a draw at one point, Ray capitalized on some poor decisions by his opponent and ended up winning a very nice game and, in the process, maintaining his full point lead with two rounds to go. Ray was in a good position, but the tournament was far from over.

For the second game of the day, Ray had the black pieces against the top seed and favorite of most spectators: 19-year-old Alex Lenderman. Lenderman had performed well at recent events, and he was ready to demonstrate his ability at this one. Although he had had a few unfortunate games, he would certainly have improved his position in this event if he could take a game away from Ray. As the game progressed, it looked like that was just what was going to happen. Lenderman seemed to have a clear advantage over the board in addition to a commanding time advantage. But it takes some luck for anyone to win a strong tournament such as this one, and luck was Ray's for that game. Alex made a few poor moves in a short period of time allowing Ray, with just a few minutes on his clock, to completely change the dynamics of the board in his favor. Despite the little time on Ray's clock, Alex had no better course of action than to resign.

So at the end of the third day, and going into the last round, Ray was still a full point ahead of the next closest contender. That person, of course, would be his opponent for the final round. The situation made it all the more exciting because if Ray's opponent, 19-year-old Sal Bercys of New York, could defeat Ray, then the two would be tied and would need to play a speed-chess playoff. And here is where having white in the last round became a factor. Sal was a very strong international master, but it would be very difficult for him to defeat Ray as long as Ray played solid moves. That was the only advice that I gave to Ray: play solid moves in good time, and everything will work out.

Although Ray did get behind on time at one point, his moves made up for the extra loss of minutes, and in a very short while he was able to secure a drawn position. With this last-round draw, Ray finished the tournament with six points out of seven (five wins and two draws), and this was enough for first place. The second place finisher, Bercys, ended up with five points, and Lenderman finished in third with four points.

What made the difference? Why did Ray win this event? The obvious response is that Ray is a capable player who was generally prepared for this event. Even though none of his preparation with Jaan ended up being a factor for this tournament (Ray was surprised nearly every round by his opponents, so his specific preparation before the tournament had no bearing on the results), I think that the training in general helped Ray. At the very least, he was thinking on a higher level when he arrived for this event, and I think that this showed in his play at the board for most of his games.

Another factor, which may have been more important than anything else, was the presence of his parents. All of the other players, with the exception of Michael Lee who came with his father, were on their own. The older kids generally hung out at a restaurant until late at night. They shared rooms together, probably stayed up later than they should have, and, for at least a few of them, missed meals. Ray, on the other hand, ate healthy meals prepared by his mom for lunch and for dinner and never missed breakfast.

For the two days when he needed extra sleep, we went down to the hotel's restaurant without him, letting him get the extra hour that he needed, and brought his breakfast up to him so that he had something hot to eat as soon as he woke up. We also made sure that he got to bed at a reasonable hour every night. On the morning when the power went out in the hotel and at least one of the players didn't wake up in time either to eat breakfast or to prepare (because his alarm clock did not go off), I made sure that Ray was up when he needed to be up. I was in the playing hall for support at the start of each game. Ray knew that he had two people there who were 100% behind him.

When the event was over and Ray had won the tournament, it was time to play. Within an hour of finishing the last-round game, Ray and two of the other players were on the tennis court. After that, Ray joined in a friendly poker game, played various blitz games, and just hung out with the other guys and had fun. Also on that last day, we made sure to join the group for a big meal at the local restaurant where the others had been hanging out each night. This was the time to socialize and to celebrate. As parents, we knew this, and I think this made a difference. In any event, Ray's victory meant good things to come. He would be the official representative of the United States for the World Junior tournament in Argentina in the fall, and he would not have to worry about whether or not he would get a wild-card spot at the 2010 US Closed Chess Championship, for he had now earned his spot well in advance of the event. As with the World Open, this, I thought, was the way to begin his fellowship.

We arrived home from Wisconsin Friday night, and by Sunday evening Ray was on a plane to Washington, DC, where he would work with Alex Onischuk for five days. This was a hectic schedule, what with the World Open followed immediately by the training with Jaan, which in turn was followed immediately by the US Junior Invitational, but I thought that the extra training would help Ray for his upcoming tournament in Norway. Added to this was the fact that Alex simply had very little time available to work with Ray. He had spent much of the summer working in chess camps, and he was not really interested in doing Internet lessons any longer. He only wanted to work with Ray in person, so we took the one week that we could squeeze into both of our schedules: the week right before we were to leave for Norway and the Arctic Chess Challenge.

Ray hadn't seen Alex since his loss to him in the last round of the US championship in May, and he was eager to work with him again. I was hoping that this training, like the training with

Jaan, would make a difference when Ray arrived in Norway for the next tournament. We would soon find out.

* * *

When Ray is gone, our yard begins to look once more like a normal yard. The grass gets cut, the weeds get pulled, the garden gets prepared for the planting season, the trees get trimmed, the birdbath gets filled with fresh water, and all of the mulch – which had long since turned back into soil – gets replenished. Twenty, thirty, and sometimes even forty garbage bags filled with weeds and leaves crowd our curb when Ray is gone. During these times, the neighbors must believe that we are getting the home ready for sale. Since we are undoubtedly considered the "bad" neighbors in terms of lawn maintenance, the thirty-bag days must excite our nameless neighbors to no end. How disappointed they must be when Ray returns and my devotion to our grounds disappears!

When Ray returned from his training with Alex, I was surprised at the negative report that he gave. The trainings were apparently filled with useful information; it was, instead, the criticism that bothered him. According to Ray, what he said was criticized, how he said what he said was criticized, and, when he didn't say anything, that too was criticized.

Whenever two people are involved in an incident, one person's report never tells a complete story – even when that person is someone you trust and love. Alex's response to my innocent "How did everything go?" e-mail added a little more to the story. From Alex's point of view, Ray wouldn't accept suggestions of any kind. He also got overly upset when he lost at something – whether it was a blitz game, a debate about the merits of a move, or even just a race in the park. In addition, Ray was uncommunicative and not so easy to get along with.

I think that Ray sees Alex as an older brother or a young uncle. And just like a younger brother hates to lose to an older brother, Ray hated more than anything else to get beat by, teased by, or criticized by Alex. Ray has this same kind of competitive relationship with the one other person whom he competes with on a regular basis: his dad. When Ray was really young and we still played chess together, he could lose gracefully to just about anyone but me. It was the same with our Ping-Pong battles and our basketball games. I eventually found a way to solve this problem by no longer keeping score in any sport we played. I think that over the past year, despite limited contact, Ray grew close enough with Alex to form this kind of competitive relationship. Added to this, Ray's knowledge of chess was good enough to legitimately challenge Alex, whether it was during a theoretical discussion or an actual blitz game.

I tried to explain to Alex some of my own understanding of the relationship. For Ray, I told him that if he didn't like hearing criticism from, or losing to, Alex, then he needed to study harder so that when he met him over the board, or on a tennis court, he would win. I really didn't want to do anything beyond this to alter the development of their relationship because I thought it was important for Ray, an only child, to have a few rivalry type relationships. And Alex was a genuinely nice guy who could handle the relationship and even feel flattered that Ray reacted strongly to him for the reasons that he did. We were lucky to have someone like Alex on our team.

28

Two days after Ray returned from his solo trip to DC to work with Alex, we were on a plane to Norway and the Arctic Chess Challenge. This would be the last trip that my wife would accompany us on because the school year would start soon after our return. We arrived five days early so that Ray could have some time to adjust to the six-hour time difference. We spent those five days vacationing in Bergen, where we hiked in the mountains above the town and enjoyed the beauty of the fjords. Aside from the rain, which appears to be present most days of the year, the only downside to the region was the exorbitant cost of everything. Eight dollars for a can of soda or a slice of pizza! Five dollars for a small bottle of water! I had to stop converting Norwegian currency into dollars or else we never would have eaten a meal. From Bergen, we flew to Tromsø in the Arctic Circle.

Jan S. Berglund, the tournament organizer, met us at the airport and drove us the one kilometer to the Scandic Hotel. The tournament wouldn't begin until the next day, so we had some time to take it easy and enjoy our new home in the north. After settling in, we walked to a market, bought groceries (and continued to marvel at the prohibitive prices!), and then ate a big dinner. Later in the day, we borrowed the bicycle that the hotel had for guests and, while Ray bicycled, Yee-chen and I walked around the area. Still later, at 11:00 p.m. when Yee-chen and Ray were asleep, I took a walk to a nearby nature preserve. The midnight sun allowed me to see everything as if it were 10 o'clock in the morning. All of the pictures that I took at that late hour did not require a flash. The sun, though low in the sky, just hung there. How strange to live in a place where for part of the year the sun never goes down and, for another part of the year, the sun never comes up.

I wondered how this bright light would affect our sleeping pattern. Although the room we slept in had two sets of curtains, we had to use some of Yee-chen's hairclips to seal the curtains as best we could in order to block out streams of light. Still, we couldn't cover everything, and the room always looked like it was about seven o'clock in the morning with the sun right outside of the curtains. Ray and Yee-chen did not seem to be affected by the light. As usual, it was only me who had trouble sleeping. At midnight, I toasted the end/start of the day with a liter of Arctic beer. There was no real change in the weather; it was still daylight.

After sleeping between 6:00 and 9:00, I got up, dressed, and then woke up Ray and Yee-chen so that they wouldn't miss our free hotel breakfast. After breakfast, Ray went right back to bed and slept for another two hours. Despite having arrived in Norway almost a week before, Ray was still adjusting to the new time zone. Of course, he was much worse earlier in the trip. When we were in Bergen, Yee-chen and I took several short walks to buy groceries, visit the fish market, and see some nearby sites while Ray remained asleep in the hotel. Even though it took some time for him to adjust, when he finally did, Ray was fully adjusted, whereas I never managed to sleep more than four or five hours at a time throughout the entire trip.

The tournament began on August 1, and Ray had the black pieces against a very cute 16 or 17-year-old Norwegian girl. I thought that this might be the most difficult pairing of all for Ray – so much for him to be distracted by! – but he played his usual solid game and so won his first round of the Arctic Chess Challenge.

For the next nine days, we fell into a pattern. I would wake Ray and Yee-chen up for breakfast. After breakfast, Ray would prepare for his next opponent until shortly before the round, when he would eat a small lunch. I would walk Ray to his 3:00 p.m. round, take two pictures, and watch the opening moves; then, while Ray played, Yee-chen and I would walk all around the island, exploring this most beautiful of places. I was glad that I had brought my recently resoled hiking boots because Tromsø was made for walking: snowcapped mountains in every direction. Between the mountains, the fresh air, the blue skies, the numerous flowers, and, of course, the Arctic Ocean, I decided that Tromsø was the most beautiful place in the world. Nothing during our trip made me alter that view. After Ray's games were over – usually around 8:00 p.m. – we would borrow the hotel bicycle for Ray, travel around the island, and then return for a late-night supper. Ray would be in bed by midnight, and the routine would begin again the following day.

For round two, Ray played his second Norwegian: a master in his 40s. That round took place on our 18th wedding anniversary, and while Ray was beating his second opponent in a row, I peddled Yee-chen on the bicycle to a pretty spot along the Arctic Ocean. The area there was particularly beautiful with clear views of several mountain peaks. It's hard to find the right words to describe just how beautiful the area was. The icy water was interspersed between landforms. In any direction I looked, I felt the urge to hike – to walk out into the wild. That feeling is what had me out under the midnight sun on the first day, walking a dirt path around a small lake, seeing the birds as clearly at 11:00 p.m. as I would in Florida at 11:00 a.m. This place made me want to walk again! By the second day, I had already taken a few long hard walks, and I didn't mind the hills one bit; in fact, I relished them and was reminded of how, as a young man, I would walk harder and faster when going uphill. This was a place for me! Yee-chen made her own connections, and at different times during the trip, each of us talked about finding a way to move to this region – if not for a lifetime, then at least for a few years.

For round three, we had a change in the schedule. While Ray prepared for his round, Yee-chen and I went on a guided walk of the town. We didn't get back until shortly before Ray's round and had, in fact, only 10 or 15 minutes with him before it was time for him to meet his Norwegian opponent. Perhaps because of the change in the routine, or perhaps for another reason, Ray didn't play very well and had to settle for his first draw. Yee-chen and I decided that for all future rounds, one of us would always be with Ray.

After round three, we all went with the group for a midnight fishing trip. Although few fish were caught, it was good for Ray to get outside and have fun with others in a casual atmosphere.

For most of our tournaments, we had missed out on local tourist events or attractions in order to focus solely on the chess. This time, however, there were just too many good opportunities to pass up. How many times in a person's life will he have the chance to go fishing at midnight with the sky as bright as it would be on any given morning?

Ray's fourth-round game was broadcast live on the Internet, so I was able to watch it and, simultaneously, use one of Ray's chess programs to analyze the positions. I watched in the comfort of our hotel room as the fairly even game turned into a win for Ray when his opponent made a blunder. Ray stayed a long time after the game had ended, analyzing various lines with his young Norwegian opponent. Later that night, after we had returned from our walk, we saw that Ray would finally be paired with a grandmaster and that his opponent was not from Norway. Grandmaster Malakhatko of Belgium would be Ray's first real test. The two had played in another cold place – Iceland – a year before, where Ray had played a solid game and drew the grandmaster.

Going into round four, only one player had 4/4 points, and Ray was among eight others who had 3.5/4. This day's game was an important one: a win was what Ray really needed. After Ray ate the lunch that I brought him, we walked down to the playing hall together. I lingered outside of the hall once the round began in order to talk with Susan Polgar who had recently arrived in Norway. I made sure to express our gratitude to Susan, for it was at her suggestion that the Tromsø organizers invited Ray to participate in the event. We were fortunate that Susan had taken a liking to Ray and appreciated his ability at the board. In addition to getting Ray an invitation to the Tromsø tournament, she had also regularly posted Ray's progress in events on her website – a popular site which helped to spread the word about Ray to a broad audience.

For better or for worse, it was one of Susan's comments that also brought a lot of extra attention to my son: namely, her comment that Ray was the next Bobby Fischer. This reference appeared in dozens upon dozens of blogs and articles that I viewed over the months after Susan had first made her statement. It appeared nearly daily in the official updates from the Tromsø event. Personally, I did not care for the comparison. One reason was that Fischer was a schizophrenic misanthrope who hated a great number of people; Ray, on the other hand, was a kind and gentle boy. Another reason was that Fischer was one of the greatest chess players of all time, and Ray was still working on his first grandmaster norm. He didn't need the distraction caused by this comparison to add more pressure to an already emotionally charged situation. Also, the more that people tried to view Ray as Fischer, the more they would miss the real Ray Robson. I didn't want Ray to be another Fischer. Ray was Ray; I wanted him to be the best Ray Robson that he could be. Of course, if the comparison was responsible for bringing us to Norway, and would be responsible for sending us to other fantastic places, then I decided that I could live with it and would continue to do what I had been doing: downplay the comparison when talking with Ray and focus on my son and his needs.

Later, when I was back in our room, I kept track of Ray's progress with the help of his chess program. At one point, the computer indicated that, with the right move, Ray would be able to turn the game against the grandmaster to his favor. I thought the move in my head, hoping to have some kind of psychic connection with Ray who was, as it turned out, already deeply into his own analysis of the benefits of that very move. And then, finally, he played it! Soon, Ray was up a pawn, then two. By this time, I was already by the board to watch the ending live. After Ray snagged the second pawn and there was no hope, the grandmaster resigned, leaving Ray in a four-way tie (with three grandmasters) going into round six.

By the time that Ray was playing his round six game against Grandmaster Rasmussen of Denmark, his round five game had been sent around the Internet, and Ray was being praised for his brilliance. As it turned out, the round six game would impress even more people. Ray prepared for this game until the last possible minute. He started preparing the night before and picked up where he had left off after we had come back from breakfast the next day. The extra time paid off, for the game progressed along the lines of Ray's preparation for the first 19 or so moves.

While Ray played his game, I climbed Mt. Storsteinen, continuing upwards at a good pace until I reached snow. I walked hard up and didn't stop much, deciding to save the peaceful viewings of the surroundings for the less strenuous return trip. On the way down, I wasn't disappointed – fjords and mountains interspersed or surrounded by the Arctic Ocean for as far as I could see in every direction. I rarely say, "Oh, my God," but that, plus "Jesus Christ," was about all I said. I decided that what I was viewing was the most beautiful scenery that I had ever seen or would ever see. Bergen, which just the week before I had called possibly the most beautiful town in the world, looked like a slum in comparison to what was before me. Tromsø had bigger fjords, more and bigger mountains, and 25% of the population of Bergen. If Yee-chen ever wanted to move to Tromsø, I would have the bags packed before she could change her mind.

Ray continued with his own highlights by beating his second grandmaster in a row (this one with the black pieces). I returned from my trip just in time to watch the final eight or nine moves. I actually went to the chess hall directly from the bus station instead of stopping in the room. I saw the final position where Ray, who had allowed himself to lose a piece, had completely immobilized his opponent's king! The result of his win was that, after six rounds, Ray and Grandmaster Monika Socko, the only female grandmaster in the event, were tied for first place and would be playing one another the following day.

After we had eaten, and after Yee-chen had left for a boat trip with some others from the group, I stayed with Ray while he prepared for about two hours for his next game. Afterwards, we went downstairs to join another group so that Ray could play in the soccer event. I hoped that he would have enough energy left over for the next day's round, but I didn't want to skip the soccer because Ray really wanted to participate. He probably would've felt worse if he had missed it even if it meant that he would have had an extra two hours to prepare for his game against Socko. Maybe Ray would have had a slightly better result, but, in the end, he would have had a worse trip if he hadn't been allowed to join the other young players. Such decisions, in the long run, are for the best. What was right to do in Wisconsin at the Junior Invitational wasn't necessarily right for the Tromsø event. Also, the soccer fit in with the pattern of hard study, followed by vigorous activity, followed by light study that he'd established with Ehlvest and continued with Onischuk. We'd continued the pattern in Tromsø with the evening bike rides/walks. So the soccer actually fit well into the schedule.

Because the activity ended after two hours (instead of the scheduled three), Ray had time to shower, prepare for another two hours, and eat the meal that I'd purchased at the closest market that was still open. Yee-chen said that Ray would never eat the big sandwich, large banana, and ice-cream treat, but I, having played hard sports as a fourteen-year-old, knew better what a teen was capable of devouring after heavy exercise. Ray ate everything.

* * *

It was while Ray was in bed, sleeping in a semi-darkened room before his big game the following day, that I sat in the adjoining suite, thinking a thought that I'd enjoyed for some years. I had been going over the Internet responses to Ray's latest win (praise from all around the chess world) while taking breaks to stare at the beautiful scenery outside of our window, clear as day at the hour of midnight, and I thought about how I had no regrets. Every action leads a person to his present experience. This I believe. I can say without any hesitation that I have no regrets because every single thing that I did in the past brought Ray into my life. Everything that seemed to be a mistake or a hardship or a sacrifice was the right thing done at the right time.

I once thought that by having a child, I would give up any chance of interesting travel and an interesting life outside of the family. It is, however, because of Ray that we have explored Brazilian beaches, visited the museums of Paris, trekked over Swiss Alps, bathed outdoors in steaming water in Iceland, swum with penguins around the Galapagos Islands, and enjoyed the scenery of the most beautiful place on earth in Tromsø. And that is just the travel part. The other, more important, part involved having another human being in my life who I could so closely connect with, admire, teach, and support. If every action and decision that I made brought me to where I am now, then I must have a charmed life. Regrets? Not a single one.

* * *

Ray hobbled down to breakfast, stiff and sore in the legs from the two hours of soccer. We didn't get back to the room until almost 11 o'clock – precious little time to finish preparing for a game that started at noon (the 3:00 p.m. rounds had given way to earlier starting times for the final days). A win today would almost assure Ray the grandmaster norm, and it would put him solidly in first place – all alone – with two rounds to play. After the round started, I watched the game on the Internet. Ray had a gift – white against a relatively weak grandmaster – but his play, combined with poor clock management, resulted in a gift for the Polish grandmaster: a draw.

Spirits were low afterwards. It took a meal, some TV, a family walk, and then a father-son talk – where I worked through the experience with Ray – for him to get back on track. By the time that the pairings for the penultimate round were posted, I felt that Ray was ready for what would come next: the final two rounds and a chance for both a grandmaster norm and a share of first place. After his last round draw, Ray was in a three-way tie for first with his Bulgarian international master opponent for round eight and also with the Polish grandmaster he had just drawn. Ray would be black against IM Petrov, and he spent the night in preparation.

Ray was excited about the surprise opening that he prepared: a French defense, which he would be playing for only the second time in his life. He was in good spirits, healthy (albeit still a little sore from the soccer), and I could just feel that it was all coming together, that he would be successful – both for the norm and for the title (or at least for a share of first place) by the time that it was all over. Ray had been on board one for round seven, and he and Petrov (one of his soccer teammates coincidently) would be there for round eight.

I stayed for the start of the game and saw the effect of Ray's surprise: Petrov appeared to have been completely caught off guard. He sat for a full 10 minutes trying to come up with a plan before he made his next move after seeing Ray's French defense. At the very least, Ray's plan had had an initial emotional impact. Perhaps that would make a difference in the long run. Of course, Ray would still have to play good moves to win any game. As it turned out, the shock soon wore off because Petrov moved ahead of Ray on time, and he eventually achieved a slightly better position on the board. I hoped that Ray would maintain his own composure and find good moves in good time.

One of the tournament directors saw me in the event room and told me that a win here for Ray would give him the grandmaster norm. This added to my own tension, but I was glad that the director shared the news with me instead of with Ray. Just over two hours into the game, our computer program said that Ray was worse; in addition, the live game site indicated that Ray was 15 minutes behind on the clock. I knew, though, that computer evaluations were not the best to follow, for humans did not make computer moves. This meant that anything could happen in the game that the two were engaged in. And as far as time went, Ray at least had a history of being able to play good moves when behind on time, though I wished that he didn't get so far behind! In any event, I decided to just put my trust in Ray. He was so sharp tactically that he could never be counted out of a game.

While watching Ray's game, I also had the television on and channel-flipped my way to a program about the comedian Mike Myers. Myers was talking about his father's attitude in general which was, essentially, "Everything's going to be okay. Let's go have fun." This was encouraging to me, and I made a mental note to share this with my own son.

Ray's game ended up being a very difficult one for me to watch. He was in a worse position for most of the game and was, at least at one point, over 20 minutes behind on time. In fact, he had several moves to make with just three or four minutes on this clock. I spent my time going back and forth between the chess room and the computer program, trying to figure out just what was going to happen in this game. At the very least, to have any chance for the norm, Ray would need a draw. When they had made time control, after move 40, the computer said that Ray was worse – possibly enough to turn the game over to Petrov.

But as I watched the first moves after the time control, that advantage, along with Petrov's extra pawn, disappeared until – after nearly 6 hours of play – they had reached a totally drawn position. I waited and waited and waited, worrying that maybe Petrov – in an equal position – would still play on thinking to drain Ray's clock. And then finally I saw the 1/2 - 1/2 symbol across their board on the computer screen: draw!

This one had made me worry, but, at the end of it all, I was very happy with the way that Ray had held the position and kept his norm hopes alive. After the game, I saw that Ray was in a four-way tie for first with Petrov, Socko, and Grandmaster Berg, who had joined the others with a win in the last round. Ray would be paired with Berg, Sweden's number one player and national champion, and he would need to draw with the black pieces in order to earn his first grandmaster norm.

Even though the next day was going to be the biggest day of all, we still took time out from preparation to enjoy Jan Berglund's barbecue party at his home. We ate lots of salmon, and I even enjoyed a few beers while Ray played soccer with some of the other participants. While Ray played and ate, I talked with some of the others who were present and received invitations for Ray to events in England and Africa. I left the barbecue thinking that exciting times were still ahead of us.

We got back in time for Ray to have an hour or so to prepare for his game against the 2600-level grandmaster. It wasn't a lot of time, but it was all that he would get because he needed his rest too. Since the final round started at 11:00 a.m., I figured that Ray would have no time to continue preparing after breakfast the next day. Everything had to be done the night before and then tomorrow over the board. My only words of advice – spoken shortly before Ray went to bed – had to do with the management of his time, with trust in himself, and with the knowledge that he was a great player. If Ray would just trust himself, he would move in the right direction.

The next morning, Ray woke up on his own at 9:30 and came over to the computer immediately to continue his analysis from the night before. I could see that his eyes were not ready to focus on the screen, so I led him into a pillow/wrestling battle on the beds. 15 minutes later, Ray was back at the computer – more alert and awake – to continue his analysis for his game against Grandmaster Berg. The extra 15 minutes of preparation time seemed to give Ray an enormous amount of comfort; he just wanted to be able to go through his own notes one more time and see if he could find any last-minute improvements.

On the walk to the tournament hall, I shared with Ray what I had heard on the Mike Myers TV show the other day – the part where Mike shares his father's general attitude towards life: Everything will be fine. Let's have some fun. I told Ray that this would be a good attitude to take now.

We arrived a few minutes late, but there were announcements, so clocks started just as Ray sat down. Berg hadn't yet arrived. In the few minutes that Ray had to wait, I took a photo and then watched as he neatly arranged each of the pieces on his side of the board. When Berg arrived, after shaking hands, the first thing he did was to neatly arrange the pieces on *his* side of the board. There were other similarities. Yee-chen said that Berg was on some of the trips that she had taken that week and noted that he generally sat quietly not talking with anyone. Although Ray can be a talk-box when he is with those he is most comfortable with, in general, he is a shy and quiet young man.

In their game, Ray played the Dragon – something he started with, was weaned from (during his sessions with his old grandmaster tutor), and then returned to on his own. He had a lot of success with this as black when he was a young player (aged 7 to 10), and he had been doing fine with it since returning to it recently. In some ways, it seemed fitting that he would play the Dragon – going back to his roots – for this game. It felt right.

On the way back to the room, I predicted that if Ray got the norm and/or first place, a lot more invitations and opportunities would appear in the near future. In fact, the invitations to England and Africa were already a sign of more of the same to come. I also thought more about how this last round was reminiscent of the United States Championship where, in the final round, Ray needed a draw with black against Alex Onischuk to secure the norm. I mentioned this to Ray the day before, and he, of course, had been thinking about it too. In that other game, Ray missed the draw. I told Ray that things had a way of coming around and that he now had a second chance under similar circumstances. I was sure that he had already considered this, a move ahead of me, as usual.

After playing for nearly 4 hours against Berg, with me watching every second of it on the Internet, I saw that the position was dead drawn, and then I watched as Ray made a mistake. Instead of moving in a way to solidify the equality of the position, Ray pushed a pawn ahead one square. Even such a tiny move as this changed the dynamics of the game in favor of the grandmaster.

The grandmaster played on, trying to ground down Ray, for another two hours. But, even though he had worsened his own position, and even though at one point – for about 10 minutes, he said – he thought that he had lost the game, Ray was able to maintain his composure at the board and find all the right moves necessary to hold the position. In the end, it was an entirely drawn position again, and the Swede had used all but 40 seconds of his clock's time in trying to find a way to get the win. They had played over 70 moves before Berg finally gave up and offered a draw.

Not only did Ray earn his first grandmaster norm with the draw, but he also shared first place since the other two leaders – Socko and Petrov – agreed to a 10-move draw (both scared, perhaps, of making a mistake and so losing a share of first). First place was just gravy, for the norm was what we had really come for. Success in Norway! Ray got a hug from me before he even left the board area, and that was quickly followed by the same from his mother. My main feeling was, "Finally!" Despite Ray's young age (14), I just felt like this first norm was long overdue. It was also a relief to have it, and I predicted that the next two would come more easily and quickly.

* * *

We hadn't been home more that two days before the news of Ray's achievement and reports on his games filled the Internet. While we were still adjusting to our own time zone, Ray's games were being posted and lectured on – particularly the two back-to-back wins over Grandmasters Malakhatko and Rasmussen. For the latter game, the talk was that Ray had come up with an entirely novel approach over the board which could mean the reevaluation of an entire system! The result of the Norway trip and the aftermath made me reflect that, while most parents with children Ray's age were dealing with issues such as marijuana, sexual activity, et cetera, my main worries had to do with making good travel arrangements for our next adventure.

The next adventure would take place in a matter of days. Ray would have five days to rest up at home before he would fly to Chicago to work with grandmaster number three: Yury Shulman, formerly of Belarus. This was a continuation of the plan to have Ray work for a week with a strong grandmaster before participating in a tournament. So far, the work with Ehlvest was followed by a win, the work with Onischuk was followed by a win and a norm, and we were hoping to keep the trend going with Shulman and the tournament that followed: a grandmaster norm event in Chicago, run by the same person – Sevan Muradian – who ran the event where Ray earned his first international master norm.

29

As with the Onischuk trip, Ray flew on his own and stayed with Yury in his home. I flew up five days later to stay with Ray in a hotel, which also served as the site of the event. Ray and Yury picked me up at the airport, and it was clear from the first moment I saw him that Ray had had a positive experience. He was talkative, lively, and seemed to be in a generally positive mood. This continued throughout dinner and on until nearly midnight, while he did some final work over the board with Yury in our hotel room.

After I had written the big check and said my own thank you to Yury, I talked with Ray about his experience that week. From what I gathered, the highlight was Yury himself, who was a good host and just a nice guy in general. I had that same impression myself just from spending part of the evening with him. Yury’s parents, who lived just down the road from him and who were frequently at the house, also made Ray feel comfortable. The downside of the visit had to do with the exercise routine. There were no tennis matches, as there were with Jaan, and there were no long runs, as with Alex; instead, Ray was mostly limited to shooting baskets with Yury's mom. Yury had recently had knee surgery and was on crutches the entire week.

When Ray wasn’t shooting baskets outside, he was training. Our plan was for Ray to learn more about the French defense from Yury, who was an expert, but it turned out that Yury may have gained more from analyzing games with Ray. He did not play the line that Ray was partial to and so the two spent more time looking at Yury's lines and Ray's refutations of some of those lines. Still, it was valuable for Ray to have high-level discussions with Yury on any topic. Also, the two worked on Ray's problem-solving ability within a certain amount of time. This was done to help Ray make complex decisions and still save some time on his clock. In the end, I felt very satisfied with the training and thought that the money was well spent.

When the tournament began, I hoped that the streak of training, followed by a strong performance, would continue. In order to do well, Ray would have to have strong games against at least three grandmasters, along with a few other international masters who, like Ray, would be trying their hardest to earn a grandmaster norm. One thing that worried me a little at the start of the event was that even a strong performance might not guarantee a norm. This was because the event was an open tournament with 30 participants. Even though the organizer had taken pains to include a number of foreigners, four grandmasters, several titled players, and players with reasonably strong ratings, everything would still have to fall perfectly into place for Ray to play all the right people in order to meet the international requirements for a grandmaster norm. In addition to getting all the right pairings, Ray would also have to play excellent chess – at the same level he had played in Norway.

For round one, we were happy with the pairing: an international master from India. This, at least, would knock out one of the four foreigners that Ray was required to play. The game itself didn't go quite like Ray would have liked. In fact, Ray was definitely worse in the game; however, his opponent got into time trouble and ended up giving the game back to Ray for his first win. It was a shaky start, but sometimes those things happen. Also, as I've said before, things have a way of coming around full circle. Ray had himself given away such games in the past and, in so doing, had hurt his own chances for norms. This time it was his turn to be on the receiving end. Such is the nature of chess matches and of norm hunts.

One other part about this tournament that was probably more challenging than anything else was the schedule itself: two rounds a day for the first four days, followed by a single round on the final day, and no rest days in between. This was an extremely demanding schedule – physically, mentally, and emotionally draining – but it was the schedule that everyone else had to follow as well. I thought that nutrition and sleep would be more important than ever, and we established a pattern on the very first day that, for the most part, we were able to maintain throughout the event.

Our hotel was located close to a number of healthy restaurants, and we started each morning with a short walk that took us alongside rich grass and several shrubs. Every day, as we walked to breakfast, we saw at least one rabbit – from the tiniest bunny that would fill up only half of my hand, to the size of rabbit you'd find roasting on a spit in another country. For breakfast, we maintained the same routine: a healthy sandwich along with a bowl of soup. Afterwards, we walked back along the bunny path to our room, looking for rabbits along the way. Back at the room, Ray would have approximately one hour to prepare for his game. This was the case before his first-round game against the Indian opponent. After his game finished, we walked immediately back to the food area, where we would try something different each day – Mexican, Mediterranean, Italian, etc. After lunch, we would head back to the room, and Ray would spend the next hour preparing for his 5:00 p.m. round. Ray would play the late afternoon round, finish at about 9:00 p.m., and then we would walk back to the food area, eat a bowl of chicken soup and maybe a cookie, and then head back "home" for bed.

By the second round of the first day, Ray was already paired with the strongest player in the tournament: Grandmaster Kacheishvili of Georgia (the country). Ray had the black pieces, so a draw would be a reasonable result. He had played Kacheishvili several times over the past year, and there had been wins on each side as well as a few draws. In every case, the grandmaster never gave an easy draw to Ray, always forcing him to earn his points. This encounter was no different, and Ray played all the right moves to secure a draw. If he were to get a norm, this was the kind of chess that he would have to play each round. I was glad that Ray had to earn his games from the grandmaster. Ten-move draws, which frequently happened in tournaments such as this, would teach Ray nothing.

For the first round of day two of the tournament, Ray had the white pieces against a lower-rated American player. Having played just one grandmaster and two foreigners, Ray still needed to be paired with two of the remaining three grandmasters and two more foreigners. Since the grandmasters were all foreigners, he would be killing two birds with one stone if he could just get the grandmaster pairings. In order to get those pairings, Ray would have to continue to win games. So Ray's fate very much rested in his own hands. His win over the American master in round three gave him one of the pairings he needed in the following round: Grandmaster Izoria of Georgia.

Izoria arrived 10 minutes late for the round and then took 10 full minutes to make his first move. I couldn't figure out if he was trying to psych Ray out in some way by sitting there so long before making a move or if, instead, he really didn't know how to proceed. Whatever the reason, I was hoping that his mismanagement of time would allow Ray to crush him in their game. As it turned out, the grandmaster did in fact dig his own grave by leaving himself too little time to find the right moves in a complicated game which Ray, who managed his time much better, took over and eventually won. This win, which came over the second highest ranked player, greatly improved Ray's chances of earning his second norm.

In order to earn a norm, one of the dozen or so requirements is that a player must perform at the 2601 level or higher, and this was no easy achievement. I knew of several cases where players had had very strong tournaments but fell short of a norm by performing just below the 2601 mark. After Ray beat Izoria, his performance rating rocketed up to 2844, well above the minimum requirement. This would be a nice cushion in case he lost or drew a game against a lower-rated player, for either result would significantly lower Ray's overall performance rating.

After two solid wins on day two, day three brought Ray's first setbacks. First, there was a draw with black against a much lower-rated player. This was followed later in the day by a second draw, also with the black pieces, and again against a lower-rated player. The only good news was that the second player was a foreign grandmaster, so Ray had at least fulfilled both the foreigner and the grandmaster requirements. His performance rating was at 2654, so he still had a little wiggle room there. With 4.5 points, he was still among those leading the tournament; however, with just three rounds to go, Ray would need at least two wins in order to secure a norm. The next round, we knew, would be the crucial one.

Ray had a nice surprise on the morning of the fourth day while he was preparing for his game against a very strong international master, Ben Finegold. Ben had long been the highest-rated international master in the United States. He was a solid player who had, amazingly, only lost once (to a grandmaster) in the past year. He had had two grandmaster norms for some time, but he had never picked up the third one, despite being a top-level player for the past decade. Both Ray and Ben were in a position to earn a grandmaster norm; a loss for one of them would mean the end of the hunt. While Ray prepared, the surprise came when Alex Onischuk called to check up on Ray. The timing was perfect, and I was glad that Ray had a chance to talk to his mentor at such a critical moment. For my part, I gave Ray only one suggestion, which I delivered on the way to the first round of the day. I said, "I suggest that you win two games today." It was a simple statement, but it had both an element of truth and an element of humor, and it seemed the right thing to say.

When the first game began, I was hoping for the best. Ray had prepared an interesting line against Ben which, if everything worked out, would give Ray a very solid position and chances for wins. Somewhere along the way, however, the game took a turn for the worse, and Ray was definitely in a poor position, if not a losing position. The only thing that could save him was a blunder. When each player's time wound down to approximately 2 minutes, Ben obliged: one poor move followed another under the pressure of time, and Ray, who played one solid move after another, was able to turn a probable loss into another win. This was the game that he really needed, and the norm hopes were still alive.

Going into the second round of the day, the penultimate round of the tournament, Ray was in first place, with a performance rating of 2700, and was one point shy of his second grandmaster norm. We thought that Ray would be black against international master Sam Shankland; however, when the pairings came out, Ray had the white pieces. Although there was some strategy in taking a draw, which would mean that Ray would only need a final draw in the last round to get his norm, I said that he should not give up his last game with the white pieces. Also, Ray had played Sam twice before and had beaten him both times – and, for whatever reason, in both games Sam had not played particularly well. Sam was another up-and-coming young player, just out of high school, who had already earned two grandmaster norms in a short time. He had told me before the round with Ray that he needed a draw with Ray and a win in the final round to earn his last norm. Apparently, he was not even thinking about winning against Ray.

Before the round started, when Ray was in the restroom, Sam came up to me and wanted to know if I thought that Ray would be willing to take a draw with him. I said that I didn't know and that he should just play the game. As it turned out, Sam's nerves got the better of him. He seemed extremely agitated throughout the game, didn't play the best moves, and then, immediately after Ray refused his draw offer, blundered a piece and had to resign. This was the second norm chance that Ray crushed in order to earn his own norm; unfortunately, that is the way things have to happen in these tournaments. With only 30 players, it is just not possible for more than one or two to earn a norm.

Of course, even with the win, we still weren't sure if Ray had earned his norm or not. Everything would depend on the final round pairing. This had to do with yet another of the seemingly endless rules related to grandmaster norms: the rule about average rating of one's opponents. In order for Ray, with 6 1/2 points, to earn his second norm, the average rating of his opponents would need to be 2434 or above. If it was just one point lower, then he would need a draw in the final round on the final day. It wouldn't be until close to bedtime before we would find out for sure who Ray would play, so we continued the routine as usual: we walked through Bunny Land, Ray had a healthy bowl of soup, and then we relaxed in the room until we learned the pairing. Whatever the pairing would be, Ray was already in a calm mood after his two important wins that day, and I had a very good feeling that, regardless of the pairing, everything would work out well.

Not long before bedtime, we learned that Ray would be playing against an international master whose rating kept us in the 2434-and-above range. In other words, Ray had already earned his norm with one round to spare! Despite this news, Ray spent the last 45 minutes before bedtime preparing for his last-round game. He did not want to take a 10-move draw, and he did not want to put in one poor game even though he had already earned everything that we had come for. He wanted to finish strong, and he wanted to win clear first place.

And that's exactly how it ended: a solid game by Ray with the black pieces which resulted in a very equal position, another half point for Ray, clear first place ahead of all four grandmasters, and the winner's check for $1500. Of course, all that we were really after was the norm. Through it all, especially during the two important rounds that resulted in the norm, Ray played with great calm and composure – even in the first game when the outcome looked bleak. Like me, I think he just felt that it was going to happen. It was time.

* * *

In reflecting on the experience, I couldn't help but notice an interesting pattern. After Ray had earned his first international master norm, the other two followed almost immediately. And the international master norms came in Chicago, Iceland (a cold place), and Texas (a state with a large Spanish-speaking population). Ray had just earned his second grandmaster norm directly on the heels of the first (within the same month even!). His first two norms were earned in Chicago and the Arctic Circle (like Iceland, a very cold place). Perhaps he would earn his final norm in October during our upcoming trip to South America, where Ray would play in norm events in both Uruguay and Argentina.

The other thing I noted in my reflections, something that Ray and I both talked about, was the incredible streak that he was on: three first-place finishes in a row without a single loss! I had one more four-day training set up with yet another grandmaster, which would be followed soon after by the South American events. If the pattern continued, then Ray would do well in Uruguay – the first of the two events – and earn his third, and final, grandmaster norm.

30

In rummaging through some of my notebooks, I found a page on which I had noted that, in the 1950s, Bobby Fischer had become a grandmaster at the age of fifteen-and-half. Neither Ray nor I had ever wasted much time in thinking about setting records or about who did what first. We'd always made our plans based on what worked for us as a family. I did, however, have a secret hope that Ray would become a grandmaster ahead of Fischer, for he had always served as our benchmark. Ray had stayed ahead of Fischer for the master and international master titles; I was confident that he would become a grandmaster at an earlier age as well. He would have a few chances to do so, and South America would serve as the location.

In preparation for the upcoming events, Ray worked for about four days in our home with Grandmaster Varuzhan "Var" Akobian, a young man who was originally from Armenia and who was now a resident of California. Of the four trainings that I had arranged, this was the one that I wondered the most about. Ehlvest was a strong grandmaster from the old school who knew his openings well. Onischuk was one of the strongest players in the United States, and he was a professional player ranked 34th in the world. Shulman was a solid player who was also among the top 100 players in the world. Var was the youngest of the four. He had earned his grandmaster title around the age of 21 and had only been a GM for five years. I wondered if the session would be as productive as the others. On the other hand, Var had come recommended by Alex Onischuk; in addition, he had had solid performances over the past year which had moved him into a very small circle of the strongest players in the United States.

The way things worked out, I was as pleased with this session as I was with any of the others. Var and Ray worked on positional understanding, openings, endgames, and clock management. In between, the young GM and the GM-hopeful battled through numerous Ping-Pong matches on the table that I had set up in the garage. It was a healthy combination of serious study and physical breaks. Var had definitely done his job well. The intellectual and physical stimulation was just what Ray needed to get him in shape for his final norm.

The training with Var was the fourth, and last, of the training sessions that I had arranged earlier in the summer. I had spent nearly one-third of the first year's fellowship funds on the training sessions alone, but, based on the results thus far, I had to admit that it was money well spent. Almost no one earns two GM norms in one month. I felt certain that the overseers of the fellowship fund would understand this and continue to work with us as the reimbursement requests were submitted one after another. I suppose that other Fellows were more careful about distributing the money over each 12-month period; however, I thought it best to give Ray as much training as possible early in the year in order to stimulate his growth and so assist with the norm hunt. By October, the beginning of our South American adventure, the funds were completely gone; most of the upcoming trip, and all future trips until year two of the fellowship kicked in, would be on me once again. And in what was a last-minute surprise for me, I learned that I would be footing the bills on half of my salary.

Literally two hours before the end of the last workday before our trip to Uruguay, I received a call from my boss and was asked to sign a contract to the effect that I would take the upcoming trip on half-salary. At the time that I was agreeing to the pay cut, I had no idea that, soon after our return from the long South American trip, I would be asked to choose between my full-time professorship (with no travel options) and a position as a part-time instructor with the flexibility to teach remotely as necessary. I viewed the last choice as one between my job and my son, and I needed less than one second to make my final decision.

I think my boss realized that there would be no end to the chess trips. As long as Ray continued to improve, invitations would come, and I would want to be with him. I could understand the move to force me to stop now or leave my post. I could also appreciate the fact that my boss was probably hearing complaints from my coworkers about my absence in general. The usual greeting from my fellow faculty members of "How are you?" had long since been replaced by "Where have you been?" I don't think it would be easy to justify my absence to the others – especially not while I was on full salary.

With the work situation settled, and with the last of the training sessions completed, we were free to focus on the task at hand: one more norm, which we hoped would come at the Pan American Junior in Montevideo, Uruguay. This event was for the best players in the Pan Am region under the age of twenty. Since the cut-off for ages was January 1, and the event was in October, most of Ray's opponents had already turned 20 and were 6 years older than he was.

The Pan Am event, unlike most norm events, operated under different rules. For example, regardless of the number of titled players participating, and regardless of the number of federations represented, the outright winner of the event would earn a GM norm. It is the same for the Under-20 European Championship and a few other events as well. We knew from having played in South America twice before that there were a number of exceptionally strong players scattered throughout the countries, including several international masters and a handful of grandmasters. Which of these would show up was a mystery to us, so Ray would just have to play whoever was there. I wasn't worried; Ray was definitely ready for the event. A clear sign of this came from a Texas event that we had squeezed in between Var's training and the Pan Am, where Ray narrowly missed the final norm. When he didn't get it there, I felt absolutely certain that it would come in Uruguay.

* * *

I was happy to have had success with my Spanish both at the immigration checkpoints and at the various offices for customs. I already had a basic knowledge of Spanish – mostly from my walk across Central America in the 1990s – and I'd spent the past month working through a high school Spanish 1 textbook. I was pleased to find that the textbook, for the most part, was just a review for me. This, I thought, is a good time in my life for me to use another language. I'm now much less anxious about making mistakes and getting laughed at for being misunderstood than at other times in my life. I tell myself that I'm 44 years old; I have no reason to be embarrassed by mistakes; just try. And then I do. And then success!

While we were waiting out the three-and-a-half hours between our arrival in Buenos Aires and our flight to Montevideo, Ray did his best to catch up on sleep by crashing on the hard metal bench in the airport, using my jacket as a pillow. The bench was just long enough for his body. Ray was now the same height as his mom and was daily measuring himself up to me, as if the passage of a single hour had propelled him one inch closer to my height. And he was nearly right! He would turn 15 at the end of the month, and I predicted that he would pass me in height maybe by the end of his 16th year. I just wished that he would fill out width-wise. He would be called “Bamboo” by his friends if he didn’t start growing outwards.

We still weren’t sure about who Ray would face in this tournament, but, based on previous events that I had looked up, I felt that Ray would have two or three major challenges and that, to get the final norm, he would probably need seven wins, no more than two draws, and no losses in the nine-round event. We also had to keep in mind that, in order to earn the norm, Ray needed to get clear first place; that was one of the rules. I figured that all Ray would have to do would be to play his normal good chess, and he would get his third norm. Of course, in any event, just one blunder or loss could make the difference. That was chess, and sometimes that was life too.

* * *

Once we finally arrived in Montevideo and found our hotel, we checked in and moved our bags to our ancient and cave-like hotel room. The room had a hairdryer nailed to the wall that looked like it had come out of the 1940s (if they even had hairdryers back then). The room was tiny, leaving us just enough room to sleep. One of the two small beds blocked the lone cabinet for clothes, so I had to move it in order to gain access to the closet. The TV was about 8 inches in both directions and needed two modern-looking remote controls to operate. There was a combination AC/heater that looked old but did not leak. The carpet was old and stained, and the lampshades had holes burned through them. The bathroom had a separate unit for washing one's backside. No washcloths, of course. Most hotels in other countries don't provide washcloths, so I had long since packed them as a matter of course. In addition to no washcloths, there was no Internet in the room, but it was available in the lobby downstairs. The room was pitch black with the lights off and cave-like with the lights on. The curtains were rusted into place and must not have been drawn for decades. When I did manage to open them and unlock and open the window, I was faced with a broken-down shutter. I was able to work that aside too, only to reveal a small square of grass scattered with miscellaneous trash. It looked like a good place for rats, so I quickly closed and locked up the shutter and window, and also closed the curtains for good measure. But of everything connected with the room, the key was the most challenging of all. We had a large skeleton key that would only unlock the loose door lock with the utmost care combined with luck. Every opening and locking was a test of patience.

By 1:00 p.m. the following afternoon, after a long rest to work out of the funk caused by 12 hours of transportation on the previous day, we were eating our first lunch in the official chess café, which was conveniently just a block and a half away from our hotel and also in the same building as the tournament. Selections for the meal were slim: a choice of two small desserts (which were served first) and a choice of three main dishes (one of which I couldn't figure out). For drinks, we had water, soda, or wine. By filling up on two baskets of bread, we were able to make a pretty decent meal. While we were eating that first meal, Andre Diamant, a Brazilian GM, showed up with his wife-to-be and their infant son. We shook hands, talked, and they – along with two compatriots – sat at the joining table. Andre, I knew, would probably be someone that Ray would need to beat – perhaps even the one player that would determine whether or not he earned the title.

After the meal, we bought some water, wafers, and oranges to keep in the room. Then we sat in the lobby, where Ray answered my e-mail messages for me. Before we knew it, it was time to go to the chess center for the 4:00 p.m. opening ceremony. The ceremony took 40 minutes and consisted of a number of speeches, only one of which I fully understood (because it was in English and directed to us). This last message was a heartfelt welcome and a wish that we would achieve our goals; everyone present knew why we were there. In addition to the kindness of the Pan Am official who recognized each of us in his speech, one of the other officials, who spoke some English, came over to tell us not to worry, and he told Ray that he should turn to him if he had any problems at the board. He was very friendly and obviously meant it sincerely when he told Ray not to be nervous and to relax – that he was among friends. This was a nice way to start a tournament, and I was beginning to think that this might be Tromsø revisited.

For round one, Ray was paired with Daniel Carlo, a Bolivian teenager whose games we didn't have time to research. When there is no time to prepare, one has to trust himself at the board. Still, even the best preparation will not prevent surprises. In chess, there are 400 different positions possible after move one, about 72,000 different positions after move two, and over 9 million different positions after move three. Surprises occur all of the time in chess! In Ray's game, on move three he was wondering if Carlo would play Nbd2; instead, Carlo played something that Ray had never seen before. This is perhaps the most difficult situation for Ray: a novel position on the board. This is when Ray's mind begins analyzing variation after variation, and his own calculations prevent him from carefully managing his time. As Ray's clock wound down, when they had reached move 28 and Ray's position wasn't particularly good, Ray just started taking control of the game. He simply outplayed Carlo and when, just a few moves later, Carlo made a mistake which led to the loss of a pawn, the game was pretty much over. Although Ray hadn't played a perfect game, he did play well enough to join 14 others with one point after round one. There were only two upsets and two draws in the first round. As I had figured out before we even left the tournament hall, Ray would be paired with the other top seeds for all of the remaining rounds.

After the three-and-a-half hour first game, we walked downstairs for dinner. They offered the same choices as for lunch, with the addition of a tiny fruit cup for dessert. Neither the lunch nor the dinner was particularly filling; it was good that I had bought the snacks to supplement our meals. Also, I guess the other chess players, like us, had been gobbling bread because, unlike at lunch, the breadbasket was not refilled on any of the players' tables.

* * *

Ray's round two opponent, Pablo Garcia Cardenas of Chile, played different openings, so we didn't know what to expect. Around move 14, Ray started thinking for a long while because he didn't know what to do. His opponent was playing good moves, and Ray wasn't happy about the position. As the game went on, Ray eventually got the initiative, and finally, around move 30, his position was better. Cardenas had his chances for a draw but didn't find the best way to proceed and all of sudden Ray had his second win, moving him into a six-way tie for first.

After the game, we ate our lunch (this time, we were limited to one entrée and four small pieces of bread). Back in the room, Ray prepared for his round-three opponent: Luis Ibarra Chami, a 20-year-old international master from Mexico. While Ray did his work, I took a short siesta. I woke up later thinking about a short story set in Mexico that I'd written nearly 20 years before. While I related the story to Ray, he knocked out one of the oranges that I had peeled along with a few wafers. Then it was time for the 5:00 p.m. round. Ray looked to be in good shape physically, psychologically, and emotionally. I was hoping for the best. A win in round three with the black pieces against the number five seed would certainly be good for him.

Chami surprised Ray in the opening and then seemed not to know the line he had chosen. Ray later told me that he thought that Chami was simply pretending, hoping that Ray would play the same moves as he had in a recently published game and allowing Chami to spring a prepared novelty on him. There is much artifice in chess; not all of the best moves are played on the board, and one must always be alert.

The game eventually moved into a drawish position, and Chami was in fact going for a threefold repetition (which would mean an automatic draw). Ray, however, avoided the repetition, for he saw that there were still some chances. It is a great psychological advantage to play on in an even position after your opponent has all but offered a draw. You are daring your opponent to match the quality of your moves and telling him that you think you can outplay him in an even game. In Ray's game, just a few moves after Ray avoided the repetition, Chami made a big mistake, leading to a better endgame for Ray and the win.

At dinner that night, the wine and the bread were both missing from the menu, but we didn't mind. We were happy with the way the tournament was going. As we moved into round four, Ray and his opponent, Ciro Diaz of Ecuador, were the only ones with three points; three others were one-half point behind.

* * *

Just prior to the start of the fourth round, Ray had a sore throat. I gave him vitamin-C lozenges to help. The day before, the chess room had been very cold, and Ray was the only player not to put on his sweatshirt (which he had) or zip up his jacket (which he had). I hoped the sore throat wouldn't affect his play. Every little thing can make a difference in important events.

We were told by one of the other players that Diaz was quite good at openings. He and Ray played into a sharp line, and Diaz's solid opening play forced Ray to give up a piece. This, followed by a terrible move, resulted in a completely lost position for Ray. Why didn't he resign? It was only the middle game, and pieces were still on the board. Where there's life, there's hope. Ray told me after the game that he never even thought of resigning. By move 12, having thought for several minutes and really needing to use the bathroom, he couldn't find a single good move. In the position, two of Ray's pieces were hanging (i.e., they could immediately be captured), and his h-pawn was hanging. Faced with one losing move after another, Ray decided that the best plan would be to move another piece so that it too was hanging. In other words, he purposefully played a bad move. Ray later told me that he decided to simply confuse his opponent.

It was a bad move, but not a bad chance. Objective moves are not always as good as practical moves. In practical games, confusion sometimes leads to more chances. Faced with the choice of three pieces and one pawn to capture, Diaz, after a long think, ended up taking nothing. If he had thought more deeply or more correctly, he would have found an easy win. And after Diaz missed his opportunity, Ray used all of his chances to create more pressure on his opponent. As the game progressed, Ray continued playing good moves and finally reached an endgame where he knew he at least would not lose the game.

Once equality was established, Ray finally took control of the board and played well enough – or his opponent played poorly enough – for Ray to win again. This was the critical game. Of all the games he played, he certainly should not have won this one, but he did. At the worst point in the game, I was thinking that a little luck is usually needed to win such tournaments and that Ray was due some luck after all of the near misses he had had in the past. Fortunately, that's just how it turned out, and Ray ended the day in clear first place. On the following day, he would have the black pieces against his main opposition: Grandmaster Andre Diamant of Brazil.

* * *

As usual, I had trouble sleeping. My only aid was the pitch blackness of the room. When I had woken up at 3:00 a.m., I did so from a dream in which Ray was obviously going to win this event. He needed just one-half point in the final two rounds to finish in clear first. I hoped that the dream would reflect reality. Ray was certainly moving in that direction as we approached the halfway point.

When I had woken Ray up and we had had breakfast and were back in the room, I moved the unused refrigerator to one side and rearranged the stuff on the desk above the refrigerator to create a workspace for Ray. This allowed him to sit up straight in a chair and keep the computer on the table instead of having to lounge on the bed and try to prepare in that way for his GM opponent. While Ray was preparing, we learned that he was a full point ahead of his next opponent – just the position to be in for a norm event. I worried, though, that Ray's health might turn out to be his main opponent. Twenty or more times during yesterday's game – reminiscent of Georgia, where Ray had become a national master – he had violent sneezing fits. I thought that it was allergies, but I wasn't sure. In any event, he refused to take medication. He didn't want anything to interfere with his preparation or his ability to concentrate at the board. But his decision resulted in more sneezing attacks and a nose which constantly ran.

Against Diamant, Ray blew his nose 40 or more times during the four-and-a-half hour game. I didn't know if the allergies were affecting his play. Ray was down material early on and was – in his words – totally lost. Diamant, needing a win, played a very sharp line. Ray played pretty well but used up too much time, while his grandmaster opponent moved quickly. And on move 20, Ray played a terrible move. He was trying to get active play but missed Diamant's response. Diamant continued to play well, but then he started thinking more, and his time gradually got lower and lower. Maybe he was nervous; this was an important game, he was behind in total points, and Ray had started playing good moves. Yes, maybe it was nerves, for Diamant went for an immediate simplifying of the position instead of a more accurate plan which would have led to a win.

By move 60, Ray had found a way to draw the game. If he could just get rid of Diamant's c-pawn, the game would be drawn. Diamant, of course, saw this too and protected that pawn but, in doing so, allowed Ray to get active pawns of his own. By move 75, the dynamics had changed to where the grandmaster was playing for the draw and Ray was playing for the win. Both players were down to one or two minutes only, and, in the end, Ray got just what he played for. In this case, the grandmaster lost because he wanted to win too badly. Emotions!

We ate afterwards – late, due to the length of the game – and were home after 10:00 p.m. Ray's nose continued to run throughout the remainder of the evening. I thought to get allergy medication, but the stores were closed. Ray wasn't able to drop off to sleep until quite late, and, when he did sleep, his nasal flow was so disrupted that it sounded like I was sharing a room with Darth Vader – particularly creepy in the pitch black room.

* * *

As Ray started his sixth-round game against Isaac Garcia Guerrero of Mexico, I made a successful trip to the pharmacy, bringing back a medicine which met the following criteria: liquid form, suitable for children, strictly for allergies (especially runny noses), non-drowsy, and not containing caffeine. Ray had the dose delivered to him by the kindly official, Ruben Hipogrosso, the one who spoke the most English and who had been keeping an eye on Ray and communicating with both of us as necessary throughout the event. It turned out that Ruben was a dentist, and I acquired the medicine on his recommendation. Later, he confirmed the drug choice with a pharmacist colleague and also with a doctor. How's that for attention and concern from the host group!

Ray's game was the longest (once again), and the medicine seemed to have only a marginal effect – less sneezing, I think, but only slightly less nose-blowing. His play, however, was not affected. Although he was playing well, by move 16, Ray had no moves, his opponent's pieces were active, and he could have taken a draw. Ray was a point ahead of the field and a draw would have been okay at this time, but he decided to play on because his opponent had a lower rating, and lower-rated players make mistakes. In chess, the winner of the game is always the person who makes the second to last mistake. On move 21, Guerrero finally made the mistake that Ray was waiting for, and Ray chased his opponent's king around the board until Guerrero finally resigned. It was another long game, another difficult game, another game that maybe should have been drawn. But it wasn't. This was his sixth win in so many games, and Ray now enjoyed a 1.5-point lead in the event.

In the short time that we had before the seventh round, Ray prepared for his 20-year-old Argentine opponent, Leonardo Tristan. A win, of course, would all but secure the norm for Ray (his opponents would still have a chance, but it would be slim indeed). Still, he could give away a draw or even a loss in this round and go into the penultimate round in clear first. The position he was in was just where he wanted to be; having that buffer of points definitely took some of the pressure off.

* * *

Round seven was probably Ray's best game. In the course of the game, he found some interesting moves, which resulted in a good position by move 16. A good position for Ray usually means an attacking position. Also, he was better on time. If you give Ray enough time and a better position, you essentially give him the game. At the end of the round, Ray was seven out of seven, two points ahead of the nearest participant, and all he needed was one draw out of the last two rounds to earn his final grandmaster norm and the title of grandmaster itself. My dream from a few nights ago had come true!

At our meal that night, I continued what had become a tradition for us: a toast to Ray’s latest victory. We’d had seven such toasts in a row. Ray pointed out that this was the first time he'd won seven games like that since he played in the elementary school national events, and that took us all the way back to grade 3 and his first national win in Chicago.

* * *

Ray dominated Andres Gallego, his Colombian opponent, in the penultimate round. Although he had all the chances for a win, Ray wisely decided not to take risks with the title on the line and offered a draw, which his opponent quickly accepted. In so doing, Ray secured clear first place and the grandmaster title . . . with one round to spare.

Back in our room, we took things easy, relaxed, and had fun. We also called home (Yee-chen was out), called Grandma and Grandpa (also out), and then shared the good news through electronic messages with Ray’s supporters: the Kempers, Susan Polgar, and the team of grandmasters who had worked with Ray most recently: Alex, Jaan, Yury, and Var.

We continued our celebration with a bear hug from me and more horseplay in the room. Around midnight, we were both still energized and ended up talking late into the night in our cave of a room. We talked about other grandmasters – how Ray had joined that elite group and could now be spoken of as a peer. We also talked about new goals: an international rating of 2600, followed by a rating of 2700, and, of course, more tournament wins along the way. It was all based on the same plan that we'd always had: continue to work hard and improve. That night, Ray told me something that I had not known before: that he was at that moment the youngest grandmaster in the world! And, at age 14, he had also become the youngest grandmaster ever to represent the United States Chess Federation.

Still later, after Ray was fast asleep, I thought about how we'd been having this experience for eight years – how he got into his first event shortly before his seventh birthday (where he lost both of his games) and how now, shortly before his 15th birthday, he had become a grandmaster. I didn't know how many fathers and sons had had such a long and deeply shared experience outside of daily life activities. I felt lucky to have shared this with my son.

* * *

After the tournament was over, we talked with people while waiting for the closing ceremony to begin (the only part of the program that did not start on time). I got in at least an hour's worth of practice speaking Spanish with some of the local chess aficionados and tournament officials. The ceremony was nice, and they took extra time with Ray's presentation, saying this was an historic moment in Uruguay's history, for it was the first time a final grandmaster norm had been awarded at an event there. Ruben, our kind friend throughout the tournament, said many good things about Ray in his speech, and then Ray was given the trophy: a beautiful local clock/plaque. Afterwards, all of the organizers wanted a photo with Ray, and then we stayed to talk with various persons. Finally, we made it to dinner, where Ruben, in true Uruguayan fashion and in what was a most touching gesture, gave Ray the traditional kiss on the cheek for a final goodbye. Back in our room, after talking with Yee-chen, we fell asleep to the Monday night football game – surely a reminder that home was not too far away.

* * *

I'd been told by others – grandmasters – that the first norm was usually the hardest and that it often happened that the others came rolling in relatively easily. For some players, though, the third norm was the biggest challenge and could take several months or even several years. This was often due to psychological factors, but, once that final norm was secured, players often went on to have other norm performances in quick succession. After his success in Uruguay, we took a week-long rest on a Uruguayan beach before heading to Patagonia for the World Junior (Under-20) Championship. Ray proved that the statements about norm performances were true, for he earned an extra norm by defeating strong players such as GM Howell, England's youngest ever grandmaster, and GM Yu, China's current youngest grandmaster.

More norm performances are certainly ahead, but none of that matters anymore. Once Ray became a grandmaster, norms became meaningless. Now the task is to continue to work hard and improve. Ray's currently ranked #4 in the world for his age group, and, also by age group, he's #1 in the world for the Pan American region and, of course, for the USA.

The key now, I believe, is to have Ray play in the strongest events possible so that he can get the difficult games and the losses that will become the basis for his future studies. As America's youngest grandmaster, the invitations to the stronger and more prestigious events, as well as other learning opportunities, are there. He has Samford Fellowship funds to support his development for one more year. I don't know where the support will come from after next year, but we'll find a way to move forward. Ray still hasn't reached his plateau yet. Let's see how far he can go.

Afterword

Grandmaster is not the goal. If that were the goal, then once you eventually arrived – after years of hard work and perseverance – you might feel that it was some sort of hoax. Is that all there is? This is why the goal is not master or grandmaster; the goal is to live a better life, which, to me, is synonymous with living more wisely. At the end of it all, if you've played the game correctly, you'll have learned as much about how to play the game of life as you have about how to play chess. And there will have been so many lessons to learn from. While I've highlighted a few that we have encountered, I have left out the family favorite: Beatenberg.

It was the year 2005, and we were in Switzerland, having taken an extra week to do some traveling before the start of Ray's second World Youth event in nearby France. We took a bus to a cable car station, paid the $100 fee for the roundtrip tickets, and rode the car to the top of a nearby mountain. All that we had noticed at the start of our trip was a sign with the word "Beatenberg" clearly displayed.

We ended up walking for 9 hours that day – only two of them by design. When we reached the point in our climb where we had to turn around to make it to the cable ride down the mountain and back to Beatenberg, Yee-chen decided that she didn't want to retrace her steps, and so instead we wound up looking for an alternate route and got lost along the way. We followed the "Beatenberg" signs religiously without ever finding Beatenberg. It wasn't until several hours later – long after we had missed the final 6:00 p.m. return cable ride, when we were hoofing it down the mountain in our exhausted state – that it occurred to me that the entire region was called Beatenberg. The signs we'd been following simply indicated that we were in yet another part of an extensive region known as Beatenberg. In other words, we had been searching for the way to Beatenberg for hours without realizing that we were in Beatenberg all along.

Once I'd figured this out and shared the news with my exhausted family, I took time to reflect on the lessons. There were the obvious ones that had to do with the blunders of making wrong conclusions and following them with great conviction. And there were the more difficult-to-see lessons along the lines of "be here now" – the idea that, yes we are lost, but look at how beautiful everything around us is! There were many other lessons too, of course, which we have reflected on both individually and as a family. To this day, any time we are in a potentially confusing situation, all one of us has to do is to say "Beatenberg" and the many lessons, accompanied by three smiles, appear. This is just what our journey has been about: life experiences and reflections on the lessons. Perhaps this kind of a lifestyle will indeed lead Ray to wisdom and a better life. At the very least, I think his present life allows for happiness. If this is so, then I guess that Yee-chen and I have done our gardening correctly; we've tended our pepper well.

Chess is a game. You play games, and you have fun. If you reach the end of it all and it's no longer a game and you find that you didn't have fun all along the way, why then you've missed the point entirely. Although there has certainly been a lot of pressure on Ray when he played the games for titles and norms, the overall experience itself has been one filled with joy. We like taking these trips. It's fun for Ray to play chess, and it's fun to play games and create amusing diversions in the time between the chess rounds. In truth, there is nothing in life that I enjoy more than these chess outings. I know that they will not last forever, and that makes them all the more valuable to me.

In the 1980s, I was a Peace Corps Volunteer. I built a bamboo hut by the side of a musical river and spent two years having one amazing experience after another every single day. During those two years, I was stimulated in every way imaginable – linguistically, intellectually, emotionally, etc. – and I still today feed off of that experience that occurred over 20 years ago. After such an unbelievable experience, I drifted from one unsatisfying situation to another. Nothing could compare with the two years that I had spent in the Philippines, and I was depressed and miserable most days. That situation, of course, reversed itself when I brought a wife and then our wonder-boy son into my life. But I have thought about this experience in terms of Ray and his own happiness.

I guess what I most worry about is that the joy might disappear if this game ever becomes a job for Ray. Going back to our first games, when Ray was just three years old, one could say that he has been feeding off of chess for over a decade already, having successes, experiencing new situations, interacting with interesting people, taxing his brain to its limit. Yes, he's worked hard and given up TV, video games, and even trick-or-treating, but he's done this out of his own desire to master the game that he loves best. Ray's never "had" to work at chess, improve, get results, et cetera; he's always wanted to do this. I wonder how things would change if he played chess for a living?

Perhaps there would be no change at all. For example, I have always loved to read books, to record my thoughts, and to reflect on lessons and experiences. I have been a teacher for over 20 years now, and, in many cases, I end up talking about books and reflection instead of reading the books and reflecting on them. But there is great satisfaction in teaching others, and I do love to teach! And while I may not read a book a night as I once did out of love for reading and learning, I still read each week, I still keep a journal off and on, and, from time to time, I still reflect on my experiences. I think that Ray is smart enough to find the kind of balance that he will need in his own life – even if his own chess games no longer become the focus of his existence.

And what if Ray were to quit chess altogether? Others have asked me this very question over the past few years. What they're really asking is, after all of the time and the expense, will it have all been for naught if he leaves chess to pursue something else? They want to know if I think it's worth it. Maybe they're remembering Josh Waitzkin, the young boy of *Searching for Bobby Fischer* fame who won several national events and generated a lot of attention. He stopped competing in his early twenties, having never made it to what must have been his ultimate goal in chess: grandmaster. He was so close, but from what I have read and heard, Waitzkin has moved on to other aspects of life and has found other interests.

Frankly, I don't think that this was ever an issue for Ray. When he was twelve years old, he was already starting to think and to play like a grandmaster. It was not a question of ability in his case; it was simply a matter of time. Just as when Ray was a Class A player, I spoke of "when" not "if" he becomes a master, so too did I later begin sentences with "When you're a grandmaster." It was just something that we both expected to happen. There was a celebration and a round of applause when it occurred, but there wasn't surprise. And as to ceilings, Ray's hasn't come into sight yet. We have no idea how far he will be able to go in chess.

But let's say for the moment that, for whatever reason, Ray decides that he's had enough of chess and wants to move on to other things. What do I think? I think that I have nothing to complain about. How can I say it was money wasted when he has college scholarships in his desk drawer? How can I say that he missed out on companionship when he gained mentors in Alex Onischuk and others as well as the friendship and respect of a number of intelligent people from all ages and from all parts of the world? How can I say that it was time wasted when he learned patience, decision making, research skills, self trust, self respect, and the value of working hard to achieve one's goals? I know with certainty that it will be Ray's love of the game that will carry him through these next years. When it's time for him to move on – if it's ever time for him to move on – he'll know it, and it will be the winning move.

And as for me? Well, what I have learned from this process – that is, the process of writing a book about my son – is that all things change over time. What is at one point in time considered an absolute tragedy, at another point becomes insignificant and barely remembered. Conversely, what at one time seems to be it – the most important event – disappears from a draft that is written two years later with two simple steps: highlight and delete.

The lesson to take from this – and the one that I have shared with my son – is that when bad things happen, if you can just wait long enough, you may realize that what once appeared to be a tragedy was not a tragedy at all. Similarly, no matter how great things are today, there are better things tomorrow. I used as an example Ray becoming World Champion – how becoming grandmaster would pale in comparison. But I also told Ray that I could imagine something that would far exceed becoming World Champion. He said that that was impossible – that I could think of nothing better than that. I said that I could, but I left the conversation there. I'll share now with you what I was thinking at that moment: better than being a World Champion is being a father to a son.

Gary Robson
Seminole, Florida
2010

About the Author

Dr. Gary Robson started his career in education as a Peace Corps Volunteer in the Philippines. Between 1987 and 1996, he taught K-12 students and trained teachers in Asia and Micronesia. Since 1996, Dr. Robson has worked in various educational settings within the United States. Although his area of expertise is ESOL (English for Speakers of Other Languages), he has worked with a variety of students and has taught multiple subjects in a number of settings. *Chess Child* is his first book.